W9-ADA-366

Poststructuralism,
Politics
and Education

Critical Studies in Education and Culture Series

Poststructuralism, Politics and Education

Michael Peters

CRITICAL STUDIES IN EDUCATION AND CULTURE
Edited by Henry A. Giroux and Paulo Freire

BERGIN & GARVEY
Westport, Connecticut • London

Library of Congress Cataloging-in-Publication Data

Peters, Michael (Michael A.)
    Poststructuralism, politics and education / Michael Peters.
       p.   cm. — (Critical studies in education and culture, ISSN
1064–8615)
    Includes bibliographical references (p.) and index.
    ISBN 0–89789–418–9 (hardcover : alk. paper). — ISBN 0–89789–420–0
(pbk. : alk. paper)
    1. Critical pedagogy. 2. Postmodernism. 3. Politics and
education. 4. Philosophy, French—20th century. I. Title.
II. Series: Critical studies in education and culture series.
LC196.P48   1996
370.11'5—dc20   95–36905

British Library Cataloguing in Publication Data is available.

Library of Congress Catalog Card Number: 95–36905
ISBN: 0–89789–418–9
      0–89789–420–0 (pbk.)
ISSN: 1064–8615

First published in 1996

Bergin & Garvey, 88 Post Road West, Westport, CT 06881
An imprint of Greenwood Publishing Group, Inc.

Printed in the United States of America

The paper used in this book complies with the
Permanent Paper Standard issued by the National
Information Standards Organization (Z39.48–1984).

10 9 8 7 6 5 4 3 2 1

Copyright Acknowledgments

The author and publisher gratefully acknowledge permission to use excerpts from the following material.

Michael Peters (1993) "Against Finkielkraut's *La Défaite de la pensée*: Culture, Post-modernism and Education," *French Cultural Studies*, IV: 91–106.

James Marshall and Michael Peters (1990) "Empowering Teachers," *Unicorn, 16,* 3:163–168.

Thomas Pavel (1989) "The Present Debate: News from France," *Diacritics, XIX,* 1. Published with permission from Polity Press.

From *The Glass Bead Game* by Hermann Hesse, translated by Richard and Clara Winston. Copyright © 1969 by Henry Holt and Co., Inc. Reprinted by permission of Henry Holt and Co. Inc. Permission for British Commonwealth granted by Jonathan Cape and the estate of Hermann Hesse.

Alain Finkielkraut (1988) *The Undoing of Thought.* trans. Dennis O'Keeffe. London: The Claridge Press.

From *The Defeat of the Mind* by Alain Finkielkraut. Copyright © 1995. Reprinted with permission of the publisher, Columbia University Press.

Mark Poster (1992) "Postmodernity and the Politics of Multiculturalism: The Lyotard-Habermas Debate Over Social Theory," *Modern-Fiction Studies, 38,* 3: 567–580.

Graham Burchell (1993) "Liberal Government and Techniques of the Self," *Economy and Society, 22,* 3: 267–282. Published with permission of Routledge.

Michael Geyer (1993) "Multiculturalism and the Politics of General Education," *Critical Inquiry, 9,* Spring: 499–533. Published with permission of the University of Chicago Press.

Gilles Deleuze (1992) "Postscript on the Societies of Control," *October, 59*: 3–7.

Detlev J. K. Peukert (1993) "The Genesis of the 'Final Solution' from the Spirit of Science." In T. Childers and J. Caplan (eds.), *Reevaluating the Third Reich,* London and New York: Holmes & Meier: 234–252. Copyright © 1993 by Holmes & Meier Publishers, Inc. Reprinted by permission of the publisher.

Gianni Vattimo (1992) *The Transparent Society,* trans. D. Webb. Baltimore: Johns Hopkins University Press. Published with permission of Johns Hopkins University Press and Polity Press.

Gianni Vattimo (1992) "The End of (Hi)story." In Ingeborg Hoesterey (Ed.), *Zeitgeist in Babel: The Postmodernist Controversy* (pp. 132–143). Bloomington and Indianapolis: Indiana University Press.

Michael Peters (1995) "'After Auschwitz': Ethics and Educational Policy," *Discourse, 16,* 1.

Michael Peters (1994) "Habermas, Poststructuralism and the Question of Postmodernity," *Social Analysis, 36,* October: 3–20.

Michael Peters (1992) "Intellectuals?" *Sites, 24,* Autumn: 21–42.

Michael Peters (1995) "Radical Democracy, the Politics of Difference and Education." In Barry Kanpol and Peter McLaren (eds.), *Critical Multiculturalism: Uncommon Voices in a Common Struggle* (pp. 43–53). Westport, CT: Bergin & Garvey. An imprint of Greenwood Publishing Group, Inc., Westport, CT.

Michael Peters (1994) "Governmentalidade Neoliberal e Educacao." In Tomaz Tadeu da Silva. *O Sujeito de Educacao, Estudos Foucaultianos.* Rio de Janeiro: Editora Vozes.

Michael Peters (1995) "Vattimo, Postmodernity and the Transparent Society," *Scottish Journal of Philosophy, Spring / Summer,* 6: 6–12.

Contents

Contents

Series Foreword

Within the last decade, the debate over the meaning and purpose of education has occupied the center of political and social life in the United States. Dominated largely by an aggressive and ongoing attempt by various sectors of the Right, including fundamentalists, nationalists, and political conservatives, the debate over educational policy has been organized around a set of values and practices that take as their paradigmatic model the laws and ideology of the marketplace and the imperatives of a newly emerging cultural traditionalism. In the first instance, schooling is being redefined through a corporate ideology that stresses the primacy of choice over community, competition over cooperation and excellence over equity. At stake here is the imperative to organize public schooling around the related practices of competition, reprivatization, standardization and individualism.

In the second instance, the New Right has waged a cultural war against schools as part of a wider attempt to contest the emergence of new public cultures and social movements that have begun to demand that schools take seriously the imperatives of living in a multiracial and multicultural democracy. The contours of this cultural offensive are evident in the call by the Right for standardized testing, the rejection of multiculturalism and the development of curricula around what is euphemistically called a "common culture." In this perspective, the notion of a common culture serves as a referent to denounce any attempt by subordinate groups to challenge the narrow ideological and political parameters by which such a culture both defines and expresses itself. It is not too surprising that the theoretical and political distances between defining schools around a common culture and denouncing cultural differences as the enemy of democratic life are relatively short indeed.

This debate is important not simply because it makes visible the role that schools play as sites of political and cultural contestation but also because it is within this debate that the notion of the United States as an open and democratic society is being questioned and redefined. Moreover, this debate provides a challenge to progressive educators both in and outside of the United States to address a number of conditions central to a postmodern world. First, public schools cannot be seen as either objective or neutral. As institutions actively involved in constructing political subjects and presupposing a vision of the future, they must be dealt with in terms that are simultaneously historical, critical and transformative. Second, the relationship between knowledge and power in schools places undue emphasis on disciplinary structures and on individual achievement as the primary unit of value. Critical educators need a language that emphasizes how social identities are constructed within unequal relations of power in the schools and how schooling can be organized through interdisciplinary approaches to learning and cultural differences that address the dialectical and multifaceted experiences of everyday life. Third, the existing cultural transformation of American society into a multiracial and multicultural society structured in multiple relations of domination demands that we address how schooling can become sites for cultural democracy rather than channeling colonies reproducing new forms of nativism and racism. Finally, critical educators need a new language that takes seriously the relationship between democracy and the establishment of those teaching and learning conditions that enable forms of self and social determination in students and teachers. This suggests not only new forms of self-definition for human agency; it also points to redistributing power within the school and between the school and the larger society.

Critical Studies in Education and Culture is intended as both a critique and a positive response to these concerns and the debates from which they emerge. Each volume is intended to address the meaning of schooling as a form of cultural politics, and cultural work as a pedagogical practice that serves to deepen and extend the possibilities of democratic public life. Broadly conceived, some central considerations present themselves as defining concerns of the series. Within the last decade, a number of new theoretical discourses and vocabularies have emerged that challenge the narrow disciplinary boundaries and theoretical parameters that construct the traditional relationship among knowledge, power and schooling. The emerging discourses of feminism, postcolonialism, literary studies, cultural studies and postmodernism have broadened our understanding of how schools work as sites of containment and possiblity. No longer content to view schools as objective institutions engaged in the transmission of an unproblematic cultural heritage, the new discourses illuminate how schools function as cultural sites actively engaged in the production of not only knowledge but also social identities. *Critical Studies in Education and Culture* will attempt to encourage this type of analysis by emphasizing how schools might be addressed as border institutions or sites of crossing actively involved in exploring, reworking and translating the ways in which culture is produced, negotiated and rewritten.

Emphasizing the centrality of politics, culture and power, *Critical Studies in Education and Culture* will deal with pedagogical issues that contribute in novel ways to our understanding of how critical knowledge, democratic values and social practices can provide a basis for teachers, students and other cultural workers to redefine their role as engaged and public intellectuals.

As part of a broader attempt to rewrite and refigure the relationship between education and culture, *Critical Studies in Education and Culture* is interested in work that is interdisciplinary and critical, and addresses the emergent discourses on gender, race, sexual preference, class, ethnicity and technology. In this respect, the series is dedicated to opening up new discursive and public spaces for critical interventions into schools and other pedagogical sites. To accomplish this, each volume will attempt to rethink the relationship between language and experience, pedagogy and human agency and ethics and social responsiblity as part of a larger project for engaging and deepening the prospects of democratic schooling in a multiracial and multicultural society. Concerns central to this series include addressing the political economy and deconstruction of visual, aural and printed texts, issues of difference and multiculturalism, relationships between language and power, pedagogy as a form of cultural politics and historical memory and the construction of identity and subjectivity.

Critical Studies in Education and Culture is dedicated to publishing studies that move beyond the boundaries of traditional and existing critical discourses. It is concerned with making public schooling a central expression of democratic culture. In doing so it emphasizes works that combine cultural politics, pedagogical criticism, and social analyses with self-reflective tactics that challenge and transform those configurations of power that characterize the existing system of education and other public cultures.

Henry A. Giroux

Preface

A preface is normally an opportunity for an author to provide a commentary or reflection upon a completed text, mentioning circumstances outside the text and external exigences that impinged upon its writing. It is literally a "pretext" for discussion of metatextual matters, including writing strategies and the organization of the book, sometimes including a list of acknowledgments and a probing of motivations. Following this convention I want to comment upon why I came to write this book, its thematic structure and the specific conditions of its production.

There is an increasing range of books available in English that provide an introduction to the concerns of poststructuralism or contemporary French thought. My concern with such texts is that they often tend, against the theoretical impulses of diverging lines of contemporary French thought, to either reduce a complex skein of thinking to a single methodology based upon a number of steps or provide a linear chronology of intellectual developments. The first extinguishes the *différend* (to use Jean-François Lyotard's term) that exists between the writings that make up the canon of what is called "poststructuralism." The second falls into the trap of establishing both a totalizing history effecting a sense of closure and an institutionalization of thought. I have tried to avoid these tendencies although their inescapable traces remain as part and parcel of the conventions that comprise the present economy of writing and publishing based on the organization and standardization of writing space. What I present here is a series of chapters, which were written at different times, often for specific audiences, revised and organized thematically around the central focus of education. I make no claims to their originality, comprehensiveness or completeness. Certainly, they are not intended to constitute a systematic introduction to the concerns of so-called French theory, nor do they pretend to have the last word. Rather, these chapters are intended as a network of ideas that thematically crisscross each other to elucidate a set of relations between poststructuralism, politics and education. In so doing they reflect my intellectual preoccupations of the past few years.

In educational theory a great deal has been written recently on social, economic and political movements predominately in Western or developed societies that have been referred to essentially in negative and reactive terms characterized by the prefix "post" — postindustrial-ism, postmodernism, post-Fordism. While much current theorizing in education has drawn upon poststructuralist approaches — deconstruc-tionism, genealogy, various forms of discourse analysis — there are few general attempts to spell out the implications of poststructuralism for educational theory by attention to the original writings that comprise the canon. This book provides something of an introduction to post-structuralism by examining a range of interrelated themes central to the field of education focusing upon the critique of reason and the problematic of the subject.

This book does not attempt to provide a systematic introduction to poststructuralism as a theory for the simple reason that what has been called poststructuralism in the academy is in reality a diverse and complex tradition of thought incapable of reduction to a stable and coherent body of theory. In fact, one might argue that once the movement has been reduced and unified, packaged into academic texts for ease of dissemination and distribution in the intellectual market-place, its time will be over. Once institutionalized and commodified, knowledge loses its power to generate new thought; it becomes fossilized and relegated to the status of the history of ideas. The label "poststructuralism" is itself a problematic one because the differences among those thinkers loosely described as poststructuralist are as important as the similarities. Accordingly, I have chosen to view poststructuralism as much a moment of French cultural history as a characterization of a distinctive critical approach in education.

Acknowledgments

There is a large number of people who have in one way or another helped me shape my ideas. James Marshall, with whom I had the pleasure of working over the last 15 years, bears at least some of the responsibility for initially recruiting me from the discipline of philosophy to the field of education. In ways too numerous to mention, he has provided intellectual support and companionship. Both Peter McLaren and Henry Giroux have provided support for the publication of this book. Colin Lankshear and Eric Brathwaite, past colleagues from the University of Auckland, helped teach me the importance of the politics of education. More recently, Bill Readings provided a constant source of inspiration and support. His tragic and untimely death in October 1994 prevented me from meeting with him when I was recently on academic leave in Canada and the United States. In recognition of his help, I have dedicated the penultimate chapter to Bill — a chapter based on a seminar Bill arranged for me to give at the Department of Comparative Literature, the University of Montreal, in December 1994.

I am also indebted to Mark Poster. His early work on contemporary French thought I studied as a graduate student. His recent works, including *The Mode of Information* and *The Second Media Age*, have greatly influenced my thinking and provide a model of clarity to which I aspire. My intellectual debt to Jean-François Lyotard is obvious from even a cursory reading of the pages that follow. His *The Postmodern Condition*, when first published in English in 1984, struck me as providing the most perspicacious account of our contemporary situation. I have now studied his work for over a decade; his style of philosophizing continues to open up new spaces for thinking.

I also acknowledge the encouragement of my colleagues and students of the Cultural and Policy Studies Group in the Education Department at the University of Auckland for their willingness to listen and to discuss many of the arguments and ideas presented here. I thank the Research Committee of Auckland University for granting me academic leave in 1994, which gave me the necessary space to complete the manuscript.

Finally, I thank Tina Besley, my partner, who gave me a great deal of support and encouragement for my academic interests during the last three years.

Introduction:
The Critique of Reason

Poststructuralist thought has its origins in Alexandre Kojève's and Jean Hyppolite's existentialist readings of G.W.F. Hegel and is foreshadowed in the structuralism of Jacques Lacan, Roman Jakobson, Claude Lévi-Strauss and others. Here the master discipline is linguistics (following Ferdinand de Saussure) in both its structuralist and poststructuralist modes and in its seemingly endless developments and theoretical refinements of analysis: semiotics, schizoanalysis, deconstructionism and discourse analysis. Poststructuralism, evidenced in the work of Jacques Derrida, Jean-François Lyotard, Michel Foucault, Gilles Deleuze and Jean Baudrillard, for instance, surfaces in the late 1960s to flourish in the French-speaking world in the 1970s and in anglophone culture in the 1980s. It is a complex skein of thought that draws its inspiration from a variety of souces: the tradition of structural linguistics, Friedrich Nietzsche's critique of occidental rationality and his attack on the Hegelian dialectic, Martin Heidegger's "destruction" of Western metaphysics, the epistemology of Gaston Bachelard and George Canguilhem, the surrealism of André Breton, and the European avant-garde more generally. These various strands of thought, as they are developed in various ways by poststructuralist thinkers, together constitute a reappraisal of the culture of the Enlightenment and its notion of a universal reason. Sabina Lovibond captures this point very clearly, although she conflates "postmodernism" and poststructuralism.[1]

The Enlightenment pictured the human race as engaged in an effort towards universal moral and intellectual self-realization, and so as the subject of a universal historical experience; it also postulated a universal human *reason* in terms of which social and political tendencies could be assessed as "progressive" or otherwise (the goal of politics being defined as the realization of reason in practice). Postmodernism rejects this picture: that is to say, it rejects the doctrine of the unity of reason. It refuses to conceive of humanity as a unitary subject striving towards the goal of perfect coherence (in its common stock of beliefs) or of perfect cohesion and stability (in its political practice). (Lovibond, 1986, p. 6)

The plurality of *reasons* — irreducible, incommensurable and related to specific genres, types of discourse and epistemes — is pitted against the Enlightenment claim to universality and the conception of a unified human reason, which, as the sole standard of rationality, allegedly underwrites all knowledge claims, irrespective of time and place, and provides the ground for the unitary subject considered as the agent of historically progressive change.

Lovibond's deceptively simple statement captures the modernist dream of "educating reason," of a universal education based on universal methods equally applicable to all nations and cultures and of a mass education operating on the principle of merit that would equip individuals with the necessary skills, attitudes and attributes to become useful citizens and good workers. Her statement also captures something of the liberal and Marxist progressive themes of Enlightenment thought based on appeals to freedom and equality organized and effected through the education of reason. The postmodern skepticism toward the Enlightenment notion of subject-centered reason recognized by Lovibond is represented explicitly by the poststructuralist critique of reason and, perhaps, most easily recognized in terms of Lyotard's (1984) typification of the postmodern attitude as an "incredulity towards metanarratives." The critique of reason centrally is a critique of education based upon Enlightenment ideals. Lyotard's *The Postmodern Condition*, a book that crystallized a form of the French critique of reason following a Kantian and Wittgensteinian line of thought, was first published in France in 1979, and was subsequently published in English in 1984. Lyotard's *The Postmodern Condition* is, above all, a critique of Enlightenment metanarratives or *grand récits*. He argues that claims for their alleged totality, universality and absolutist status in effect render these notions ahistorical, as though their formation took place outside of history and of social practice. Lyotard wants to question the dogmatic basis of these Enlightenment metanarratives, their "terroristic" and violent nature, which, in asserting certain "Truths" from the perspective of one discourse, does so only by silencing or excluding statements from another.

Lyotard, in a now often quoted passage, uses the term "modern": "to designate any science that legitimates itself with reference to a metadiscourse . . . making an explicit appeal to some grand narrative, such as the dialectics of the Spirit, the hermeneutics of meaning, the emancipation of the rational or working subject, or the creation of wealth" (Lyotard 1984, p. xxiii).

In contrast, he defines "postmodern" elliptically as "incredulity towards metanarratives," by which he means to point to "the obsolescence of the metanarrative apparatus of legitimation," to which corresponds "the crisis of metaphysical philosophy and of the university institution" (p. xxiv). Lyotard (1984) challenges the two grand Hegelian metanarratives: the emancipation of humanity and the speculative unity of knowledge. Lyotard's indirect assault is against the concept of "totality" — he elsewhere announces "a war against totality" — and the notion of autonomy as it underlies the sovereign subject. While Lyotard returns to Kant and Wittgenstein to mount his argument against a monocultural and universal reason, the attack on occidental rationality originates with Nietzsche, which serves as a source of inspiration for poststructuralism. Lyotard's notion of the *différend* clearly bears a family resemblance to Derrida's notion of *différance* and Foucault's *genealogy*.

One of the inaugurating moments of poststructuralism is surely Deleuze's *Nietzsche and Philosophy* (1983), originally published in 1962; both Derrida and Foucault occupy a strategic relation to Nietzsche. At one point Derrida, for instance, is driven to write, in the now famous essay "Différance": "Is not all of Nietzsche's thought a critique of philosophy as an active indifference to difference, as the system of adiaphoristic reduction or repression?" (1982a, p. 17). While other poststructuralists read Nietzsche in the late 1950s and early 1960s and interpreted him as a means to escape Hegelianism and Marxism — a matter I discuss fully in Chapter 1 — Foucault studied Nietzsche in the early 1950s and used his work to displace the constitutive subject of phenomenology. Although he wrote very little directly concerned with Nietzsche's work ("Nietzsche, Genealogy, History" is his best-known piece), a number of scholars view Foucault as Nietzschean through and through. Michael Mahon, for example, begins his major study of Foucault with the following remark: "Foucault saw himself in the tradition that extends from Hegel through Nietzsche and Max Weber to the Frankfurt School and more generally in the tradition of anti-Platonism" (1992, p. ix). Whatever the interpretation of Foucault regarding Nietzsche, it is clear that Nietzsche's critique of reason is fundamental to poststructuralism.

Magnus Bernd (1989) usefully interprets postmodern philosophy or criticism within the interpretive space of a cluster of concepts originating with Nietzsche: a putative anti (or post) epistemological standpoint, antiessentialism, antirealism about meaning and reference, antifoundationalism, a suspicion of transcendental arguments and viewpoints, the rejection of the picture of knowledge as accurate representation, the rejection of truth as correspondence to reality, the rejection of canonical descriptions and final vocabularies and, finally, a suspicion of metanarratives.

He characterizes postmodern philosophy as insisting on the fact that all vocabularies are optional and contingent, drawing a moral from the history of our own philosophical practice: "The history of philosophy counts against the metaphysical realist precisely because there is not now nor has there ever been a canonical consensus on *any* 'philosophical' question" (Bernd, 1989, p. 304). He identifies seven themes central to Nietzsche's writings which, taken collectively, may be thought of as elective affinities that have helped to shape postmodern discourse either directly — as in the case of Heidegger, Derrida, Foucault, Lyotard, Paul de Man, Deleuze and Felix Guattari — or indirectly, as in the case of Hans-Georg Gadamer, Jürgen Habermas, Richard Rorty, Wilfred Sellars, Willard van Quine, Paul Feyerabend and Hilary Putnam. He specifies these seven elective affinities as: perspectivism; the diagnosis and critique of binarism, along with the metaphysics of presence; the substitution of genealogical narratives for ontology; a diagnosis of the power-knowledge connection, as well as the structures of ideological domination; an erasing of the boundaries between philosophy and literature; the disarticulation of the self; and the self-consuming, self-deconstructing character of Nietzsche's own discourse and categories.

A number of these Nietzschean features are already evident in the critique of the culture of the Enlightenment undertaken by Max Horkheimer and Theodor Adorno, the founding fathers of the Frankfurt School, in their book *Dialectic of Enlightenment*. The Nietzschean influence upon Horkheimer and Adorno is evident in their analysis of the "dark side" of the Enlightenment, which, in their interpetation, has lost its liberating force and relapsed into mythology: they argue, "Myth is already enlightenment; and enlightenment reverts to mythology" (1972, p. xvi). Reason stripped of its normative aspects surfaces as modern science, which is best exemplified in terms of logical positivism — a scientific reason interested only in questions of pure technical utility. This analysis, of course, is the basis of the critique of instrumental reason in Horkheimer and Adorno. In cultural modernity, reason has been assimilated into sheer power and enlightenment has been reduced to a form of domination over an external world. Art has become a form of infotainment in the development of mass culture and thereby loses all critical force. It is perhaps no surprise, then, that Foucault situated himself in relation to the tradition of Critical Theory or that numbers of commentators have drawn strong parallels between the preoccupations of poststructuralism and the founding fathers of the Frankfurt School.

Adorno begins the first chapter of his *Against Epistemology*, based on a manuscript produced at Oxford during the first years of his emigration (1934–37), with the following statement:

Since Descartes' time a contradiction has come to the fore in the relations between philosophy and the sciences, though it was already implicit in Aristotle. Philosophy seeks to think the unconditioned, to transcend positivity and the accepted existence of sciences . . . and to contrast the scientific domain with the unfettered truth. Yet philosophy takes science as its model. . . . The possibility of metaphysics as a science is a transcription not merely of the themes of the Kantian critique of reason as epistemology. It also points up the impulse behind modern philosophy as a whole. (1982, p. 48)

Against Epistemology aims to broach the question of "the possibility and truth of epistemology in principle" (Adorno, 1982, p. 1) through a critique of Husserl's phenomenology. Later, after World War II and repatriation to Germany to found the Frankfurt School, Horkheimer and Adorno (1972) were driven to abandon Marxist social theory for a total critique of the Enlightenment. They were in step with very different philosophical tendencies — Heidegger's (conservative) "destruction" of Western metaphyics and the radical Cercle Communiste Democratique, founded by Georges Bataille. David Ingram states: "These too drew inspiration from Nietzsche's critique of occidental rationality, but differed from critical theory in their rejection of the bourgeois ideal of emancipation and self-realization" (1987, p. 75). He claims that poststructuralist thought is informed by the Nietzschean dream of overcoming modernity in an anarchistic, aesthetic avant-garde that, in the will to power, forges its own values and projects its own interpretations onto an otherwise chaotic experience. Poststructural thought maintains that the cultural value of the Enlightenment — and of the process of modernization — linking subjective freedom to a "scientific" reason "conceals a will to power that ultimately binds the individual to the technological apparatus."

Derrida recasts the critique of reason and metaphysics in terms of structural linguistics. Focusing on an essay, little known and unpublished during Nietzsche's lifetime ("Truth and Morality in an Extramoral Sense," 1873), Derrida, in effect, fuses Nietzsche's attack on the correspondence theory of truth with Saussurean linguistics. The arbitrary relationship of signifier to signified is the central epistemological insight that inspires a view of language as an endless chain of signifiers, a completely enclosed, self-referential system of signs that is cut off from presenting the world. Such a view involves the radical decentering of the subject in relation to language, because "the subject, and first of all the conscious and speaking subject, depends upon the system of differences and the movement of *différance*" (Derrida, 1981, p. 29).

Derrida claims that the illusion of Western metaphysics is grounded in a logocentrism that has privileged speech over writing. In *Of Grammatology* Derrida (1976, p. 3) focuses our attention on the ethnocentrism that has controlled the concept of writing. Logocentrism

— the metaphysics of phonetic writing — Derrida claims is "nothing but the most original and powerful ethnocentrism," which has controlled the concept of writing, the history of metaphysics (assigning the origin of truth to the logos) and the concept of science (which has always been determined as logic). Grammatology — the science of writing — glimpses the closure of a historical-metaphysical epoch that privileges the meaning of being in general as presence — a self-identical, transparent self-presence. In the Western tradition, "the formal essence of the signified is *presence* and the privilege of its proximity to the logos as *phonè* is the privilege of presence" (1976, p. 18). Following Nietzsche and Heidegger, Derrida attempts to demonstrate that writing is not subordinate to the logos or to truth: "this subordination has *come into being* during an epoch whose meaning we must deconstruct" (1976, p. 19). Philosophy in one form or another has tried to freeze the play of *différance*: clear and distinct ideas, ideal Platonic forms, an ultimate referent or "transcendental signified" (Being), absolute knowledge, the logical form of propositions, and so on — all devised to freeze meaning and its circulation within closed systems of truth. But such closure, Derrida argues, is impossible because philosophy cannot reach outside language. The claim to have done so rests on excluding or assimilating whatever escapes the grids of intelligibility it imposes on the movement of *différance*. In Derrida's eyes, philosophy, as a kind of writing, is essentially predicated on logo- and homocentric illusions that deny the play of *différance*.

While poststructuralism is opposed to many of the things that the Frankfurt School and Jürgen Habermas oppose — in particular, the bureaucratic colonialization of the life-world and the subordination and assimilation of dissident subcultures to the dominant scientific culture — it "blames this impulse toward systemic closure and social homogeneity on the rational demand for unity, purity, objectivity, universality, and ultimacy" (Ingram, 1987, pp. 77, 78). This is, in part, the alleged basis for Habermas' claim that the French poststructuralists juxtapose to instrumental reason "a principle only accessible through evocation, be it the will to power or sovereignty, Being or the dionysiac force of the poetical" (1981a, p. 13). Habermas attributes the term "postmodernity" to the French current of thought, the tradition, as he says, "running from Bataille to Derrida by way of Foucault" (it is to this line that Lyotard also belongs), and he compares the critique of reason of these French philosophers to the "Young Conservatives" of the Weimar Republic: "The *Young Conservatives* recapitulate the basic experience of aesthetic modernity. They claim as their own the revelations of a decentered subjectivity, emancipated from the imperatives of work and usefulness, and with this experience they step outside the modern world" (1981a, p. 13).

Habermas may be astray in christening Foucault "a postmodernist." Foucault, in an interview with Gérard Raulet, professes not to understand what either the term "modernity" (at least, after Baudelaire) or "postmodernity" means or what kind of problem is common to postmodern or poststructuralist thinkers. His interviewer, Raulet, however, has no such problem. In putting the question to Foucault of whether he belongs to such a current, Raulet sketches his own understanding of postmodernity: "It is the idea of modernity, of reason, we find in Lyotard: a 'grand narrative' from which we have finally been freed by a kind of salutory awakening. Postmodernity is a breaking apart of reason; Deleuzian schizophrenia. Postmodernity reveals, at last, that reason has only been one narrative among others in history; a grand narrative, certainly, but one of many, which can now be followed by other narratives" (1983, p. 205).

While Foucault professes not to understand the problem behind postmodernism, his sympathetic critics certainly take him to be a poststructuralist/postmodernist thinker who, along with Derrida and Lyotard, teaches that the values of the modern era were essentially logo- and homocentric illusions. Certainly both Mark Poster (1981) and Nancy Fraser (1981) understand Foucault's examination of "the philosophy of the subject" — by which he means a *problematique* dominating the modern *épistème* that privileges the subject as the foundation of all knowledge and signification — as bearing centrally on discussions of modernity. Both argue that Foucault's genealogical analysis of modern power operates on the basis of a radical decentering that denies an epistemic or historical privilege to either the traditional Cartesian notion of a "centered" subjectivity or the humanist ideal of a rational, autonomous and responsible self. Poster, for instance, writes: "In place of the continuous chronology of reason ... there have appeared scales that are sometimes very brief, distinct from one another, irreducible to a single law, scales that bear a type of history peculiar to each one, and which cannot be reduced to the general model of consciousness that acquires, progresses and remembers" (1981, p. 138).

They understand that Foucault's method allows us to see power very broadly in the development of a plurality of incommensurable discursive regimes, each with its multiplicity of "micropractices," which ultimately directs us to study the "politics of everyday life" and suspends the problematic of legitimacy understood in terms of the standard modern liberal normative framework with its talk of rights grounded as it is in the nature of persons.

The issue between Habermas and Foucault, at least as Habermas sees it, concerns their respective evaluations of modernity. Habermas, locating himself in the tradition of Marxist social criticism reflected in the work of the Frankfurt School, argues that we should attempt to preserve the "emancipatory impulse" behind the Enlightenment:

The project aims at a differentiated relinking of modern culture with an everyday praxis that still depends on vital heritages ... this new connection, however, can only be established under the conditions, that societal modernization will also be steered in a different direction. The life-world has to become able to develop institutions out of itself which sets limits to the internal dynamics and to the imperatives of an almost autonomous economic system and its administrative complements. (Habermas, 1981a, p. 19)

In contrast, he sites Foucault and Lyotard in a tradition of a line of thinkers, including Nietzsche, Heidegger and the French poststructuralists, who wish for a total break with the Enlightenment, and thereby allegedly criticize the very constitutive norms of modernity that make critique possible. The problem that Habermas identifies is that Nietzsche's critique of reason involves a criticism and rejection of the constitutive norms of modernity — truth, rationality and freedom. These are the very norms, Habermas claims, that alone make critique possible. In other words, Nietzsche's critique of reason faces a self-referential paradox and is unable to appeal to reason in order to legitimate itself on rational grounds.

The problem over rationality between Habermas and Lyotard is explained further by Rorty:

From Lyotard's point of view, Habermas is offering one more metanarrative, a more general and abstract "narrative of emancipation" than the Freudian and Marxian metanarratives. For Habermas, the problem posed by "incredulity towards metanarratives" is that unmasking only makes sense if we "preserve at least one standard for (the) explanation of the corruption of all reasonable standards". If we have no such standard, one which escapes a "totalising self-referential critique", then distinctions between the naked and the masked, or between theory and ideology, lose their force. (1985, p. 163)

Habermas argues that to accept Lyotard's argument would be to strip ideology-critique of its principal function. Unless there is a universal metadiscourse, the possibility of legitimizing validity claims in a theoretical manner disappears. Yet for Lyotard, seemingly, the very opposite appears to be the case. Universal metadiscourses cannot theoretically effect a closure: practically and empirically they betray their own ahistoricism in the experiences of recent contemporary history (e.g., the Gulags, Auschwitz, May 1968). As van Reijen comments, "Lyotard accuses Habermas of wanting to revive the terror of reason" (1988, p. 97).

French poststructuralism, David Wellbery argues, thus involves a rejection of the narrative of history "conceived as the story of a single logical-temporal movement that embraces and renders intelligible all individual histories" (1985). It is a view of history that arises in the eighteenth century with the work of Kant, Herder, Condorcet and Hegel. Significantly, Habermas sees his work as a continuation of this tradition.

In France, by contrast, Wellbery maintains that this narrative of history is viewed with extreme skepticism. It is seen rather as "a ploy, an ideology, the very function of which is to deny the reality of history in order to celebrate such mythical heroes as Man, Reason or Consciousness." The rejection by French poststructuralists of a philosophy of history is a rejection of a philosophy that has dominated Western thinking since the Enlightenment.

From the vantage point of poststructuralist thought, the classical philosophy of history, which has since the Enlightenment presented itself as the ultimate horizon of all interpretations, appears simply as *one* way of making sense among others. It functions as myth describing the progress of a universal subject — "the hero of knowledge and of liberty" — and serves to legitimate and to protect from criticism a specific set of cultural values that are deeply embedded in the West. Wellbery comments further:

Whether these values are defined as the foundational concepts of the discourse of metaphysics since Plato, as in the case of Derrida, or as the elements of the anthropological humanism that developed in the late eighteenth century, as in the case of Foucault and Lyotard, matters little. The essential point is the shared rejection of the Great Narrative, a rejection that is by no means a flight from the historical world, but rather the first step toward comprehending our historicity without mythical distortion. (1985, p. 233)

Habermas' (1981a) rhetoric, it is argued, disguises the real philosophical differences between himself and the French poststructuralists, which concern the theme of discourse and ultimately views on the nature of language itself. Wellbery claims it is hard to imagine a view of language or discourse that is more removed from Habermas' ideal of a universal norm of communicative action, which is said to be immanent in speech itself and which allegedly enables participants to arrive at consensus without distortion or external constraint. Wellbery maintains that all postmodern philosophers "*repudiate the dream of an innocent language*" (1985, p. 233) and contrasts Habermas' modernist, universalist vision of a "noise-free," fully transparent sphere of communication based on consensus with the view of language and discourse developed by the French poststructuralists — a view that investigates the opacities inherent in language and holds that consensus can be established only on the basis of acts of exclusion.

This difficulty, then, goes right to the heart of the issues. It goes to the heart of the polemical debate between poststructuralism and the French critique of reason, on one hand, and Critical Theory, Habermas' "project of modernity" and his goal of preserving the "emancipatory impulse" behind the Enlightenment, on the other. Further, the difficulty and the questions it engenders focus the debate on rationality and respective evaluations of modernity and postmodernity. Foucault's response, based on a reading of one of Kant's minor texts, is to argue that the thread connecting us to the Enlightenment is *not* "faithfulness to doctrinal elements, but rather the permanent reactivation of an attitude — that is, of a philosophical ethos that could be described as a permanent critique of our historical era" (1984, pp. 42–43). Defining the Enlightenment in this way, he suggests, "means precisely that one has to refuse everything that might present itself in the form of a simple and authoritarian alternative. You either accept the Enlightenment and remain within the tradition of rationalism . . . ; or else you criticize the Enlightenment and then try to escape from its principle of rationality."

The debate includes a set of issues intimately connected with the problem of the subject, of subject-centered reason that directly impinges upon the question of education and the functions that it serves. To what extent have education and schooling been shaped by the culture of the Enlightenment? To what extent do modernist educational ideals and the principles and methods of mass schooling depend upon the Enlightenment notions of a universal reason and a universal subject? If modern education has been and is still legitimated by "metanarratives of emancipation" that have been unmasked as ideological, how might education be legitimated in the postmodern condition? Given the poststructuralist critique of reason, what new forms might educational theory take? These questions, which form the substance of this book, can be supplemented by another related but wider set that focuses clearly upon politics and carries strong implications for educational theory. To what extent does the decentering, deconstruction of the subject deny a theory of agency necessary for political change? Does poststructuralism lack a coherent politics? Is it essentially conservative or nihilistic? Relevant to these questions are Fredric Jameson's (1983, 1989a) and David Harvey's (1989) critique of postmodernism as the culture of late consumer capitalism and the critique mounted by feminists (e.g., Mascia-Lees et al., 1989) who argue that postmodernism hypothesizes the "death of the subject" at precisely that point, historically, when others (women, ethnic groups, gays, and so forth) have begun to speak for themselves and to (re)claim themselves as historical subjects. The question of the subject and political agency for the left is, of course, strongly bound to both the Hegelian and Marxist traditions. The poststructuralist critique of the subject, discussed fully in Chapter 1, impinges upon the reevaluations of these traditions and the viability of models of political change and agency. The significance and the consequences of this critique, because it is so recent, are, historically speaking, still being worked through and occasion little agreement.

On the one hand, the effects of a full-fledged historicization of culture and philosophy is lamented by Habermas, who fears that the social hope nurtured by the Enlightenment will disappear. On the other hand, left-wing scholars like Stanley Aronowitz (1983) embrace the historically specific new social pluralism, turning it into an opportunity for the critique of orthodox historical materialism to argue that Marxism has denied its own historicity. Historical events, Aronowitz maintains, have escaped Marxism's basic principles (structured around the paradigm of production), to express a radical heterogeneity of social resistance that can no longer be captured by a single ruling or master discourse of liberation. Aronowitz's revisionism is directed not only at the concept of class (which postulates a transhistorical subject) but also at the scientism which vitiates historical materialism. "My argument may be expressed in one final principle: the counterlogic of the erotic, play, and the constituting subject may not be reduced either to the mode of production of material life or the mode of social reproduction (family, school, or religion in their capacity as ideological apparatuses of the state). Political economy ends when theory seeks to specify the conditions of transformation" (1983, p. 196).

Aronowitz's line of argument is extended in a different direction and given a practical orientation by Iris Marion Young, who relates how the concept of oppression has been used among radicals since the 1960s partly in reaction to some Marxist attempts to reduce the injustices of racism and sexism to the effects of class domination. She argues:

From often heated discussions among socialists, feminists, and anti-racism activists in the last ten years, a consensus is emerging that many different groups must be said to be oppressed in our society, and that no group's form of oppression can claim causal or moral primacy. The same discussion has also come to understand that group differences cross individual lives in a multiplicity of ways that can entail privilege and oppression for the same person in different respects. Only a plural explication of the concept of oppression can appropriately capture these insights. (Young, 1988, p. 276)

She suggests that only a plural concept of oppression can capture such insights, and elaborates "five faces of oppression," including *exploitation, marginalization, powerlessness, cultural imperialism* and *violence*. Limits of space preclude their full explication in this Introduction, but these "faces" are designed to function as criteria of oppression, which "help show that while no group's oppression is reducible to or explained by any other group, the oppression of one group is not a closed system with its own attributes, but overlaps with the oppression of other groups" (Young, 1988, p. 288). This is a theme that I pick up to examine in the final chapter, concerning democracy and the "politics of difference." Young (1992) shows how the ideology of group difference as Otherness exhibits a logic of identity such that it represses difference by asserting a unity that actually generates dichotomies of the included and the excluded. Anna Yeatman (1992), following the same orientation toward a "politics of difference," elaborates a critique of the liberal discourse of citizenship. The ontological approach to citizenship of liberal discourse, she maintains, dictates a notion of civic community based upon the bounded and coherent identity of *one group*. She points out that liberal discourse shares the assimilative ideal with both the republican and welfare state discourses of modern citizenship. The republican ideal postulates a "public" that comes into being through reason, a rational consensus that assimilates substantive cultural differences and denies the hetero-geneity of social life. The welfare state discourse of citizenship identifies "the model citizen with the formal individuality of the rationally-oriented, freely contracting subject" (p. 6), bracketing out interdependence and what is substantively needy about our lives.

More recently, Yeatman has turned her attention to a postmodern revision of the political, arguing that "Where moderns turn their enquiry on the question of the conditions of right reason, postmoderns interrogate the discursive economies of the different versions of right reason that we have inherited" (1994, p. viii). She suggests that postmodern emancipatory politics do not offer a utopian future but rather work to open up new public spaces by contesting the core assumptions and values of discourses of modern democracy, including the construction of the foundations of political communities by reference to an order of being given privileged ontological status, a univocal construction of reason and consensus as a regulative ideal, and the "construction of the subject of politics as subsumable within an uncontested universal and impartial subject" (p. x).

This book is comprised of chapters which, in the main, work directly from first sources, from the texts of French poststructuralist thinkers as they have been translated into English, rather than the large and growing secondary literature utilizing poststructuralist approaches within the field of education. This has been a deliberate decision. I have not, for instance, engaged with the work of Madan Sarup (1993), Rex Gibson (1984) or Cleo Cherryholmes (1988), all of whom have written useful introductions to structuralism or poststructuralism in relation to the study of education. I have not, except in passing, mentioned the substantial feminist literature in education that has adopted poststructuralist approaches, such as Patti Lather's *Getting Smart* (1991). Neither have I attempted to discuss the work of critical educationists, such as Peter McLaren (1989, 1994) who usefully reformulates the project of critical pedagogy in the postmodern condition. My intention has been rather to elucidate some of the main aspects of poststructuralist thinking, providing appropriate historical and philosophical background where necessary, in order to elaborate a series of political themes with special relevance for the field of education: the critique of universal reason and of the subject; the role of intellectuals; the relations between poststructuralism, education and postmodern culture; the neoliberal doctrine of the self-limiting state and its construction of "market" subjects in education; education and the "politics of space"; ethics and education policy "after Auschwitz";

science, education and technology in the information society; the critical role of the mass media in the transition to postmodern society; cybernetics, cyberspace and the university; democracy, education and the politics of difference.

While the overriding impetus of French poststructuralism has been toward general questions concerning the problematic of the subject, politically speaking, much of the emphasis revolved around the escape from certain brands of Hegelian and Marxist thought dominant within postwar French left intellectual culture. My emphasis has been toward marshalling poststucturalist resources for a sustained attack upon and a philosophical critique of neoliberalism, which is the reigning political philosophy in Western liberal-capitalist states, rather than reappraisals of Marxism per se, and I have tended to focus upon the political consequences of the most recent technological developments accompanying the so-called "information society." Frankly, I do not believe that the Marxist tradition is dead or that the power of Marxist political economy has diminished. Nor do I believe that poststructuralism stands opposed to contemporary forms of Marxist analysis. Such alleged opposition is a product of a kind of binary thinking that poststructuralism is an attempt to escape. Certainly, in historical terms it is a product of a particular phase of French intellectual culture in rebelling against the hard-line doctrinaire Stalinist Marxism that prevailed in the immediate postwar environment. Indeed, it is my opinion that there are grounds for a "poststructuralist Marxism," but that is another story and the subject of another book.

Briefly, to recapitulate, my overwhelming emphasis is upon a critique of political reason as it has been construed by contemporary forms of neoliberalism and I have recruited the poststructuralist critique of reason and of the subject as the means to deconstruct and criticize neoliberal constructions of the subject in education and in social policy more broadly. Questions concerning the ideological reproduction of the subject and, in particular, the tremendous conceptual weighting neoliberalism invests in a rejuvenated *Homo economicus* are thrown into sharp relief when investigated against a transformed environment variously referred to as the "information society," "information economy" or "communications society." In this respect the modernity/postmodernity debate, which is best exemplified through the writings of Lyotard and Habermas, constitute an essential aspect of the theoretical background against which I carry out my investigations. This theoretical context brings together the critique of subject-centered reason with the search for viable political forms, and it raises fundamental questions concerning language and communication central to societies obsessed with the speed and efficiency of information exchange. In terms of the debate, as will be clear from what follows, I side with Lyotard against Habermas. While I think that the oppositional tendencies in their thinking has been greatly overplayed both by them and their commentators, the genuine philosophical differences that divide them over the nature of language and the central values of consensus and transparency incline me to Lyotard's position rather than that of Habermas.

The first chapter is both historical and philosophical. It examines the history of poststructuralism in terms of the broader canvas of European formalism, futurism, surrealism and structuralist poetics, following an observation made by Foucault. The chapter's subtitle, "The Games of the Will to Power against the Labor of the Dialectic," taken from a work by Gilles Deleuze, is meant to encapsulate the French Niezschean critique of Hegel as a basis for the "liberation" of the logic of difference and for the poststructuralist reappraisal of the philosophy of the subject.

Deleuze's Nietzschean critique of the Hegelian dialectic is one of the major keys to understanding French poststructuralism and serves as a basis and starting point for an alternative radical theorizing. The chapter provides an introduction to politics of poststructuralism through a critical appreciation of a history of structuralism that is interpreted within the broader horizon of European formalism. The Deleuzean interpretation of Nietzsche is situated within the wider reaction to Hegelianism in contemporary French thought in order to characterize poststructuralism's rejection of the dialectic and the notion of totality. Finally, the chapter indicates the significance of post-structuralist critique of the subject for analyzing contemporary forms of the ideological construction of the liberal subject of education.

The second chapter focuses upon the notion of intellectuals and examines this idea in relation to postmodern culture. I argue that postmodern culture and, in particular, the democratization of (consumer) culture has led to a problematization of the modernist notion of the intellectual, and I briefly examine three poststructuralist accounts of the "intellectual": those given by Foucault, Lyotard and Julia Kristeva. These accounts emphasize a limited, more specific, local role for intellectuals, one sensitive to the institutional sites of power/knowledge that form dominant discourses and regimes of truth. The poststructuralist conception of the specific intellectual presents a politics of intellectuality which recognizes both that the question "who speaks?" is inherently a political one and that "speaking for" is a (representational) act of violence.

The third chapter continues the emphasis on culture to examine one of the most influential and virulent attacks upon postmodern culture and, implicitly, poststructuralism. The decline of the European, universalist, rationalist world-view and the concomitant rise of cultural pluralism signifies for Alain Finkielkraut (1988) the most dangerous trend of modern times. Finkielkraut's *Undoing of Thought* is an attack on the notion of culture that embraces everyday life and practice as against "life with thought" or Enlightenment reason. The latter sense is associated with "the higher life," with the separation of history and reason, with universalist values; the former is both local and particularistic. For Finkielkraut, postmodernism is both fragmentary and inauthentic, leading to a "pedagogy of relativity" and a "raging nihilism" that levels all distinctions between cultures. His complaint against postmodernism is that it no longer sees culture as a means of emancipation or democracy as the access to culture for everybody. On this basis he ascribes "the present crisis" to education, arguing: "The school in the modern sense of that word is a product of the Enlightenment, and it is dying today because the authority of the Enlightenment has been called into question" (Finkielkraut 1988, p. 124).

Finkielkraut's book is also an attack on poststructuralism. He belongs to a group of French neoliberal thinkers who have developed a new philosophical agenda: in the words of Thomas Pavel (1989, p. 20), the end of "nihilism, antihumanism, and the critique of identity and the subject" as viable alternatives for French thought; and a return to individualism and humanism, the recovery of human agency, intentionality and consciousness.

In Chapter 4 I address the neoliberal notion of the "market," utilizing Foucault's work to understand what I call the *paradox* of the neoliberal State: the paradox is that while neoliberalism can be regarded as a doctrine concerning the self-limiting state, under neoliberal market policies the state has become more "powerful." This paradox is approached through Foucault's notion of governmentality, which permits us to view the minimal state as promoting a new form of individualization where human beings turn themselves into market subjects under the sign of *Homo economicus*. This is the basis for understanding the "government of individuals" in education as a technique or form of power that is promoted through the adoption of market forms. Foucault's work can be understood as a critique of the subject and of the liberal metanarrative of the self: an autonomous, rational and full transparent individual self, standing both separate to and logically prior to society, able to make choices in the market in accordance with its desires. The chapter investigates the ways in which education has been discursively restructured under the sign of *Homo economicus* as a form of neoliberal governmentality.

Chapter 5, also taking its inspiration from Foucault, is an attempt to overcome the despatialized nature of critical educational theory. Foucault calls the present epoch the "epoch of space" in contrast to the nineteenth century, which was obsessed with the question of time, and he observes how "disciplinary power" depends upon "a politics of space." I have titled the chapter "Architecture of Resistance," after the architectural theorist Kenneth Frampton, because it seems to me that architectural theory and its metaphors, along with geography, are centrally concerned with questions of space. When it comes to the politics of space, educational theory can learn from these disciplines. The relevance of the politics of space to education, I argue in this chapter, can be illustrated in terms of the "postmodernization" of education based upon understandings of recent conceptions of both postmodern geographies and architectures. The architectural metaphor is important for understanding the way in which educational institutional spaces are built to permit a kind of internal control with the power to transform individuals. That is certainly so because Foucault's disciplinary power is based on the instruments of observation, judgment and examination made possible by institutional architecture designed to permit a kind of knowledge through surveillance. The school, for example, is organized as a spatial mechanism for training the individual, for individualization. In the final section of the chapter I follow Deleuze (1992), who uses the term "societies of control" to denote a set of new forces and processes of free-floating control, which Foucault foresaw as the basis of the immediate future society.

Chapter 6 also bears the unmistakable imprint of Foucault. The theme of the chapter is based on the highly charged metaphor of "after Auschwitz," which, following Adorno and Lyotard, I take to signal a historical watershed in the critical self-understanding of the social sciences as part of the culture of modernity. The phrase "after Auschwitz" serves to emphasize the critical approach I take to the social sciences in relation to ethics and public policy. First, I explore the revival of Holocaust memories and what is known as the "historian's debate." Next, I examine Adorno's and Lyotard's use of "after Auschwitz" as a metaphor that signals, in emblematic fashion, "an incredulity towards metanarratives." Finally, and in terms of this theoretical background, I advance the controversial thesis of the late German social historian, Detlev Peukert (1993), in relation to the history of "social-welfare education" and its contribution to the genesis of the "Final Solution" in the Third Reich. Peukert's work suggests a shift to a paradigm of "biological politics" in the historical under-standing of "Auschwitz" and has significant parallels to Foucault's twin notions of "governmentality" and "bio-power."

Science, education and technology have a special place in the new economic order. Restructured and fully rationalized public good science and state education have been commercialized and commodified in the name of increasing national competitive advantage. Within the infor-mation society, science and education are hypothesized as the principal forces of production. Within the context of transformation wrought by the new information technologies, knowledge becomes an informational commodity indispensable to the economy and the future basis of international competitive advantage. Science and education become the main "knowledge industries" within an "information state." This is the thesis of Chapter 7. The neoliberal discourse of economic rationalism restructures public good science and state education and recuperates it into the economic system as its leading sectors. This chapter begins by scrutinizing the notions of postindustrialism and the information society with the explicit aim of highlighting the political questions it raises for science and education. It provides an account of postmodern science based upon the work of Stephen Toulmin and others, who signal a "reenchantment" of science or a "return to cosmology" in order to argue the case for a view of science inextricably bound up with social, political and ethical responsibilities. The chapter extends the emphasis on the political by examining a poststructuralist account of science in the postmodern condition, drawing particularly on Michel Foucault's "power/knowledge" and Lyotard's thesis in *The Postmodern Condition*. Under the ideology of economic rationalism, science and education are construed as *reasons* of state. Their purposes have been reduced and they have been encompassed by and put in the service of the economic system.

Chapter 8 extends and develops the emphasis on the politics of the information society by examining the work of the Italian postmodern philosopher Gianni Vattimo. Vattimo's work, steeped in interpretations of Heidegger and Nietzsche, is constructed at the intersection between hermeneutics, nihilism, and postmodernity. I have included a chapter on Vattimo because he still sees a residue of foundationalism in Heidegger's "destruction" of Western metaphysics and post-Wittgensteinian analytic philosophy, and he points to hermeneutics as the only nonmetaphysical way of resolving it. In addition, Vattimo identifies a problem in Lyotard's work, namely that the dissolution of metanarratives is itself a kind of metanarrative. The criticism briefly is that Lyotard uses a procedure of *historical* legitimation, and yet Vattimo indicates that this does not entail the rejection of Lyotard's position. Indeed, it is only by recognizing the paradoxical nature of the problem that Habermas' criticisms can be met and the problem of legitimation solved.

This chapter first discusses the "crisis of reason" referred to by Italian philosophers and Vattimo's contribution to this debate — his notion of "weak" reason — before examining his interpretation of the idea of the "end of history." It is in his major recent work *The Transparent Society* that Vattimo (1992) builds upon his thesis of the "end of history" to link the birth of postmodern society with the decisive role that mass media plays in the transition. He argues in the opening pages of *The Transparent Society* that modernity ends when it no longer seems possible to regard history as unilinear. History can no longer be regarded as the progressive realization of emancipation, and the evolutionary assumptions that underlie a view of the West as the apex of civilization to date have become problematic. Vattimo reasons that the mass media do not make society more "transparent." On the contrary, they make society more "chaotic," and in this relative "chaos"

— a profusion of multiple perspectives — our present hopes for emancipation lie. This is a view that he tracks out by reference to the role of the human sciences in a "communicational" society, a view that has obvious consequences for educational theory.

The theme of communication and the dream of a universal language constitutes the subject-matter of Chapter 9, which I investigate in terms of the metaphor of Hermann Hesse's *The Glass Bead Game*. Specifically, I use this metaphor as a framework to examine the place of the university in the cultural history of symbolic logic and cybernetics, both of which underlie the present incipient development of the "mode of information" — to employ Mark Poster's (1990) characterization — "the Information Superhighway" and "cyberspace." I treat these new information technologies as aspects of late modernity. The central symbolism of *The Glass Bead Game* squarely relates to the modernist dream of a universal language, a form of symbolic exchange guided by the telos of consensus and is clearly much closer to Habermas' "ideal speech community" based upon the stable bourgeois subject than to Lyotard's conception of the *différend* and multiple, hybrid, cultural subject-positions. Hesse's *The Glass Bead Game* belongs to the tradition of the German *Bildungsroman*, and it is no accident that the ethos of the German educational tradition historically defined by the *Bildungsroman* informs Habermas' conception of a humanist pedagogy and the ideal of the liberal university based on the stability of the universal subject of communication.

The metaphor of *The Glass Bead Game* is used as a cultural lens for investigating the dream of a universal language and for examining, in more practical terms, the place of the university in cyberspace. Recently, strong claims have been made for the remarkable convergence of democracy, technology and the university curriculum (Lanham, 1993). These claims require the most careful evaluation. This literary excursus is also designed to demonstrate that educational theory can benefit from forms of literary analysis and theory as much as from "scientific" pursuits.

The introduction of the new information technologies has brought about the age of telepolitics: a new media-based mode of electoral politics based on intensive public opinion polling and the techniques of mass marketing. Democracy has become commodified, public opinion has been privatized, the potential for active participation in the political process has been minimized and public education as the means for pursuing the social goals of democracy has been greatly compromised. It is the media-based apparatus of the Right that has been so influential in politicizing American higher education by shifting the emphasis in politics away from an exclusive focus on the economy to questions of culture. In the final chapter I turn to, perhaps, *the* question of the day in American higher education — multiculturalism — to examine the variety of political positions taken on this issue. I trace the emergence of cultural conservatism and claims concerning the notion of "political correctness" in the American academy. I examine the "new liberal alliance," focusing on Charles Taylor's (1994) important essay on the "politics of recognition," comparing it to claims made on behalf of the new cultural "politics of difference." The force of my argument is that the communitarian project to reform liberalism has been unsuccessful precisely to the extent that it has ignored the poststructuralist critique of subject-centred reason, although I point out, following Mark Poster (1992), that the alliance between "postmodernists" and "multiculturalists" is also a troubled one, troubled to the point that either position can free itself from the politics of the Enlightenment.

NOTE

1.   The uses of the terms "postmodernism" and "poststructuralism" are now so commonly conflated that I have not bothered to consistently differentiate throughout the text. To some degree the matter is further complicated by the fact that a number of poststructuralists, including both Lyotard and Baudrilllard, have systematically engaged the term "postmodernism," while others, such as Foucault, have confessed that they do not know what the term and its associated notion "postmodernity" mean or what problems they are expected to address. In general, I regard the term "postmodernism" as a broad cultural and aesthetic phenomenon with its original home in the American and European avant-gardes, in poetics and literary criticism and architecture. The use of the term has been considerably expanded since its early use in the 1950s to apply more broadly to a set of cultural changes. By contrast, the genealogy of the term "poststructuralism," at least in its initial and developing formations, is clearly a distinctively French phenomenon, tied to innovations in structural linguistics and closely related to the Nietzschean critique of both Hegel and occidental rationality, as I have sought to explain in this chapter. I have restrained the urge to be pedantic by accepting the use of "postmodern philosophy" to include "poststructuralism," although it is clear that such a move homogenizes the differences among poststructuralist thinkers.

1

Poststructuralism and the Philosophy of the Subject: "The Games of the Will to Power against the Labor of the Dialectic"

Since we take nourishment from the fecundity of structuralism, it is too soon to dispel our dream. We must muse upon what it *might* signify from within. In the future it will be interpreted, perhaps, as a relaxation, if not a lapse, of the attention given to *force*, which is the tension of force itself. *Form* fascinates when one no longer has the force to understand force from within itself. That is, to create.

— Jacques Derrida[1]

INTRODUCTION

There is a cartoon drawing by Maurice Henry titled "Le Déjeuner des Structuralistes." The cartoon, published in *La Quinzaine Littéraire*, July 1, 1967, pictures Michel Foucault, Jacques Lacan, Claude Lévi-Strauss and Roland Barthes sitting, right to left, cross-legged in a semi-circle. They are all wearing grass skirts with chests bare, and their environment is obviously a tropical island. Foucault is holding forth while Lévi-Strauss is busy taking notes and both Lacan and Barthes are listening intently, if not critically. The ironic allusions to Manet and *Tristes Tropiques* aside, Henry's cartoon depicts a common view held by the French public and, subsequently, by many English-speaking academics: that there was something called "structuralism" — a uniform intellectual and specifically French movement that existed for roughly a decade from 1958 to 1968 — that could be identified with a "tribe" of certain French intellectuals. Although from different fields — history, philosophy, psychoanalysis, anthropology, Marxism and literary criticism — their tribal affiliations constituted a single doctrine, theory or approach.

From the article, "Education and Empowerment: Postmodernism and the Critique of Humanism" first published in *Education and Society*, 9, 2, 1991. Copyright © 1991 JAMES NICHOLAS PUBLISHERS, Melbourne, Australia. Used with permission. All rights reserved.

Maurice Henry's first mistake was to exclude Louis Althusser from the group and his second was to suggest that they formed a *homogeneous* group called "structuralists." The first mistake, historically, has been well and truly rectified; the second has been compounded indefinitely, so much so that now, in the 1990s, we repeat the mistake in the same way with respect to a group that has been christened "poststructuralists." "Poststructuralists," according to this common view, are a group of contemporary French intellectuals, who come *after* the structuralists and constitute a homogeneous group espousing a common theory or approach.

There is also, paradoxically, something essentially correct in this view. "Poststructuralism" ought to be studied or understood *against* the background context of structuralism. The tribal analogy also is a useful one in that it focuses upon kinship patterns of influence and "family resemblances," to use a Wittgensteinian term, without stamping a single face upon the theoretical contributions of those we have come to call poststructuralists. I want to argue that we ought not to repeat the intellectual mistakes of the past: that we should respect "tribal differences" and that we should understand poststructuralism, in its specific French historical development, essentially as both a reaction against and an escape from Hegelian thought. This reaction or escape, to summarize in Deleuzean terms, essentially involves the celebration of "the play of difference" against "the labour of the dialectic." Hence the title of this chapter, which is taken from the conclusion to Gilles Deleuze's *Nietzsche and Philosophy* (1983, p. 197). Deleuze's *Nietzsche et la Philosophie* was originally published in 1962. It represents one of the inaugurating moments of French poststructuralism providing as it does an interpretation of Nietzsche that highlights the play of difference, using it as the central underpinning of a polemic attack on the Hegelian dialectic. Deleuze writes in summary form:

Three ideas define the dialectic: the idea of a power of the negative as a theoretical principle manifested in opposition and contradiction; the idea that suffering and sadness have value, the valorisation of the "sad passions", as a practical principle manifested in splitting and tearing apart; the idea of positivity as a theoretical principle and practical product of negation itself. It is no exaggeration to say that the whole of Nietzsche's philosophy, in its polemic sense, is the attack on these three ideas. (1983, pp. 195–96)

Deleuze's radical questioning of the dialectic, its negative power and its purely reactive predisposition — the positive is achieved only through the double negation, "the negation of negation" — is contrasted with the purely positive power of affirmation inherent in "difference" as the basis of a radical thought and philosophy that is not Hegelian or Marxist. In a forceful passage Deleuze encapsulates his interpretation: "The Hegelian dialectic is indeed a reflection on difference, but it inverts its image. For the affirmation of difference as such it substitutes the negation of that which differs; for the affirmation of the self it substitutes the negation of the other, and for the affirmation of affirmation it substitutes the famous negation of negation" (1983, p. 196).

Deleuze's Nietzschean critique of the Hegelian dialectic, as one of the major keys to understanding French poststructuralism, should be more fully acknowledged as a basis and starting point for an alternative radical theorizing. This chapter moves in that direction. First, it provides an introduction to politics of poststructuralism through a critical appreciation of a history of structuralism that itself is interpreted, following Foucault, within the broader horizon of European formalism. Second, it returns to the Deleuzean interpretation of Nietzsche to situate it within the wider reaction to Hegelianism in French thought, in order to characterize French poststructuralism in its rejection of the dialectic and the notion of totality. Third, the chapter briefly indicates the significance of poststructuralist critique of the subject for analyzing contemporary forms of the ideological construction of the liberal subject of education.

FOUCAULT AND THE POLITICS OF FRENCH STRUCTURALISM

It is perhaps ironic that, at the point when Jean Piaget published his *Le Structuralisme* in 1968, structuralism had already become identified with outdated and suspect political positions and attitudes. Many interpreted the spontaneous events of May 1968 as a refutation of the structuralist critique of bourgeois humanism. In essence, at the point when Piaget[2] (1971) renamed structuralism in terms of "wholeness," "transformations" and "self-regulation," the movement was dead and the structuralists — those mentioned by Henry — had all denied that there was ever a common venture called structuralism, while at the same time attempting to disassociate themselves from the label. Thus Lévi-Strauss, rejecting the public perception represented by the Henry cartoon, commented that he saw himself in the tradition beginning with Georges Dumézil and Emile Benveniste and further developed by his colleagues at the Centre de Recherches Comparées sur les Sociétés Anciennes at the École Pratique des Hautes Études (Champagne, 1990, p. 131).

Foucault, in interviews with both the Italian communist Duccio Trombadori in 1978 (Foucault 1991c) and his fellow countryman Gérard Raulet (1983), declared that he was not a structuralist. Asked about the meanings of the terms "modernity" and "postmodernity," Foucault confessed that he did not understand clearly what they meant, what kind of problems were intended by the terms or how they were common to postmodernists. He was to comment: "While I see clearly that behind what was known as structuralism, there was a certain problem — broadly speaking, that of the subject and the recasting of the subject — I do not understand what kind of problem is common to the people we call post-modern or post-structuralist" (Raulet, 1983, p. 205).

In the interview with Raulet, Foucault makes it clear that structuralism was *not* a French invention and that the French movement of structuralism during the 1960s should be properly viewed against the background of European formalism, starting, perhaps, with the impulse of Russian modernism, focused around the forces of the combined movements of futurism and formalism. Asked the origin of the global term poststructuralism early in the interview with Raulet, Foucault responds by saying that "none of the protagonists in the structuralist movement . . . knew very clearly what it was all about." He qualifies this statement by exempting those applying structural methods in lingusitics and comparative mythology and then goes on to relocate French structuralism within the broad current of formalism that runs through twentieth-century Western culture. In this context he makes the following remark:

I am struck by how far the structuralist movement in France and Western Europe during the sixties echoed the efforts of certain Eastern countries — notably Czechoslovakia — to free themselves of dogmatic Marxism, and towards the mid-fifties and early sixties, while countries like Czechoslovakia were seeing a renaissance of the old tradition of pre-war European formalism, we also witnessed the birth in western Europe of what was known as structuralism — which is to say, I suppose, a new modality of this formalist thought and investigation. That is how I would situate the structuralist phenomenon: by relocating it within the broad current of formal thought. (Raulet, 1983, p. 190)

Foucault indicates the way formalist culture in the early years of the twentieth-century, and especially in Russia and Czechoslovakia, was associated with Left political movements and even a revolutionary impulse which was concealed by Stalin's brand of dogmatic Marxism. He comments with some irony that thirty years later, structuralism as a new modality of formalism, indebted to its Eastern European inspiration, develops types of analysis to unsettle the dogmatic Marxism of parties and institutions. Clearly, he has in mind the Parti Communiste Français.

To anybody with a passing familiarity with the modern history of linguistics, Foucault's remarks would seem perfectly in place. The internal textual evidence clearly supports Foucault's interpretation, as do recent histories. In 1958, Lévi-Strauss published *Anthropologie Structurale*, (a decade earlier than Piaget's treatise), which comprises a collection of papers written between 1944 and 1957. Lévi-Strauss acknowledges his debt to Saussure and Jakobson, and goes on to define the structural method in terms of the programmatic statement made by Nikolai Troubetzkoy, a member of the Prague School and founder of phonology.[3]

Jakobson is a central influence on Lévi-Strauss and, indeed, on the historical development of structural linguistics. Lévi-Strauss studied with and was introduced to structural linguistics by Jakobson at the New School for Social Science Research in New York in the early forties, and, in fact, published his first article, which related structural linguistics and ethnology and became an early chapter of *Structural Anthropology*, in Jakobson's newly established journal *Word* in 1945. Jakobson's position in the history of structural linguistics is pivotal. He is an instrumental figure in Russian formalism, helping to set up both the Moscow Linguistic Circle and the Society for the Study of Poetic Language (OPOJAZ) in St. Petersburg (which also included Boris Eykhenbaum and Victor Shklovsky, among others), before moving to Czechoslovakia in 1920 to establish, with people like Jan Mukarovsky, the Prague Linguistic Circle.

Jakobson's formative years were greatly influenced by the tradition of the Kazan School (de Courtney and Mikolaj Kruszewski on the notion of the phoneme), Saussure (whose work was brought back to Moscow by Sergej Karcevskij in 1917), the strong Russian tradition of Hegelian and post-Hegelian dialectics, the phenomenology of Husserl and the work of Anton Marty on universal grammar and Gestalt psychology.[4] Jakobson not only helped found the Prague Linguistic Circle in 1926 but also served as its vice-president until his departure from Czechoslovakia in 1939. It was Jakobson who first coined the term "structuralism" in 1929 to designate a structural-functional approach to the scientific investigation of phenomena, the basic task of which was to reveal the inner laws of the system. Jakobson, following the success of the First Prague International Slavistic Congress, came to frame his program-matic statement in these terms:

Were we to comprise the leading idea of present-day science in its most various manifestations, we could hardly find a more appropriate designation than *structuralism*. Any set of phenomena examined by contemporary science is treated not as a mechanical agglomeration but as a structural whole, and the basic task is to reveal the inner, whether static or developmental, laws of this system. What appears to be the focus of scientific preoccupations is no longer the outer stimulus, but the internal premises of the development: now the mechanical conception of processes yields to the question of their functions. (1973, p. 11)

Jakobson continues this statement by emphasising the way in which the Prague Linguistic Circle was closely linked with contemporary streams of both Western and Russian linguistics: "the methodological achievements of French linguistics," German phenomenology (Husserl) and the attempted synthesis of the Polish (de Courtenay) and Russian (Fortunatov) schools. It is important to note that Jakobson defined his theory of language structure against Saussure's, which he found both too abstract and static. Jakobson treated

Saussure's dichotomous formulations (langue/parole, synchrony/ diachrony) dialectically, insisting on the close relationship between form and meaning within a state of dynamic synchrony (Waugh and Monville-Burston,1990, p. 9).

The development of Russian formalism began around 1914 under the influence of futurism, a movement whose origins were firmly rooted in European and Russian avant-garde art (impressionism, postimpressionism, primitivism, cubism) in its aim to establish the immediacy and autonomy of art (Pike, 1979, p. 3). Russian futurist poets wanted to establish a new, pure poetry, based on the foundation of the word and purged of psychological, religious and mystical elements. In this they were reacting against the dominant cultural traditions (Pushkin, Tolstoy, Dostoevsky) to build a new culture where art not only was part of the life of the masses but actually corresponded to their reality. Formalism was united by the interest in language and the application of the newly developing science of linguistics to literature, inspired by Jan Baudouin de Courtenay and Ferdinand de Saussure.[5] Jackson writes: "Russian Formalism, closely allied with Russian Futurism, came into being in 1914–1915, flourished in the 1920s and disappeared in Stalin's countercultural revolution of the 1930s. Revolutionary in its ethos, it was an integral part of the great Russian modernist movement in literature, linguistics, art, music and culture . . . that came to define, briefly if paradoxically, the innermost aspirations of the Russian Revolution" (1985, p. xi).

Russian formalism was an attempt to establish a "literary science." It brought together diverse works from a range of different epistemological and methodological viewpoints to focus on "literariness": what Jakobson took to be the characteristics that made any given work a *literary* work. In this assertion of the object of literary science, Russian formalism can be interpreted as a reaction and negation to the "civic realism" as it had come to predominate in the main approaches to literature: the biographical, with a strong focus on the author; the sociohistorical, as the mirror of its time; and the philosophical, as an illustration of an interpreter's assumptions. With the 1917 revolution both the futurists and the formalists found themselves in a more congenial setting in instituting a now recognized archetypal modernist tradition of breaking with the past, only later to become embroiled in a doctrinaire debate over Marxist proletarian culture in the period after the revolution.[6]

The Bolshevik criticisms focused on the formalist dichotomy between literature and life, but such criticisms, as Pike points out, were "based on the polemics of formalism, rather than its reality" (1979, p. 20). The formalists had never denied the connection of literature to society, asserting only that it was not an object of study for literature, which must concern itself with the work itself and its "literariness." G. Conio explains:

[The] connection between literature and society lies at the very heart of the debate, and is violently denounced by those who favour an autonomy, a "sovereignty" of the science of literature, while it is accepted by certain "sociologists" vainly seeking to reconcile the two terms; it is this connection between literary creation and social demands, between art and revolution, which lies at the heart of, and determines official Marxist criticism and its conception of a directed, committed "party" literature. (1979, p. 41)

Despite moves in the early twenties to incorporate sociology into literature through concepts such as Eykhenbaum's "literary mores" or methods like Shklovsky's "formo-sociological" approach, the critics were relentless and the debate became increasingly rigidified. With the state takeover of ideology in 1934, formalism was seen officially as counter-revolutionary and the objectives of the formalist science of literature became subordinated to the dogma of Stalinist Marxism.

Foucault's remarks made in the interview with Trombadori, seen in this light, are provocative but at the same time have a great lucidity:

What happened in the East and West was essentially the same kind of thing, within certain limits. Because what was at stake was this: to what extent is it possible to constitute forms of thought and analysis that are not irrational-istic, that are not coming from the right, and that moreover are not reducible to Marxist dogmatism? These are complex problems, with all the devel-opments they have had, that are included in the vague and confused term of "structuralism". And why did this term appear? Because the debate on structuralism was actually the central position at stake in the USSR and Eastern Europe. And on the other hand, something about structuralism was in question there that was analogous to what was being proposed in France, which is to say: to what extent is it possible to conduct a theoretical, rational, scientific program of research that can surpass the laws of dialectical materialism? (1991c, pp. 94–95)

Foucault (1991c, p. 88) refers to the "problem of structuralism" in France as a consequence of more important problems in eastern Europe, a deeper history to which most of the French academic community was blind. And yet, he suggests, Communists and other Marxists must have had a premonition that structuralism was about to bring to an end traditional Marxist culture in France: "*A left culture that was not Marxist was about to emerge*" (Foucault, 1991c, p. 90).

The *problem* of structuralism is one that Foucault discusses in terms of a single point of convergence for otherwise completely different kinds of investigations: the focus on a philosophical opposition to "the theo-retical affirmation of the primacy of the subject," which had dominated in France since the time of Descartes. It had served as the fundamental postulate for a range of philosophies and approaches during the thirties, forties and fifties, including phenomenological existentialism, "a kind of

Marxism that agonizes over the concept of alienation" (Foucault, 1991c, p. 86) and tendencies in psychology, which denied the unconscious.

NIETZSCHE VERSUS HEGEL IN CONTEMPORARY FRENCH THOUGHT

Truly to escape Hegel involves an exact appreciation of the price we have to pay to detach ourselves from him.

— Michel Foucault[7]

The history of contemporary French philosophy, like, in part, the complex history of the reception of Hegel, is a theme now scholastically well established. It is the ground established in the English-speaking world by Mark Poster (1973; 1975) who argues, following Lefèbvre, that the decisive philosophical event in the postwar years was the discovery of the Hegelian dialectic, which provided a direct link between "the collapse of the old bourgeois world, the expectations of socialism and the emergence of interest in Hegel" (Poster, 1972, p. 110).[8]

Vincent Descombes (1980) notes a change in the connotation undergone by the term dialectic as characteristic of the "return of Hegel": "Before 1930 it was understood pejoratively. . . . After 1930, on the contrary, the word was almost always used in a eulogistic sense" (p. 10). Descombe attributes the resurgence of interest in Hegel to the "renewal of interest in Marxism that occurred in the wake of the Russian Revolution" (p. 9) and the influence of Alexandre Kojève's course on Hegel at the École Pratique des Hautes Études from 1933 to 1939.[9] Jean Wahl's (1984) *Le malheur de la conscience dans la philosophie de Hegel* marked the beginning of a Hegel renaissance with a reading of the *Phenomenology* rather than the later systematic works. The "unhappy consciousness" is based on the awareness that all human development and personal growth is a product of alienation of the subject from what it desires. The dialectic, thus, in Wahl's terms, is understood from an existentialist viewpoint. History is the story of moral progress that offers the prospect of reconciliation. Kojève also taught his students that the dialectic was to be understood in existentialist terms as the process both of self-transformation and, in class terms, as the "absolute negation" of the Masters' world. This emphasis on the dialectic as alienation, a process whereby the self engages with an Other in a discursive struggle for mutual recognition, is the essence of Hyppolite's interpretation. John Smith comments: "In his interpretation, Hyppolite emphasized not the systematic and logical necessity of the dialectical method but Hegel's own characterization of the *Phenomenology* as the history of the *Bildung* of consciousness, i.e. a process by which the 'authentic individual' develops as 'an unstable synthesis of the particular and the universal . . . which incorporated alienation as an essential moment'" (1987, p. 239).

Jean Hyppolite published the standard two-volume translation of the *Phenomenology* in 1939–41 and in 1947 brought out his own commentary, *Genèse et structure de la Phénoménologie de l'Esprit*. Both the translation and the commentary had an immense influence on Michel Foucault, Gilles Deleuze, Louis Althusser and Jacques Derrida, who attended his seminars at the Collège de France.

Mark Poster (1975) in an influential interpretation, states that the reading of the *Phenomenology* by Kojève and Hyppolite was an intellectual source for the renewal of Western Marxism, for Sartre's existentialism, and even for the structuralism of the 1960s. The first generation of French interpreters, steeped in both Marxism and existentialism, read the *Phenomenology* "as a critique of the notion that reason and history were antithetical. The error of the social scientists lay in their methodology and theory of knowledge. Their idealism situated the knower outside the field of knowledge, outside history" (Poster, 1975, p. 7).

Hegel was given an "existentialist" reading. Poster (1975) remarks how every page of Kojève's and Hyppolite's commentaries on the *Phenomenology* was loaded with existentialist concepts. The reason was clear enough: Hegel's dialectic of reason and history enabled Marxists to focus on the rationality of history in a conceptualization of advanced industrial society that captured the existentialist emphasis on the temporal nature of human consciousness and reason. Existentialists stressed the subjective, individual experience of being in time and the active creation of the world in terms of subjective meanings. This meant that existential Marxism looked to *all* the relations of daily life, and not just to the relations of production, in order to explain society, the intellectual's position within history and her role in the elimination of society's alienating structures. Sartre's existentialism emphasized a philosophy of consciousness that made humanism consistent with Marxism and avoided the reductive and mechanical dialectical materialism (Stalin, Lenin) that, in terms of the gulags, implied a suppression of individual human freedom according to the goal of establishing a socialist state.

Poster's (1975) argument is that French structuralism of the 1960s must be understood as complementary to existential Marxism. He quotes Derrida in support of his view, referring to the well-known lecture delivered in 1966 at the International Colloquium on Critical Languages and the Sciences of Man, Johns Hopkins University: "The paradox is that the metaphysical reduction of the sign needed the opposition it was reducing. The opposition is part of the system, along with the reduction" (Derrida, 1978a, p. 281). By defining itself against the philosophies of consciousness, Poster maintains, structuralism inevitably shapes itself in relation to those philosophies and can never succeed in simply surpassing them.

Louis Althusser is, perhaps, the best known of French Marxist structuralists to attempt to surpass philosophies of consciousness, with their humanist emphasis on the subject as the agent of history and social transformation. Althusser's theory of ideology was an attempt to provide Marxism with a philosophy "without succumbing to the pitfalls of humanism, that is, without lending support to the liberal politics of bourgeois individualism and without undermining the Communist party as the vanguard of the revolution" (Henriques et al., 1984, p. 95). Althusser's "theoretical anti-humanism" rejects the status of the knowing human subject as nothing other than a bearer of structural relations: "The structure of the relations of production determines the *places* and *functions* occupied by the agents of production, who are never anything more than the occupants of these places" (1970, p. 180).

The rejection of the early Marx as ideology with its humanist or anthropological problematic is the source of Althusser's (1969) theoretical antihumanist bias. On the basis of a "symptomatic" reading of Marx, Althusser argues that there is a clear epistemological break between the early Marx of the *Manuscripts* and the later Marx — a break representing a clear separation between a science (based on the concepts of historical materialism, i.e., the relations and forces of production) and its humanist ideological predecessor. For Althusser, the later Marx's greatest theoretical debt to Hegel is not a simple inversion of the dialectic, but the notion of history as *a process without a subject* — one powered by its own internal contradictions. Thus, in the mode of production (or practice) of theory, "The whole process takes place in the dialectical crisis of the mutation of a theoretical structure in which 'the subject' plays, not the part it believes it is playing, but the part which is assigned to it by the mechanism of the process" (Althusser, 1970, p. 27).

Educational theorists will recognize the philosophical importance of Althusser and structuralist arguments, more generally, in the work of Samuel Bowles and Herbert Gintis (1976), *Schooling in Capitalist America*, which is the origin of the "correspondence" (social reproduction) theory in education. They will also recognize such influence in the important contributions of both Kevin Harris (1979) and Michael Matthews (1980) to a "knowledge as production" thesis. The genesis of the modern structure-agency debate in social theory and in education, particularly, dates from this period. The work of early *resistance theorists* such as Henry Giroux (1983), Paul Willis (1977) and Peter McLaren (1985), are attempts to overcome the somewhat over-deterministic and reductionistic economism and classism that motivates the account of social reproduction by Bowles and Gintis, stressing "the *partial autonomy* of the school culture and . . . the role of conflict and contradiction within the reproductive process itself" (McLaren, 1989, p. 187).

In a strong sense, the move of resistance theorists in education into the realm of cultural reproduction and to recognizing the importance of language in this process represents a poststructural reevaluation of the role of agency — some might argue an overly romantic reevaluation of the humanist subject, symbolized in the working class student antihero, who, in her resistance to dominant school culture, tragically reinforces her own class position. Althusser's major contribution was to provide an account of ideology that, although determined "in the last instance" by the economic, was in practice "relatively autonomous." He provided a formulation that showed how Ideological State Apparatuses (the family, the church and the school) "produced individuals as subjects in such a way that they participated in reproducing capitalism" (Henriques et al., 1984, p. 96).

Yet, as Poster remarks, Derrida reminds structuralists of their dialectical dependence on a metaphysics of subjective meaning: "The intelligibility of the signifier appears only in relation to the doctrine of the intelligibility of the signified" (1975, p. 354). Derrida, in the essay "The Ends of Man," addresses himself to the question, "Where is Franco, as concerns man?" in a way that sheds some light on our purposes here. He writes: "After the war, under the name of Christian or atheist existentialism, and in conjunction with a fundamentally Christian personalism, the thought that dominated France presented itself essentially as humanist" (1982a, p. 115).

While humanism or anthropologism was the common ground of the various existentialisms, of the philosophy of values, of personalisms and of Marxism in the classical style, Derrida comments, "The history of the concept of man is never examined. Everything occurs as if the sign 'man' had no origin, no historical, cultural or linguistic limit" (1982a, p. 116). Humanism, as embodied in the transcendental ego, in the speaking subject, was the all-powerful motif of postwar French philosophy, an over-riding motif that was authorized by anthropoligistic readings of Hegel (Kojève, Hyppolite), Marx (especially the *Manuscripts*, rediscovered in the 1960s), Husserl and Heidegger. Yet Derrida asserts and attempts to demonstrate how this anthropological reading was a serious mistake. It was based on serious misreadings of Hegel's *Phenomenology* and Heidegger's *Being and Nothingness*, (which was, self-consciously, antihumanist) and reflected the humanist-existential understandings of the then practicing French philosophers rather than adopting a more scholastic approach. The critique of humanism and anthropologism is, as Derrida states, "one of the dominant and guiding motifs of current French thought" (1982a, p. 119) — yet, even so, such critique is more a product of an *amalgamation* of Hegel, Husserl and Heidegger (as the source or warranty of critique) with the old metaphysical humanism, rather than a central requestioning of humanism.

Derrida challenges Hegel's anthropological assumptions through a critique of the principle of identity, which in Hegel's theory of the sign is able to effect a closure in the symbolic relationship of sign to signified. Hegel's opposition of sign and signified is established as internally related features of a unified reality through a process of dialectics where "every concept is to be negated and lifted up to a higher sphere in which it is thereby conserved" (see Bass' note 23, pp. 19–20 to Derrida's 1982c, "Différance"). This preserves the unity of consciousness, projected and yet recovered, as self-presence. Yet for Derrida *différance* ruptures the relation between sign and signified; reference to the signified is always displaced and the unity of the subject as self-presence is simply the fiction of linguistic practice. Derrida writes: "Contrary to the metaphysical, dialectical 'Hegelian' interpretation of the economic movement of *différance*, we must conceive of a play in which whoever loses wins, and in which one loses and wins on every turn. If the displaced presentation remains definitively and implacably postponed, it is not that a certain present remains absent or hidden. Rather, *différance* maintains our relationship with that which we necessarily misconstrue, and which exceeds the alternative of presence and absence" (1982c, p. 20).

The alterity of the unconscious is not a *hidden* self-presence. It is a *trace*, that, as Derrida expresses it, "differs from, and defers, itself" (1982c, pp. 20–21). "Trace", as Gayatri Spivak (1976) explains in her Preface to *Of Grammatology*, in French carries connotations of track, footprint, imprint. Spivak continues: "Something that carries within itself the trace of a perennial alterity: the structure of the psyche, the structure of the sign. To this structure Derrida gives the name 'writing.' The sign cannot be taken as a homogenous unit bridging an origin (referent) and an end (meaning), as 'semiology,' the study of signs, would have it. The sign must be studied 'under erasure,' always already inhabited by the trace of another sign which never appears as such" (Spivak, 1976, p. xxxix).

Derrida (1978a) in the now classic early essay "Structure, Sign and Play in the Discourse of the Human Sciences" (often taken as one of the inaugurating moments of poststructuralism), questions the "structurality" of structure and the way in which conceptual resources for the "decentering" of structure, of the transcendental signified, can be found in Nietzsche, Freud and Heidegger. He distinguishes two interpretations: one, which is Hegelian in origin and exemplified in Lévi-Strauss' work, "dreams of deciphering a truth or an origin which escapes play and the order of the sign" and which seeks the "inspiration of a new humanism"; the other, based on "Nietzschean *affirmation*, that is the joyous affirmation of the play of the world and of the innocence of becoming, the affirmation of a world of signs without fault, without truth, without origin which is offered to an active interpretation," tries to pass beyond man and humanism (Derrida, 1978a, p. 292). In "'Genesis and Structure' and Phenomenology" (an allusion to Hyppolite's interpretation), Derrida had already laid out major elements of his philosophical program. The essay is concerned with Husserl's treatment of the sign and there is an (early) attempt to develop a "deconstruction" of Western metaphysics by recognizing reason as the *logos* produced in history, which has been determined as self-presence on the model of speech. From 1959, the date Derrida delivers his lecture on Husserl, to 1968, when he formulates the notion of *différance,* it has taken some nine years. In an interview with Jean-Louis Houdebine and Guy Scarpetta, Derrida comments: "If there were a definition of *différance,* it would be precisely the limit, the interruption, the destruction of the Hegelian *relève* wherever it operates" (1972, p. 40).

As Derrida makes clear in the interview, *relève* is his interpretation and translation of the Hegelian *Aufhebung.* Combining insights from Heidegger and Saussure that emphasize, respectively, a temporal and a spatial dimension, Derrida arrives at the notion of *différance,* which he says is the most general structure of economy, in the sense established by Georges Bataille. Derrida argues in a reading of Bataille ("From Restricted to General Economy: A Hegalianism without Reserve"), "The Hegelian *Aufhebung* is produced entirely from within discourse, from within the system or the work of signification" (1981, p. 275), and, therefore, it remains within restricted economy. Michèle Richman explains further: "*Economy* in this context refers to the production of values within language as determined by a system of differentiation, but Derrida also evokes the prejudice of economy as economizing: the minimum expenditure for maximum gain, or in this case, the capacity of a finite set of phonemes to generate unlimited combinations" (1982, p. 141).

Différance, according to a relatively stable interpretation of Derrida's (1981, pp. 8–9) "refers to the . . . movement that consists in deferring by means of delay, delegation, reprieve, referral, detour, postponement, reserving"; the movement of *différance* is "the common root of all the positional concepts that mark our language" and the production of those differences that is the condition for any signification. Finally, it is "the unfolding of difference," of the ontico-ontological difference, which Heidegger named as the difference between Being and beings.

Derrida's early text on "genesis and structure" in Husserl's phenomenology was published some three years before Deleuze's *Nietzsche et philosophie,* breaking new ground and conceptually creating a "clearing" for Deleuze, who, as Vincent Pecora notes "powerfully introduced Nietzsche into the problematics of structure outlined earlier by Derrida" (1986, p. 38). Pecora continues: "For Deleuze will read Nietzsche as the one who provides the alternative not only to the 'unhappy consciousness' that is one moment of the Hegelian dialectic, but to dialectics as the medium and support of that consciousness — to dialectics as the suffering, guilty, *negating* thought of *ressentiment* which can only affirm by negating twice" (1986, p. 38).

Pecora argues that Deleuze's use of the notion of difference to elaborate the will to power in Nietzsche is a way of reinterpreting "Nietzsche's attempt to cure the 'bad conscience' of his time through the transvaluation of all values to Deleuze's own particular and political circumstances" (1986, p. 39). Pecora establishes clearly the limits of Deleuze's interpretation emphasizing the way in which the substitution of the "play of difference" for the "labour of the dialectic" establishes a radical reinterpretation of Nietzsche's work, becoming a turning point for postwar European philosophy and critical theory. Yet he is troubled by Deleuze's devaluing of "desire" in Nietzsche and the confinement of desire and struggle to the reactive history of *ressentiment*. He asserts that Deleuze, in celebrating the play of pure difference, has sacrificed or censored the "complexity of tone" and the "intellectual tension" in Nietzsche's work, ignoring the suffering and despair against which playfulness appears. Deleuze's *idealization* of Nietzsche's work, Pecora suggests, is at the bottom of "many of our present difficulties with 'poststructuralist' thought" (1986, p. 47). He sums up his criticism of Deleuze by arguing:

To the degree that thinkers like Derrida have elaborated "difference" as a "discipline and preparation" for the ability to control values, rather than be controlled by them, Nietszche's work has been actively, fruitfully extended. But to the degree that "difference" has come to signify a freedom of play that does not in fact exist, and that does not seem capable of reflection upon such a condition, Nietzsche's work has only been turned into a fantastic escape from "history, nature, man himself." (Pecora, 1986, p. 47)

To a large degree this kind of criticism of poststructuralism is now commonplace. More often than not it is accompanied by a line of thought that wants to recover the unity of Hegelian subject as the basis for political agency. Thus, for instance, Thomas McCarthy (1989) accuses Derrida of the "politics of the ineffable." There is something curious, however, about Pecora's approach, because, while based on a sophisticated understanding of poststructuralist criticism, it appears that Pecora wants to assert a determinant reading of Nietzsche against Deleuze's creative appropriation and upon that reading to base the "reality" of history as struggle.[10]

Deleuze's interpretation of Nietzsche and his Nietzschean critique of Hegel serves as the conceptual grounding for poststructuralism. As one commentator has forcefully argued: "The political implications of all their work could even be argued to be directly rooted in their critiques of the Hegelian and Marxist dialectics" (Carroll, 1984, p. 79).

Judith Butler in a lucid explanation of contemporary French theory as a series of reflections on Hegel, begins her final chapter with the following interpretation: "The twentieth-century history of Hegelianism in France can be understood in terms of two constitutive moments: (1) the specification of the subject in terms of finitude, corporeal boundaries, and temporality and (2) the 'splitting' (Lacan), 'displacement' (Derrida), and eventual death (Foucault, Deleuze) of the Hegelian subject" (1987, p. 175).

Both Foucault and Derrida, in seminal essays ("Nietzsche, Genealogy and History" and "The Pit and the Pyramid: An Introduction to Hegel's Semiology"), begin with Hegelian themes to suggest a radical departure. Foucault questions the unilinearity of an implicit and progressive rationality and the way in which the dialectical explanation of historical experience assumes a single origin and cause. Narratives of historical experience, which draw on the theoretical fiction of an immanent rationality, disguise and attempt to rationalize an original multiplicity of events and forces that resist the demands of a unifying dialectic.

Historiographers have masked and rationalized this original and radical heteronomy of events and forces through the "imposition of orderly theoretical forms." Butler suggests that Foucault's analysis of modernity "attempts to show how the terms of dialectical opposition do not resolve into more synthetic and inclusive terms but tend instead to splinter off into a multiplicity of terms which expose the dialectic itself as a limited methodological tool" (1987, p. 180). Foucault pretends not to understand the problem behind postmodernism or postmodernity. Yet some of his critics certainly take him to be a poststructuralist/ postmodernist thinker who, along with Derrida (and others), teaches that the values of the modern era were essentially logo- and homo-centric illusions. For instance, both Poster (1981) and Fraser (1981, 1983, 1985) understand Foucault's examination of "the philosophy of the subject" — by which he means a problematic dominating the modern episteme that privileges the subject as the foundation of all knowledge and signification — as bearing centrally on discussions of modernity. They argue that Foucault's genealogical analysis of modern power operates on the basis of a radical decentering that denies an epistemic or historical privilege to either the traditional Cartesian notion of a "centered" subjectivity or the humanist ideal of a rational, autonomous, and responsible self.

They argue, that Foucault's method allows us to see power very broadly in the development of a plurality of incommensurable discursive regimes, each with its multiplicity of "micropractices," which ultimately directs us to study the "politics of everyday life." Such an approach suspends the problematic of legitimacy understood in terms of the standard modern liberal normative framework with its talk of rights grounded as it is in the "nature of persons."

Butler comments that for both Derrida and Foucault "the Hegelian theme of relational opposition is radically challenged through a formulation of difference as a primary and irrefutable linguistic/ historical constant" (1987, p. 183). The projection and recovery of the subject in Hegelian terms, thus, for Derrida and Foucault set conditions for an exercise in self-deception. Butler plots the growing instability of the subject in the work of Kojève, Hyppolite and Sartre and summarizes the progression in French thought as a series of reflections on Hegel's "anthropocentrism."

While the subject in Hegel is projected and then recovered, in Sartre it is projected endlessly without recovery, but nevertheless *knows itself* in its estrangement and so remains a unitary consciousness, reflexively self-identical. In the psycho-analytic structuralism of Lacan and in the Nietzschean writings of Deleuze and Foucault, the subject is once again understood as a projected unity, but this projection *disguises* and falsifies the multiplicitous disunity constitutive of experience, whether conceived as libidinal forces, the will-to-power, or the strategies of power/discourse. (Butler, 1987, p. 185)

Certainly it is the case that Foucault (along with Deleuze and Derrida) rejects both the normalizing and totalizing tendencies of the Hegelian dialectic and their anthropological expression in foundational assumptions of the human subject. Foucault (1989a) tells us that he begins to study Nietzsche (outside the academy) as early as 1953 and that Nietzsche, Blanchot and Bataille permitted him to free himself from the confines of a French university education that, in philosophy, was "a Hegelianism deeply penetrated by phenomenology and existentialism, which hinged on the theme of the 'unhappy consciousness'" (Foucault, 1991c, p. 45). Nietzsche represented for Foucault an "invitation" to call into question the category of the subject. There was also an important relation between Foucault's theoretical work and his (local) politics — "politics," he suggests at one point, became "a way of testing how much I was maturing in my theoretical reflections" (1991c, p. 47). Given Foucault's Nietzschean genealogical critique, which aims at revealing the contingent and historical conditions of existence, it ought not to be surprising that Foucault does not separate out questions of "history," "politics" and "philosophy" in the case of his own intellectual development.

The ultimate effect of Nietzsche on Foucault's construction of politics is given strongly by Foucault in the Preface to the English edition of *Anti-Oedipus: Capitalism and Schizophrenia* where he writes: "Do not demand of politics that it restore the 'rights' of the individual, as philosophy has defined them. The individual is the product of power. What is needed is to 'de-individualize' by means of multiplication and displacement, diverse combinations. The group must not be the organic bond uniting hierarchized individuals, but a constant generator of deindividualization. Do not become enamoured of power" (Deleuze & Guattari, 1983, pp. xi–xiv).

In the Translator's Introduction to Deleuze's *Foucault* (1988), Séan Hand records the ultimate impact of a Nietzschean antirationalism on the work of Deleuze and Foucault and on Kantian philosophy as the "liberation of pure difference," which, he suggests, "leads to the abandonment of dialectics and a move to an affirmative thought of disjunction and multiplicity" (Hand, 1988, p. x). Hand here is noting the emergence of a new form of post-Kantian philosophy, where, as Foucault comments in regard to Deleuze's work, "thought is again possible" (cited in Hand, 1988, p. x). It is primarily a philosophy that represents "the abandonment of categories and the move to an acategorical thought." By this Hand means that Foucault and Deleuze have moved beyond the *concept* to a philosophy of the pure event — "to an ontology of the present that works against the dialectic." In these terms, theory is no longer a totalizing force. It is a *practice* that resists all unitary thought to celebrate multiple potentialities. As Foucault himself expresses it, in his Preface to *Anti-Oedipus*: "Free political action from all unitary and totalizing paranoia. Develop action, thought and desires by proliferation, juxtaposition, and disjunction, and not by subdivision and pyramidal hierarchization. . . . Prefer what is positive and multiple: difference over uniformity, flows over unities, mobile arrangements over systems" (cited in Hand, 1986, p. vii).

In order to understand the poststructuralist critique of the subject it has been necessary to retrace briefly the reception of Hegelianism in contemporary French thought, from a historical moment of popularity among the first generation of interpreters (Hyppolite and Kojève) to one of rebellion of the second generation (Butler, 1987).

The attempt to escape Hegel is also clearly evident in the work of Jean-François Lyotard. In a relatively early essay, "Adorno as the Devil," Lyotard (1974) argues that negative dialectics suffers from a fatal weakness in that it is forced through negation to take on its adversary's position. Lyotard simply does not believe that a political, philosophical or artistic position is abandoned because it is "sublated": it is not true, according to Lyotard, that the experience of a position means its inevitable exhaustion and necessary development into another position where it is both conserved and suppressed. As J. M. Fritzman has recently argued, adopting Lyotard's position: "A rhetorical reading of the Hegelian corpus shows that while Hegel assumes that the end of communication is consensus, consensus is not the goal of communication, but rather its death. Discourse can be kept alive once it is seen that disagreement, paralogy, is its end. Disagreement as the end of communication allows a transversing of the Hegelian dialectic that succeeds in escaping its recuperative moment" (1993, pp. 57–58).

Deleuze's interpretation of Nietzsche occupies a special place in the canon of French poststructuralist philosophy. Deleuze's interpretation, historically speaking, provides the philosophical and political means to displace the earlier preoccupations of postwar French philosophy, based around the Hegelian subject and the unquestioning acceptance of the dialectic, simultaneously inventing a lineage of "counter-philosophy" and reactivating the French tradition of vitalism going back to Bergson. Petra Perry (1993) argues that Deleuze never really surpasses his early reading of Nietzsche; that while he continues to memorialize Nietzsche and, ultimately, attack him in the later collaborative work with Félix Guattari, Deleuze is largely responsible for the advocacy of the new Nietzsche and its positive reception by his fellow poststructuralists. Even if one agrees with Perry that this reception reaches its high-water mark in 1972 with the Cerisy-la-Salle colloquium on Nietzsche, or one agrees with others (e.g., Houlgate, 1986) that Deleuze's interpretation is misleading in scholastic terms, the fact is that Deleuze's "manu-facture" of Nietzsche effectively becomes a turning point for French philosophy, opening new spaces for philosophizing, helping to reinstate an outlaw tradition, and providing the basis for an alternative mode of critical thought both inside France and beyond.

LIBERALISM, EDUCATION AND THE CRITIQUE OF INDIVIDUALISM

My starting point for this book is the exhaustion of the philosophy of the subject and the bankruptcy of one particular set of liberal capitalist practices and institutions based on this paradigm, where the subject is construed in individualist and consumerist terms. Fredric Jameson distinguishes two clear positions on the critique of individualism. The first is a historical thesis closely connected to the changing conditions of modern capitalism. He suggests that "in the classical age of competitive capitalism, in the heyday of the nuclear family and the emergence of the bourgeoisie as the hegemonic social class, there was such a thing as individualism, as individual subjects. But today, in the age of corporate capitalism, of the so-called organization man, of bureaucracies in busi-ness as well as the state, of demographic explosion — today, that older bourgeois individual subject no longer exists" (1985, p. 115).

The second position Jameson identifies — that of the poststruc-turalist critique — is regarded as more radical: "It adds, not only is the bourgeois individual subject a thing of the past, it is also a myth; it *never* really existed in the first place; there have never been autonomous subjects of that type. Rather, this construct is merely a philosophical and cultural mystification which sought to persuade people that they 'had' individual subjects and possessed this unique personal identity" (1985, p. 115).

Of the two positions, the latter is more philosophically interesting and productive, for it exposes or unmasks the individualism of liberal-ism, and its rejuvenated form in neoliberal thinking as ideological at the stage of history when this form of ideology has achieved hegemonic proportions. That the philosophy of the subject is at an end, however, is not in dispute. It is a theme that runs through much German and French contemporary philosophy. Seyla Benhabib, for instance, writes: "No idea has been as central to the tradition of critical social theory as the belief that the exercise of human reason is essential to the attainment of moral autonomy and fulfilment, public justice and progress. This idea, which critical theory showed with the great thinkers of the bourgeois Enlightenment from Hobbes to Kant, was never really repudiated" (1986, pp. 343–44).

Benhabib charts a series of movements leading to an impasse: Hegel's critique of Kant's pure reason, which emphasized the unfolding of reason in history; Marx's critique of Hegel, initiating the turn from the *reflexive* to the *productive* subject; the early Frankfurt School's appropriation of insights from both Hegel and Marx to emphasize "that the autonomous subject was not an isolated Cartesian ego, but a historically and socially *situated*, concrete, and embodied self" (1986, p. 344).

The period of the 1960s and the early 1970s witnessed a series of cultural crises heralding the triumph of principles of liberal humanism. The civil and human rights movements, the growth of antiestablishment postwar youth cultures, the revitalization of ethnic minorities, the peace movement and, in particular, the Vietnam protest movement, the antiapartheid movement and the student movement — all these so-called cultural crises that posed problems of social legitimation for then existing civil institutions — resulted in significant gains in personal rights.

However, in the late 1970s and the 1980s there was a revival of the main articles of faith of market liberalism. The so-called new right is now the ascendant sign and, under strategies of privatization designed to restructure capital — to provide favorable public conditions for the new re-accumulation of capital under conditions of declining productivity — the definitions of "public" and "private" are being redrawn. The historical struggle continues, perhaps as an indication of the contradiction in liberal capitalist democracies between the demands for capital accumulation, on the one hand, and those for democratic legitimation, on the other, as neo-Marxists claim. To a large extent we are experiencing the contradiction between the imperatives of a liberal humanism underlying the role of government and the traditional welfare state, and that of a market liberalism that seeks to reduce direct government intervention both in the economy and in society more generally and yet to maintain control through other means.

More cryptically, to the so-called death of the subject corresponds the intellectual demise of the project of liberal capitalist schooling and education. Historically, *liberal institutions* (prisons, courts, psychiatric institutions and so forth), including that of the school and the modern university, have legitimated themselves and their practices by reference to the discourse of subject-centered reason. The Cartesian-Kantian tradition conceived of the epistemological subject as the fount of all knowledge, signification and moral action. In transhistorical terms, liberal philosophers pictured the subject within a set of highly individualistic assumptions as standing separate from, and logically prior to, society and culture.

These same assumptions vitiate the planning and policy documents of liberal capitalist and democratic societies. The individual is conceptualized in theory, and seen in practice, as the primitive unit of economic and political analysis, the ultimate beyond which one cannot go. These same assumptions, but in a revitalized form, now surface in the neoliberal (and neoconservative) critique and reform of the welfare state and of education. Underlying these reforms of education in countries like the United States, the United Kingdom, Australia and New Zealand are a set of assumptions that reify a form of individualism. Sometimes this form of individualism is referred to as abstract individualism; more commonly it has been christened possessive individualism. The notion, irrespective of nomenclature, has surfaced most obviously in the behavioral postulate of a renewed classical liberal economics, which has guided neoconservatives in policy arrangements to redraw the boundaries between the public and the private, in setting the parameters for easing the transition toward the so-called postindustrial and information society. The postulate of *Homo economicus*, one of the main tenets of new right economic thinking, holds that people should be treated as "rational utility-maximizers" in all of their behavior. In other words, individuals seek to further their own interests, defined in terms of measured net wealth positions in politics as in other aspects of their behavior.

The project of liberal capitalist mass schooling and higher education in the late twentieth century is built on the liberal intellectual authority inherited from the Enlightenment. It is grounded in a European universalism and rationalism heavily buttressed by highly individualist assumptions. It is these assumptions and the authority that rests upon them that is now being called into question and, with it, both neoconservative and left radical attempts to reform education. Poststructuralism is a theoretical strand, a moment in the broad movement of European formalism, that best typifies this questioning and the attempt to find new cultural and political orientations.

At one level, poststructuralism has come to refer to forms of philosophical analyses focusing on the critique of the subject, including changes in modes of production and consumption. It is closely related to a break with foundational philosophy and with the rejection of universalist claims of totalizing social theory. Specifically, poststructuralism as a basis for the critique of modernist social theory serves to radically decenter the subject, the cornerstone of both liberalism and Marxism (though in different ways).

Specifically, I want to suggest that the discourse of liberalism is concerned with the ideological reproduction of *us* — of human beings — as individuals. This is a difficult thesis to develop, because historically liberal discourse since the French Revolution has shaped the concepts — the institutions and practices by which new members of Euro-centric–based societies came to view and understand themselves. Liberalism, I am claiming, has shaped and determined to a very large extent understandings of ourselves as rationally autonomous individuals. Liberalism has "manufactured" the notion of a human being as a rationally autonomous person (post-Kant) and liberal discourse (and practice) has constructed us accordingly.

Against these common-sense (or theoretical) institutions that we have about ourselves as individuals, I wish to make the case that we are socially constructed, in a strong sense, as individuals, and that this process is in part one of ideological self-production. In general terms the major task is to problematize the category of the individual as the central underlying category of liberal discourse and to show how human beings are constructed as "consumer" individuals.

What has this to do with educational philosophy? The philosophy part is, perhaps, not hard to grasp, because we are dealing with the philosophy of the subject and how subjects become individuals. But why *educational* philosophy? Because education is concerned with understanding the principal socializing means in our society and, in particular, that of schooling. The school, along with the family as an institution, constructs us as "individuals" through a network of educational practices, including, for example, examinations, forms of surveillance, records, reports, competitions and so on — practices that are part of both the formal and the informal or hidden curriculum (Illich 1973).

NOTES

1. Jacques Derrida. (1978). Force and Signification. In Alan Bass (trans.), *Writing and Difference*, (pp. 4–5). Chicago: University of Chicago Press.

2. In Chapter 7, "Structuralism and Philosophy," Piaget discusses the relations between structuralism and the dialectic: "To the extent that one opts for structure and devaluates genesis, history, and function or even the very activity of the *subject* itself, one cannot but come into conflict with the central tenets of dialectical modes of thought" (1971, p. 120). In this context Piaget, first, arbitrates in the debate between Lévi-Strauss and Sartre to conclude that there is no inherent conflict between structuralism and dialectic; and, second, discusses Foucault's "structuralism without structures," which he takes to demonstrate "that there cannot be a coherent structuralism apart from constructivism" (p. 135).

3. Lévi-Strauss writes, "First structural linguistics shifts from the study of *conscious* linguistic phenomena to the study of their *unconscious* infrastructure; second, it does not treat *terms* as independent entities, taking instead as its basis of

analysis the *relations* between terms; third, it introduces the concept of *system* . . . ; finally, structural linguistics aims at discovering *general laws*" (1968, p. 33).

4.   For a synoptic intellectual biography of Roman Jakobson, see Linda R. Waugh and Monique Monville-Burston (1990), who provide a clear chronology of Jakobson's intellectual life and an assessment of his influence. They write: "The strongest influence on Jakobson's thinking was 'the turbulent artistic movement of the early twentieth century'" (p. 4), including the work of the literary and artistic avant-garde: Picasso, Braque, Stravinsky, Joyce, Xlebnikov, Le Corbusier.

5.   The classic text on Russian formalism is Victor Erlich's (1969) *Russian Formalism*. In this respect see Jackson and Rudy's (1985) retrospective on Russian formalism, a *Festschrift* in honor of Erlich. See also Peter Steiner's (1982) collection of original essays from the Prague School and his recent reassessment of Russian formalism (1984). Jurij Striedter (1989) provides a reconsideration of Russian and Czech structuralism, indicating the importance of the native Czech tradition, the centrality of Hegel to that tradition, and the way in which it goes beyond Russian formalism. Interestingly, he mentions the neglect of the Prague School by both American and English literary theorists, including Fredric Jameson and Terry Eagleton. On the relation of Russian formalism to Russian futurism, see the introductory essay by Christopher Pike (1979) to a collection of original essays in English translation.

6.   Bakhtin, Volosinov, Medvedev and Vygotsky were to criticize the formalists for their neglect of the ideological and social aspects of language and literature. Mikhail Bakhtin, in particular, was to insist that language was inherently "dialogical." As Eagleton explains: "The sign was to be seen less as a fixed unit (like a signal) than as an active component of speech, modified and transformed in meaning by the variable social tones, valuations and connotations it condensed within itself in specific social conditions. Since such valuations and connotations were constantly shifting, since the 'linguistic community' was in fact a *heterogenous* society composed of many conflicting interests, the sign for Bakhtin was less a neutral element in a given structure than a focus of struggle and contradiction" (1985, p. 117).

7.   Michel Foucault, "Orders of Discourse." Inaugural Lecture Delivered at the Collège de France, trans. Rupert Sawyer, *Social Science Information* 10, April 1971:28.

8.   In fact the reception of Hegel in contemporary French thought predates World War II considerably. The surrealists, under the influence of André Breton, based their revolutionary practice on an understanding of Hegel. Poster (1973) is somewhat dismissive of the surrealists, especially considering that the movement achieved a unique synthesis of Marx, Freud and Rimbaud, which was, perhaps, the most important basis, along with Marxism itself, for the emergence of a postwar left culture in France (see Lewis, 1988). The surrealists joined the French Communist Party in 1927 and demonstrated their adherence to dialectical materialism by embracing all the theses: "the primacy of matter over thought; adoption of the Hegelian dialectic as the science of the general laws of movement of the external world as well as of human thought; the materialist conception of history . . . ; necessity of social revolution as the resolution of the antagonism . . . between the material productive forces of society and the relations of existing production" (Breton, 1978, p. 147). Well before Reich or Marcuse attempted a productive synthesis of Marx and Freud, Breton had emphasized a *critical* psychoanalysis. The union of surrealism with Marxism was possible precisely because of their common point of departure in Hegel. The dialectic for Breton was the theoretical means for interpreting "the interior reality and exterior reality as two elements in a process of unification," which, at one point at least, he considered the "supreme aim of surrealism" (1978, p. 116).

9.   Among those attending Kojève's seminar were Georges Bataille, Raymond Aron, Alexandre Koyré, Pierre Klossowski, Jacques Lacan, Maurice Merleau-Ponty, Eric Weil and, as Descombes (1980, p. 10, n.1) notes, André Breton less frequently.

10.   Where Pecora (1986) tackles Deleuze's interpretation by arguing that it distorts Nietzsche, Stephen Houlgate (1986) argues from the other side of the question. He thinks that Deleuze has been unfair to Hegel and he accuses Deleuze of failing to see Hegel's point. In Houlgate's view, Deleuze's criticism of Hegel is based on the way the dialectically constituted Hegelian self is the "product of a wholly negative mode of will to power — one which conceals the specific differences between forces beneath abstract, and therefore fictional, concepts such as 'non-ego.' Such a procedure, in Deleuze's view, is uncritical because the other is reduced to an abstraction which, though conceptually *opposed* to the self, is nevertheless legitimated by being treated as a necessary moment in the dialectical construction of the self" (1986, p. 6).

2

Poststructuralism, Intellectuals and Postmodern Culture

INTRODUCTION

Perhaps now more than at any time in the past, the question of the intellectual demands a response.[1] The title of this chapter symbolizes everything I discuss in relation to the topic of intellectuals: Who are they? Do they still exist, or does the term simply signify an empty set? What role might they still play within postmodern culture? Where does their legitimacy reside today? In short, I problematize and interrogate the category intellectuals by reference to poststructuralist theory.

This activity is a rather belated attempt to come to grips with a changed set of socio-economic conditions within which the intellectual now finds herself.[2] At the very historical moment when the new right — in the ascendant sign — has initiated policies that redefine the parameters of the social, the status of knowledge and the idea of the university, the intellectual — on one conception, at least — must contemplate the possible end to her labors, must renounce a position of privilege. At a time when the grand metanarratives (*récits*) have been revealed as yet another self-deceptive ideology based on an active mythologizing that subjugates local knowledges, what roles are there now left to play? At this exact point of the media saturation of society when celebrity broadcasters, TV journalists and frontmen jostle with the stars of popular culture to read events, set trends, break a story, champion a cause — what public space remains for the activity of intellectuals?[3] At a stage when the new social movements have developed agendas specific to the politics of gender, class, ethnicity, peace and the environment, as much outside the walls of the academy as within it, to what extent do the loyalties and affiliations of intellectuals intersect or contradict one another?

This welter of crisscrossing questions may indicate something of the confusion and ambiguity that today weighs heavily on the category of intellectuals. This chapter seeks to address and explore these questions. It does so by describing a shift in both the notion and conditions of "culture" and by examining different conceptions of the intellectual in relation to "postmodern culture." The drift of argument is that post-modern culture and, in particular, the democratization of (consumer) culture has led to a problematization of the notion of intellectual, of both the status and identity of the intellectual defined in traditional modernist terms. The second half of the chapter is devoted to briefly reviewing three poststructuralist accounts of the intellectual. The thought of Foucault, Lyotard and Kristeva are distinguished and examined.

INTELLECTUALS AND POSTMODERN CULTURE

One author, Andrew Ross, intending to resituate intellectuals in relation to popular culture, says, "Today, a code of intellectual activism which is not grounded in the vernacular of information technology and the discourses and images of popular, commercial culture will have as much leverage over the new nomination of modern social movements as the spells of medieval witches or consultators of the *I Ching*" (1990, p. 212).[4] He notes that intellectuals have found it necessary to reexamine their institutional affiliations in order both to understand and transform the codes of power, "which are historically specific to their disciplinary discourses," and mentions in this regard the influence of Michel Foucault's studies on the disciplinary nature of "regimes of truth," Derrida's deconstruction of the university institution, Lacan's challenge to the rationality of science, and Bourdieu's work on the notion of symbolic capital.

For Ross, the new intellectuals "are uneven participants on several fronts who belong to different social groups and have loyalties to differ-ent social movements" (1990, p. 230). He suggests that intellectuals today will be guided by "the pragmatic, democratizing possibilities ushered in by the new technologies and new popular cultures in a hegemonic capitalist society." They are unlikely to understand the new politics of knowledge if they do not recognize why so many cultural forms "draw their popular appeal from expressions of disrespect for the lessons of educated taste" (p. 237).

Ross (1990) clearly feels that if intellectuals have a role to play today it is in respect to popular culture. Their role is informed by the same matrix of power and desire experienced by other consumers and their task is to begin to rearticulate the popular in ways that confront its worst excesses. To this degree, then, he not only accepts the "postmod-ern" collapse of the distinction between high culture and popular culture but also firmly locates the new intellectual's primary critical role in relation to popular culture.

Surveying a collection of essays devoted to examining the politics of postmodernism, Ross notes that for some theorists a politics of difference and a politics of the local and particular "are not only symptoms of, but also essential strategies for coping with a postmodernist culture that advertises itself as decentered, transnational, and pluralistic" (1988, p. vii); he sees postmodernism as "a belated response to the vanguardist innovations of high modernism . . . the continuation of modernism by other means" (p. ix).

Another critic, Chantal Mouffe (1988), describing the reformulation of the socialist project attempted in an earlier work (Laclau and Mouffe, 1985), indicates how such a project demands a nonessentialist epistemological perspective. This reformulation, while acknowledging the role that the epistemological perspective of the Enlightenment played in the emergence of democracy, now sees it as an obstacle in understanding the new form of politics that is characteristic of our times. An appropriate understanding, we are told, is to be gained from using "the theoretical tools established by different currents of what can be called *the postmodern in philosophy* and of appropriating their critique of rationalism and subjectivism" (Mouffe, 1988, p. 33; emphasis added). By "the postmodern in philosophy," Mouffe clearly means poststructuralism, the philosophy of language of the later Wittgenstein and post-Heideggerian hermeneutics, as she acknowledges in a footnote. She writes: "To be capable of thinking politics today, and understanding the nature of these new struggles and the diversity of social relations that the democratic revolution has yet to encompass, it is indispensable to develop a theory of the subject as a decentered, detotalized agent, a subject constructed at the point of intersection of a multiplicity of subject-positions between which there exists no a priori or necessary relation" (p. 35).

This reappraisal represents, of course, a revision of the Marxist concepts of class and class struggle. To a large degree these notions were important in helping to inspire and to formulate the philosophies of feminism and decolonialization, in elevating them to *universal* concerns. With the continued growth and fragmentation of the new social movements, which have taken place largely outside organized class interests and institutions, traditional Marxist notions increasingly seemed to be reductionistic. The emergence of social and cultural difference could not be captured theoretically or explained adequately in terms of simple "class interests." In one sense this juncture represented a conceptual shift from class to a more anthropologically differentiated notion of culture.

The view of the intellectual implied by Ross and Mouffe in one sense is a direct consequence of the rise of cultural studies as a distinct field of academic endeavor and a number of significant related changes in the appraisal of the notion of culture more generally. If one looks across the range of humanities and social sciences it is clear that over the last twenty years there has been a remarkable shift in the centrality of the notion of culture in recent theorizing.

In sociology, for example, Mike Featherstone has described the way in which an interest in culture up until the mid-1970s was "considered eccentric, dilletlantish, and, at best marginal" (1989a, p. 148). He charts the astonishing rise in the number of journals in the English-speaking world concerned with theorizations of culture and indicates how "feminism, Marxism, structuralism, post-structuralism, semiology, critical theory, and psychoanalysis also helped to raise the profile of cultural questions" (p. 6). Eisenstadt has more precisely detected a shift in the notion of culture with recent sociological analysis away from culture conceived as "fully structured according to clear principles, embedded in the very nature of the human mind, which, through the medium of a series of codes, regulate human behaviour" (1989, p. 6) to one that emphasizes, in a hermeneutical manner, the symbolic and expressive dimensions. Both the structuralist-functionist and the symbolic-expressive conceptions are motivated by underlying theories of language, giving the cultural a greater importance in social theory than was previously the case. The shift itself from strictly structuralist accounts (based, historically, on the work of Saussure and others) to interpretivist, symbolic and hermeneutical models is directly related to developments in the theory of language and, in particular, those developments attributable to the work of Saussure, Heidegger, Gadamer and Wittgenstein, among others.

To some degree this new interest in culture, as Stuart Hall notes, has been "an attempt to address the manifest break-up of traditional culture" (1990, p. 12), especially traditional class cultures. To some degree in Britain (and in its ex-colonies) it has reflected the profound crisis of national identity and culture under a new-right ideology.[5] To a very large extent, undoubtedly, it also reflects the crisis of the humanities under late capitalism. Holland and Lambropoulos make the point extremely clearly:

The very market forces that dissolved theocratic society and may at one time have fostered autonomous reason in free individuals now pulverize individuality and obliterate independent rationality. Scientific reason appears inseparable from the technological domination of nature worldwide and is deployed in all-pervasive technologies of social domination serving the nation-state; critical reason seems finally unable to counteract the subordination of rationality to the market calculations of the "cash-nexus" and the power calculus of state reason. Even outside the natural and social sciences, the realm of aesthetics is increasingly recuperated and refunctionalized by institutions ranging from campaign management and museum sponsorship to advertising. The institutions and modes of thought that once sustained the humanities . . . have deserted, leaving it to face crisis without apparent intellectual resources or sacrosanct cultural domains: this time, the crisis is not for, but of, the humanities. (1990, p. 1)

They go on to remark how commonplace it has been among intellectuals to regard high culture in the West, since the Enlightenment, as the countercultural critique of the existing order. It becomes puzzling, then, for intellectuals and the supposedly avant-garde to realize that the projects of liberal humanist critique "have lost their critical edge and end up serving the very social order they were meant to contest" (Holland & Lambropoulos, 1990, p. 1).

The turn to culture and to the attempt to retheorize culture as a central category in the humanities and social sciences is primarily a response to changing historical conditions that allegedly have given the notion of culture an autonomy and potential basis for a new politics, while emphasizing a historicism that denies claims to universality, to universal experience and to universal history. Culture, in other words, has become more anthropologically differentiated and a much more complex concept. I elaborate this point further.

The seminal works of Raymond Williams and E. P. Thompson — and before them, though in different ways, Richard Hoggart and F. R. Leavis — had the combined effects of devising new approaches to the study of cultural history and helping to initiate and delineate cultural studies as a field of legitimate academic interest (Johnson, 1986; Hall, 1990).

Indeed, it was Raymond Williams who first took a "democratic" approach to the definition of culture and emphasized the modern diversity of cultural experience in which "working-class culture" could no longer be denied its own existence. In a later work, Williams (1983, pp. 87–93) maps the range and overlap of meanings of the word "culture": its early use as a noun of process; its metaphysical extension to human development through the late eighteenth century and its status as an independent noun for an abstract process, which marks the history of its use in modern times. His analysis is comprehensive and now also well known, such that it need not detain us here, except to say that it became possible to speak of cultures in the plural: "the specific and variable cultures of nations and periods, but also the specific and variable cultures of social and economic groups within a nation" (Williams, 1983, p. 89). The dominant sense of the word as it prevails in modern social science can be traced first to Klemm's "decisive innovation" and later, following Klemm, to Tylor's usage.

In addition to these usages, Williams also identifies a third and relatively late use of culture as an "independent and abstract noun which describes the works and practices of intellectual and especially artistic activity" (1983, pp. 90–91). He indicates that the opposition between "material" and "spiritual" that bedevilled its earlier usage is repeated in modern terms in the disciplines: archaeology and cultural anthropology refer to *material* production, whereas history and cultural studies make reference, instead, to signifying or *symbolic* systems. To his mind this confuses and conceals the central question of the relations between material and symbolic production that Williams (1981) develops in providing a socialist theory of culture.

This kind of understanding is prevalent in the attempt to define the focus of cultural studies in the local context as both "situated forms of everyday culture" related to questions of social identity and more abstracted forms that are represented as accounts of social life by public media. It is also reflected in the concept of multiculturalism, as a code word in the international context that represents an ideological construction of cultural diversity.

Williams' observations are important not only for their theoretical contributions but also because they offer a standpoint to recognize the complexity of actual usage, the problems that arise from the conflation of different senses and the way in which the history of the word culture is still active, still in the making. Thus, he notes the coining of *culchah* (a class mime-word) and *culture-vulture* (American) as signs of hostility to the notion when it has been used as a basis for making claims to superior knowledge, refinement and "high" art; and, at the same time, he indicates how this hostility has diminished as the sociological and anthropological uses of the term (e.g., in subculture) have been steadily extended.

To these specifically modern developments we can now add enormously: "the culture industry" (Horkheimer and Adorno); "mass culture" (Irving Howe); "consumer culture"; "the culture of narcissism" (Lasch); and even more recently "information culture," "popular culture" and, most recently, "enterprise culture,"[6] and "global culture." What these terms variously attempt to describe is culture in its ambiguous relationship to late capitalism or advanced industrial society. In a word these epithets attempt to characterize (what I will call) postmodernism. It is a word to which Williams (1989, p. 48) himself takes exception. He regards postmodernism as "a strictly ideological compound from an enemy formation." In taking this position he is not alone. In a now classic formulation, Jameson (1984; 1985) theorizes postmodernism as the cultural logic of late capitalism, although, significantly, he leaves open the possibility that it may have the double capacity to also resist that logic. Hal Foster (1983) was perhaps the first to name this ambiguity by announcing a "postmodernism of reaction" and its antithesis in a "postmodernism of resistance." Others, such as Linda Hutcheon (1989, p. 21), have taken his lead to emphasize the complicity of postmodernism with late capitalism while seeking an agenda for resistance, maintaining that since the advent of postmodernism representation can "no longer be considered a politically and theoretically innocent activity."

Hutcheon, strongly influenced by poststructuralist developments, understands culture as the *effect* of representations (as opposed to their *source*) and asserts that the primary agenda of postmodernism is "the investigation of the social and ideological production of meaning" (1989,

p. 27). Under the influence of new developments in semiotics, structuralist Marxism, feminism, psychoanalytic theory and poststructuralism, traditional concerns of language as an innocent representing activity have given way to an interest in the production and reproduction of "meanings" more generally, which are seen to be embodied, and both socially and economically situated. To that extent the politics of postmodern representation, as Hutcheon explains, is concerned with "the ideological values and interests that inform any representation" (1989, p. 7).

The early work of Jean Baudrillard is exemplary here. In the essay "Towards a Critique of the Political Economy of the Sign," Baudrillard builds on a line of reasoning developed in *La société de consommation* (1970), where he views "consumption" as an active labor involving the manipulation of signs. He writes: "Today consumption — if this term has a meaning other than that given it by vulgar economics — defines precisely *the stage where the commodity is immediately produced as a sign, as sign value, and where signs (culture) are produced as commodities*" (1981, p. 147).

Clearly, in this early text, Baudrillard has made use of Saussurean insights to interpret consumer society as a semiological system of signs where commodities, differentially related to other, comprise a signifying system and the consumer consumes not the object itself, but the whole system. As Levin puts it in his Introduction to Baudrillard: "It is this very condition of semiosis, engendered by the universalization of commodity relations, which privatizes experience in the first place. As we 'consume' the code, in effect, we 'reproduce' the system" (1981, p. 5). Baudrillard's interpretation brings into focus the relations of language and culture for consumer society and is understood in terms of a linguistic system. It also reminds us of its theoretical debt to Saussurean linguistics, which first problematized referential theories of meaning. On the model of structural linguistics, semiology taught us to regard meanings not in terms of relations between language and the world but rather as a differential system where nothing is regarded as meaningful in and of itself but only as it differs from other elements in the system.

Jameson (1989a; 1989b; 1990) has had cause to modify the "starkness" and purity of his original position. He indicates that his thoughts are to be understood "as an attempt to theorise the specific logic of the cultural reproduction of that third stage" of capitalism, following Mandel, and not as "yet another disembodied cultural critique." He calls for "the renewal of historical analysis itself" and confronts the paradox of asserting a totalizing, unified theory of differentiation by challenging the levels of abstraction: "a system that constitutively produces differences remains a system" (Jameson, 1989a, p. 34). The logic of capital, he maintains, is "a dispersive and atomistic, 'individualistic' one," which, contradictorily, stems from its own systemic structure: "the very concept of differentiation . . . is itself a systemic one" (p. 35). Even so, he argues, the mode of production is not a "total system" in the forbidding sense alluded to by Foucault and Weber, because it "includes a variety of counterforces and new tendencies within itself, of 'residual' as well as 'emergent' forces, which it must attempt to manage or control (Gramsci's conception of hegemony): were those heterogeneous forces not endowed with an effectivity of their own, the hegemonic project would be unnecessary" (1989a, p. 39).

In this transitional period in which earlier economic forms are being restructured on a global scale, he maintains, a new international proletariat will eventually emerge. Does Jameson here betray a sense of a pluralism that admits of a distinctively postmodern politics of resistance? He asserts elsewhere (1989b, p. 11), in an interview with Anders Stephanson, that the idea of a cultural dominant does not exclude forms of resistance, and he emphasizes that postmodernism has both positive and negative interpretations. He suggests, for instance, that the democratization of culture "cannot be altogether bad" and that "even heterogeneity is a positive thing." He adds, "The point is that many of these seemingly negative features can be looked at positively if they are seen historically" (p. 13). His major emphasis is on the fact that "these developments have to be confronted as a historical situation rather than as something to be morally deplored or simply celebrated" (p. 12).

This would seem to imply a quite distinct role for intellectuals. It implies, for instance, that it is not enough for intellectuals simply to engage in text-based forms of discourse analysis of cultural products from the safety of institutional sites, however critical and self-reflexive these projects might be. It requires, minimally, that the intellectual make a political commitment, take sides, contest and resist the exercise of power in a way that bears on historical situations. To that extent Jameson is tied to the traditional Marxist notion of the universal intellectual.

In an interview with Stuart Hall in *Marxism Today*, Jameson (1990, p. 28) elaborates his analysis. Within a "relatively anonymous systemic culture" it becomes "problematic to talk about ruling classes in the old way." A sign of postmodernism as a "tendentially complete modernisation" is the "plebianisation of culture": "the way in which much larger sections of the public now consume culture on a regular basis and live within culture in ways that they didn't have the occasion to do before. That's a crucial part of post-modernism, which underscores its ambiguity. One cannot object to the democratization of culture, but one must object to other features of it. Those mixed feelings have to be preserved in any analysis of the postmodern" (p. 29).

It seems that the notion of class culture becomes less applicable in new circumstances emphasizing a systemicity. Rather, looked at from the outside, from the perspective of the non-West, the old term "cultural imperialism" is more relevant. In this sense the real object is North American culture as an expression of corporate capitalism, "which is exported and implanted by way of media technology" (Jameson, 1990, p. 30). The crucial point is that such consumer culture is now more systemic, more regulated and nationalized than it has ever been before. Cultural production has reached a stage where reflexive, critical distance from it is both less obvious and less possible. Even oppositional and critical forms have become fully enmeshed or fully integrated into the system of cultural production, to the point where there is no public space left for critical reflection on the system or its relation to the economic and political systems.[7]

Stuart Hall, in conversation with Jameson, advances the central problem in lucid terms. The question is "whether what is going on in the postmodern is simply a dominant system producing marked differentiation as part of its own logic of domination: or whether there really has been a shift, representing the power of the marginalised or subordinated cultures and people to make what you called, earlier, a real difference" (Jameson, 1990, p. 30).

If it is the case that the system is producing its own differentiation, "then the 'logic of history' in a classical marxist sense is still operating, while going through one of its many epochal changes" (Jameson, 1990, p. 31). If, on the other hand, the second scenario holds true, then these changes may in fact represent the suspension of the "logic of history" and the end of the metanarrative of classical Marxism. (On this question see the collection of essays on Jameson edited by Kellner, 1989. See also McLennan, 1991).

Jameson is certainly clear on the fact that it is politically positive that subgroups and subcultures have been able to attain "a certain collective existence that they didn't have before" (1990, p. 30). And yet at the same time he comments on how these developments clearly fit into "a kind of cultural commodification on the part of the industries that now have a new submarket and produce new things for it" (p. 30). He is pessimistic about a purely cultural politics and agrees with Hall that the sense of totality, collective action and solidarity has been undermined by the new logic of difference. Yet he is adamant, nevertheless, that the new phase of global capitalism also carries with it a new class logic that "has not yet completely emerged because labour has not yet reconstituted itself on a global scale" (p. 31). I think Jameson is too optimistic about the emergence of a global reconstituted labor, especially in view of the dominance of multinational enterprises in the process of the globalization of markets — their increasing interdependence and interpenetration (see Eden, 1991). In my view Jameson tends to ignore the differences in labor both globally and locally and to minimize the role and existence of the new social movements and the potential for a politics of difference (Radhakrishnan, 1989; Peters, 1991).

Others have recognized the tension (contradiction?) between forces of cultural homogenization and those of cultural heterogenization within "the global cultural economy" (Appadurai, 1990). In this context some theorists have sought to emphasize "a postmodernism of resistance." Mike Featherstone, for instance, embraces a positive and optimistic reading of postmodernism. He writes:

Postmodernism is both a symptom and a powerful cultural image of the swing away from the conceptualization of global culture less in terms of alleged homogenizing processes (theories which present cultural imperialism, Americanization and mass consumer culture as a proto-universal culture riding on the back of Western economic and political domination) and more in terms of the diversity, variety and richness of popular and local discourses, codes and practices which resist play-back systemicity and order. (1990, p. 2)

From his perspective, intellectuals must develop new modes of investigation, and this necessity renders problematic not only conceptions of society tied exclusively to the bounded nation-state but also assumptions inherent in Western models of rationalization, modernization and industrialization. "In effect," he writes, "the assumption is that we have moved beyond the logic of the universal 'iron cage' rationalization process" (1990, p. 3), and he encourages us to discard the binary logic that seeks to understand culture in terms of mutually exclusive opposites: homogeneity/heterogeneity, integration/disintegration, unity/diversity.

The *problem* of intellectuals — their identification, their function, their history — has become now a field of academic specialty in itself. There are those who have attempted to provide definitions of intellectuals focusing on their role in society (Shils, Debray). Others have adopted a psychological approach attempting to delineate behavioral characteristics (Coser). In general, as Eyerman and others (1987) maintain, sociologists have adopted one of two broad approaches to defining intellectuals: the phenomenological, which starts from the individual's own self-understandings and the structural, which begins with an analysis of the intellectual's class position. As regards the latter perspective, the towering figure of Antonio Gramsci still retains its attraction for many. Gramsci, it may be remembered, maintained that intellectuals were incapable of formulating a set of common interests. They had to align themselves with the interests of labor or capital. Organic intellectuals, those associated with working-class interests, served to articulate those interests in the domain of problems of culture as against traditional intellectuals, who, reflecting their dominant class position together with its control over the institutions of culture, served to reproduce their class hegemony.

An increasing number of scholars and commentators have argued that the world is a different place from that experienced by Gramsci. The old class allegiances have become more fragmented with the rise of the new social movements, and the status of knowledge has altered as societies move into the postindustrial era and cultures move into the postmodern age. The field of cultural studies reflects these changes and tensions. Pickering (1991, p. 19), for instance, while elaborating the working-class interests that inspired the founding texts of Williams, Hoggart and Thompson and approving of its critical impulse, at the same time demonstrates his deep ambivalence concerning postmodernism and postmodernist theory. On the one hand, in one form at least, postmodernism is complicit with late capitalism, displaying "a self-conscious delight in mass-produced art, kitsch and vernacularism, in the play of surfaces, in anti-realism and anti-historicism"; on the other hand, postmodern theory has "made important contributions to the ways we see and understand the consumer culture of (late) capitalist societies" (p. 15). On the one hand, as Pickering argues, postmodernism lacks an effective theory of political agency and the resources to provide a basis for a critical stance on contemporary culture; on the other hand, its decentering of the subject, its emphasis on difference, accommodates the political will of antiracist and antisexist struggles. The resolution of this apparent contradiction for Pickering is in the fact that postmodernist theory has no clear or definable object of critique. While I share Pickering's ambivalence about postmodernism (in particular about its reactionary and conservative forms — the way in which neoliberalism has appropriated aspects of postmodernism for its own agenda), I do not share his belief in the resolution, because if one distinguishes poststructuralist from postmodernist theory it is clear that such theory does indeed have a definable object of critique: the critique of reason (construed in modernist terms) and the related critique of the philosophy of the subject.[8] Both critiques, I would argue, are centrally important to the interests of cultural studies.

The changed set of cultural conditions has prompted one sociologist to argue that intellectuals, once legislators in the modern age, are now to be regarded as interpreters in the postmodern age (Bauman, 1987). The postmodern situation presents a crisis of confidence for the modernist intellectual and an end to the intellectual conceived of as the legislator of knowledge and power — as the creator of public opinion, of freedom of thought and of human rights. From the vantage point of postmodernity, Bauman proclaims "the end of the exploration of the ultimate truth of the human world or human experience, the end of the political or missionary ambitions of art, the end of dominant style, of artistic canons, of interest in the aesthetic grounds of artistic self-confidence and objective boundaries of art" (1987, p. 118).

The end of the intellectual of modernity, based on those seductive metanarratives that glorified the mythical entities of Man, Reason and

History in universalist terms, coincides with the end of the epoch of European world history. Such history served only to subjugate local history and local knowledge. As David Roberts expresses the point:

The unfulfilled task of modern intellectuals in face of the rationalization, which has fragmented authority and left the market as the only link between sub-systems, is thus to combat the dominant mode of the social integration (privatization) of individuals as consumers by the discursive redemption and reconnection of personal autonomy and social rationality. The post-modern conclusion recognizes only a failed project of modernity. The intellectual can no longer identify any agent of Reason. The inner-directed Puritan has been turned into a consumer, the poor have lost their attraction. The vision of a good society is undercut by an ongoing anonymous process of rationalization which has no need of "transparent" legitimation. (1989, p. 147)

Under these latter conditions Bauman (1987) argues for the view of postmodern intellectuals as interpreters, as "cultural hermeneutists" (Roberts, 1989, p. 146), who, deprived of the claim to authority based on the universality of truth, judgment and taste, now lapse into the lesser roles of facilitator and negotiator within local contexts, translating and interpreting "the multiplicity of life-worlds and language games from the human cultural archive" (Featherstone, 1989b, p. 133). Post-modernism, in these terms, represents a crisis of identity for modern intellectuals, who increasingly (and as a result, in part, of "the democratizing effect of being drawn into a wider cultural consumption market") must now engage in a "searching reconsideration of the value, ends and purpose of their endeavours" (p. 133). As Featherstone (1990, p. 134) acknowledges, while some are willing so to reexamine their status and identity in these changed conditions and, like Bourdieu, embrace the idea of the emergence of particular as opposed to universal intellectuals, others, such as Jacoby, see the demise of the universal intellectual project as cause for alarm.

POSTSTRUCTURALISM AND INTELLECTUALS

Over against the teacher, who is on the side of speech, let us call a *writer* every operator of language on the side of writing; between the two, the intellectual, the person who prints and publishes his speech. Between the language of the teacher and that of the intellectual there is hardly any incompatibility (they often co-exist in a single individual); but the writer stands apart, separate. Writing begins at the point where speech becomes *impossible* (a word that can be understood in the sense it has when applied to a child).

— Roland Barthes[9]

Commenting on the role of the intellectual following the events of May 1968, Foucault, in discussion with his friend and colleague Gilles Deleuze, argued: "The masses no longer need him [sic] to gain knowledge: they know perfectly well, without illusion; they know far better than he [sic] and they are certainly capable of expressing themselves" (1972, p. 207).

For Foucault,[10] then, the intellectual's role is not to elucidate knowledge in abstract symbols, to pose alternative world views, or to express for the masses what they either do not know or cannot articulate well; rather, it is "to sap the power, to take the power, it is an activity conducted alongside those who struggle for power, and not their illumination from a safe distance" (p. 207).

Gilles Deleuze comments in this discussion that Foucault was the first to teach us about "the indignity of speaking for others" (Foucault, 1972, p. 209). It is not the intellectual's form of discourse then that matters, nor the ability of the intellectual to articulate or totalize a world view for the oppressed, but the discourse against power developed by the oppressed. It is a counter-discourse of the oppressed and not a discourse developed by intellectuals about why they are oppressed. Thus, for Foucault and his work in *Le Group sur l'Information des Prisons*, it is the prisoners' discourse, forged in the prisons as a counter-discourse to the discourses of jurists and penologists (no matter how sympathetic) that is important. Yet, somewhat paradoxically, the discourses about prisons and prisoners formed by jurists and penologists are necessary to force and forge the resistance and the discourses of the oppressed prisoners.

What had been conceived as universal and theoretical becomes local, regional and practical in Foucault's approach. Far from proposing a universal world view in theory, a specific *practice* against power emerges. As opposed to Gramsci's organic intellectual, Foucault talks then of *specific* intellectuals, contrasting their role with the role of the traditional intellectual:

In general, I think that intellectuals — if this category exists or if it ought still to exist, which is not certain and perhaps not even desirable — are renouncing their old prophetic function. And in saying that I'm thinking not only of their pretension of saying what is going to happen but also of the legislative function to which they have aspired for so long: "Here is what has to be done, here's what's good, follow me. In the confusion you're all in, here's the fixed point, it's where I am". The Greek sage, the Jewish prophet and the Roman legislator are still models which haunt those who nowadays make speaking and writing their profession. I have a dream of an intellectual who destroys self-evidences and universalities, who locates and points out in the inertias and constraints of the present the weak points, the openings, the lines of stress; who constantly displaces himself, not knowing exactly where he'll be nor what he'll think tomorrow, because he is too attentive to the present. (1989c, pp. 154–55)

These remarks can be understood in terms of Foucault's project of writing the history of rationality, of reason, from the point of view of the making of the human subject. More precisely, his interest revolved around the forms of rationality, which human subjects applied to themselves — the way in which reason was and is self-created. In an interview in the year of his death Foucault describes his researches in the following terms: "How does it happen that the human subject makes himself [sic] into an object of possible knowledge, through which forms of rationality, through which historical necessities, and at what price? My question is this: How much does it cost the subject to be able to tell the truth about itself?" (1989a, pp. 245–46).

In this enterprise, Foucault understands the historical emergence, since Kant, of multiple forms of rationality that, through the power-knowledge discourses of the human sciences, invested themselves in a variety of practices and institutions: the school, the military, the clinic, the psychiatric institution, the court.

Where Critical Theory recognizes the bifurcation of reason into an instrumental technical rationalism and a practical-moral reason, and seeks to judge and rehabilitate the former from the perspective of the latter, Foucault recognizes multiple bifurcations, multiple forms — each of which demands its own analysis and institutional focus.[11] He writes: "I believe there is a self-creation of reason and therefore I am trying to analyse the forms of rationality: various proofs, various formulations, various modifications by which rationalities educe each other, contradict one another, chase each other away, without one therefore being able to designate a moment in which reason would have lost its basic design or changed from rationalism to irrationalism" (1989a, p. 244).

On this view there is no universal reason — moral-practical, critical or otherwise — that intellectuals can identify with; there are only forms of rationality (involving different modes of subjection) that intellectuals can oppose. This may explain Foucault's enigmatic comment: "The word 'intellectual' is foreign to me. I have never encountered any intellectuals" (1989d, p. 194).

The comment above indicates Foucault's suspicion of the totalizing force of reason and of those who prosecute and proselytize in its name. In terms of Foucault's position, then, the ethics of an intellectual are centrally related to "modifying one's own thought and that of others" (1989b, p. 303). It is not "to mold [sic] the political will of others" but "to re-examine evidence and assumptions, to shake up habitual ways of working and thinking, to dissipate conventional familiarities, to re-evaluate rules and institutions and starting from this re-problematization (where he [sic] occupies his specific profession as an intellectual) to participate in the formation of a political will (where he [sic] has his role as citizen to play)" (pp. 305–6).

Jean-François Lyotard (1993) raises similar arguments to Foucault against the traditional notion of the intellectual's role, though he believes that Foucault still grants too much privilege to the intellectual.

Indeed, he believes the traditional position of the intellectual to be no longer tenable.

Lyotard (1993) responds to the then socialist government's call for support from its intellectuals. He does so by distinguishing experts from intellectuals. The former group are contained within their own specialist field and governed by the performativity criterion; that is, they are governed by the demand to achieve the best possible performance in their field. The latter, on the other hand, are quite different. Bennington explains that in traditional terms Lyotard views an intellectual as "someone who identifies . . . with a collective subject given a universal or potentially universal value (humanity, the nation, the proletariat etc.), who analyses a situation in terms of that subject and prescribes what should be done for it to flourish, accompany its destiny, or at least proceed toward some such accomplishment" (1988, p. 5).

Over and above these two groups, Lyotard (1993) introduces a third group (although it is not clear why they are said to constitute a group): artists, writers and philosophers. They have different responsibilities in the sense that their *raison d'être* is encapsulated by a unique question: respectively: What is painting? What is writing? What is thought? They do not identify with any collective universal subject or progress toward an emancipatory goal. Their purposes preclude the subordination of experimental activity to political or cultural demands. Their functions are, what is more, heterogeneous and cannot be reduced one to the other.

Further, Lyotard (1993) claims that the traditional notion of the intellectual is no longer coherent. It could function only on the basis of a totalizing unity — within a common teleology such as the emancipation of the proletariat or a universal education for Enlightenment thought. In the postmodern age, Lyotard claims, there is no such totalizing unity. It is no longer possible to identify with a universal subject. Bennington explains further: "the signs which were to legitimate the idea of the emancipated proletariat (i.e., international solidarity of the workers) are fewer and farther between than ever, and any ideal of universal emancipation through education is nowadays apparently strictly subordinated to the production of experts and thereby to the improvement of performativity" (1988, p. 7).

While there are still victims and injustice and, therefore, also the responsibility to address and act on questions of oppression, this can no longer be legitimated on the basis of a grand narrative of emancipation or the historical fulfillment of a universal subject. Such activity "can only legitimate local and essentially defensive interventions" (Bennington, 1988, p. 8).

Julia Kristeva (1977) might also be seen to share the same suspicion of the traditional intellectual's role as that which characterizes the work of Foucault and Lyotard.[12] Kristeva (1986) begins by questioning the opposition between the masses and the individual — a dichotomy on which the notion of the intellectual (including Gramsci's "organic intellectual") rests. It is an opposition that is said to be governed by the master-slave dialectic (which generates pity and guilt) and thus induces "a kind of pro-slavery mentality in the intellectual, who represents the supreme product of the systematic conjunction of Christianity and capitalist production" (p. 293).

For Kristeva, the future of Western society depends greatly upon a reevaluation of the dialectic opposition that governs the relationship between the masses and the individual — the intellectual and society — and "on our ability to break out of the dialectical trap between these oppositions and to recast the whole relationship" (1986, p. 293).

Kristeva's analysis is based on a psychoanalytic diagnosis and reassessment of the relationship. Nietzsche is, in part, the source for this reappraisal, because it was he, in *The Genealogy of Morals*, who first questioned the old prophetic functions of the disciple to the masses. This revolt is also represented in what Kristeva calls "the eruption of the languages of modernity," by which she means the breakdown of the master discourses (and of the cultural and institutional coherence they commanded) and the emergence of new languages (presumably those of psychoanalysis, semiotics, genealogy, deconstruction, semanalysis), which permit "the group to question particular forms of subjectivity or the unconscious" (p. 294). The emphasis on the "large history," on what Lyotard has called the "metanarrative" with its self-seducing commitment to honoring the mythical entities of Reason, History, Consciousness and Truth has, in Kristeva's terms, excluded "the specific histories of speech, dreams and *jouissance*" (pleasure) (p. 294).

The new type of intellectual, then, adopts the dissident function, which produces the right to speak, to voice these specific histories and to assess their political value. Kristeva writes: "Give voice to each individual form of the unconscious, to every desire and need. Call into play the identity and/or the language of the individual and the group. Become the analyst of every kind of speech and institution considered socially impossible. Proclaim that we reveal the Impossible" (1986, p. 295).

As Toril Moi (1986, p. 8) comments, Kristeva is, in effect, presenting "a politics of marginality" as a basis for renewed intellectual activity. This may reflect her own experience as both an exiled foreigner and her marginalized position as an intellectual woman in Paris in the late sixties.

Kristeva (1986) identifies three groups of intellectual dissidents: the rebel who attacks political power; the psychoanalyst who transforms the master-slave dialectic and the writer who experiments with the limits of identity. The first is still caught up in the Hegelian dialectic and remains within its limits. The second is able to transform the dialectic and remain a site of active dissidence. The third is able to undermine the law of symbolic language. In addition, Kristeva identifies the subversive potential of women based on sexual difference.

A full analysis of Kristeva's position would require an understanding of her semiotics, her psychoanalysis and, in particular, her notion of the subject-in-process and her relation to feminism. These are well beyond the scope of this chapter. But enough can be gleaned from this skeletal compromise to serve as a basis for making some general points about the intellectual from the perspective of poststructuralism.

All three thinkers demonstrate a suspiciousness of the grand narratives and their legitimating functions. Against the ahistorical and universalist pretensions of these totalizing master narratives, they assert a belief in difference, in the local and particular, in the singular. Lyotard, for example, counterposes the notion of singularity against that of totality — the singularity of the event — and even suggests that it is the guiding thread of poststructuralism. Kristeva writes at one point:

A woman is trapped within the frontiers of her body and even of her species, and consequently always feels *exiled* both by the general clichés that make up a common consensus and by the very powers of generalization intrinsic to language. This female exiled in relation to the General and to meaning is such that a woman is always singular, to the point where she comes to represent the singularity of the singular — the fragmentation, the drive, the unnameable. This is why philosophy has always placed her on the side of that singularity — that fragmentation prior to name or to meaning which one calls the Daemon — she is demonic, a witch. (1986, p. 296)

The emphasis on singularity is also a motif symbolizing a new space for *thought*, for thinking, which has always been the true threshold for dissidence and resistance.

All three thinkers, as now must be obvious, question the traditional notion of the intellectual. All question the "universalist" intellectual in terms of his or her refusal to recognize the specificity of historically rooted practices, especially those intellectual practices that comprise traditional liberal institutions like the university and serve as the basis of the authority and epistemic privilege for theoretical pronouncements. By contrast, they emphasise a limited, more specific, local role for intellectuals who can engage in a politics of resistance or a politics of marginality that is sensitive to the institutional sites of power and knowledge in forming the dominant regime of truth and yet refrains from the indignity of speaking for others.

This conception of the specific intellectual, while not immune to criticism (see, for instance, the instructive essay of Radhakrishan, 1990), at least presents a politics of intellectuality which recognizes both that the question Who speaks? is inherently a political one and that "speaking for" is a (representational) act of violence. Given the kinds of changes I have been describing under the banner of postmodern culture — and, in particular, the heterogeneity of subject-positions — the challenge that this view of the intellectual represents to the traditional intellectual of modernity should recommend a reconsideration of conceptions of intellectual practice and their central-ity within cultural studies. In postcolonial countries like Canada, Australia and New Zealand, where the question Who speaks? has been repressed in official and academic discourses alike and only now is beginning to be heard, where those who chose to speak in their native tongue were ignored, punished or penalized, the politics of intellectuality takes on a new urgency.

NOTES

1.   This chapter is based on a paper first presented at a staff-student M.A. seminar program in the Education Department at the University of Canterbury, May 2, 1991. I acknowledge the constructive criticisms of participants at the seminar and also the helpful suggestions made by a member of the editorial board of *Sites* on an earlier version of this chapter.

2.   I have self-consciously chosen to identify the intellectual in female terms not simply out of respect for the feminist subject and against the demands of sexist language. This form of address is also meant to symbolize (following Smith, 1988, p. 152) how "feminism's critique of patriarchal culture has been perhaps the most effective and sustained contestatory discourse of the last twenty years or so." Feminism, according to Smith (p. 150), has been so effective precisely because of its "double strategy" of critiquing the fixed patriarchal subject inherited from traditional humanist thought while accepting from poststructuralism the notion of the dispersed or decentered subject. By deploying both strategies simultaneously, Smith argues, feminism is uniquely able (among the various discourses of resistance) to formulate the subject both "in terms of its experience as dominated 'subject' and also as an active contestatory social agent" (p. 152). The notion of intellectual provisionally subscribed to is (loosely) meant to refer to what Aronowitz and Giroux (1985) call "transformative intellectuals."

3.   See Dana Polan (1990) who coins the phrase "mediatization of the intellectual."

4.   It could be argued within liberal-capitalist states that the introduction of the new information technology demands that intellectuals address themselves not only to its uses and products — "images of popular, commercial culture" — but also to a critical approach to the now prevalent notions of "information society" and "information culture." For recent critical approaches in this area see Poster (1990), Luke (1991) and Raulet (1991).

5.   This is not to suggest that the crises experienced by Britain and, say, New Zealand are the same. Under Thatcherism it is a question of national identity from the point of view of a declining world power. In New Zealand, on the other hand, it is more a question of the cultural redefinition of national identity from the perspective of an ex-colony. While the new right, in universalist terms, wants to reduce us all to "rational utility-maximizers" in a way that is both gender- and culture-blind, resist-ance against this new hegemony is framed by questions of a small country still trying to come to terms with its colonial, white-settler past.

6.   Keat and Abercrombie state that the idea of enterprise culture "has emerged as a central motif in the political thought and practice of the Conservative government

in Britain" (1991, p. 1). The task of constructing such a culture has involved remodelling institutions along commercial lines and encouraging the acquisition and use of enterprising qualities. In accordance with this ideology, both the welfare state and the education system have been criticized for leading to the "culture of dependency." There are clear signs that the Thatcherite notion of enterprise culture has been adopted by the New Zealand government as part of official discourse designed to represent issues of economic and institutional reform in cultural terms. In part, the use of enterprise culture has been devised as a new-right counterpoint and strategy to a (new-right defined) culture of dependency.

7.   Interestingly, Flower, reviewing the question of intellectuals in recent French thought, refers to Henri Lévy's claim that the crisis of intellectuals is so critical "that historians will regard the intellectual as no more than a curious passing feature of twentieth-century social and cultural history" (1991, p. 278). In Lévy's neo-liberal eyes, Flower reports, the democratization of culture is to blame.

8.   Poststructuralism has an important historical and conceptual place in any discussion of the two paradigms of cultural studies — culturalism and structuralism. While Pickering (1991, pp. 19ff) acknowledges the move to poststructuralism, he does not emphasize how it superseded the structure-agency debate or the way in which it predates, considerably, the emergence and delineation of the two paradigms in cultural studies. The deliberations of Derrida (1978a) seem most appropriate here, in particular his early seminal essay, "Structure, Sign and Play in the Discourse of the Human Sciences," originally delivered as a lecture at Johns Hopkins University in 1966. The essay, which some commentators interpret as marking the moment when poststructuralism as a movement begins, opposes both classical structuralism (and particularly that of Lévi-Strauss) and traditional humanism.

9.   Roland Barthes (1983). "Writers, Intellectuals, Teachers." In Susan Sontag (Ed.), *Roland Barthes: Selected Writings* (pp. 378–403). New York: Fontana. Aronowitz and Giroux (1985), in their chapter "Teaching and the Role of the Transformative Intellectual," analyze the social function of educators as intellectuals in terms of the following categories: transformative intellectuals, critical intellectuals, accommodating intellectuals and hegemonic intellectuals. The significant contribution revolves around the first category, which attempts to articulate a view that unites the language of critique with that of possibility by recognizing how teachers are tied to a specific social formation although able to perform a function that is expressively political in nature. The authors are aware that the language of critique has eliminated room for hope and institutionally focused struggle. Their view is what might be termed a "reformed Deweyism," still framed within the tradition of a critical education or pedagogy. To that extent the authors have not come to terms with the poststructuralist critique. See Giroux and McLaren (1991) for an explicit attempt to go beyond a pedagogy of reproduction and resistance on the basis of poststructuralist insights. See also Muller and Cloete (1987), who, in the South African context, argue for a view of "intellectual labor" which, based on the work of Foucault and Derrida, recognizes forms of *popular* knowledge production as a means of empowerment for the working class. Specifically they challenge participatory action research and Touraine's intervention sociology as being wedded to metaphysical assumptions about the nature of consciousness and knowledge framed in terms of hierarchical binary opposites. The engagement of intellectuals is not to be seen in terms of either the "handmaiden" or "conscientization" models, but rather as a means that simultaneously releases subjugated knowledges (Foucault's "counter-memory") while setting in train a process of empowerment.

10.   Part of the discussion of Foucault's notion of intellectual is drawn from an earlier paper written in collaboration with James Marshall (Marshall and Peters, 1990). I thank him for allowing me to use part of that text in this chapter.

11.   Foucault, referring to the Frankfurt School and French structuralism, acknowledges the "remarkable problem of non-penetration of two forms of thought, which are akin to each other" and remarks, "If I had known the Frankfurt School at the right time, I would have been spared a lot of work" (1989a, pp. 241–43).

12.   It is important to note also "Kristeva's skepticism toward the taking of political positions, her dismissal of collective feminist organization, her privileging of dissident individualism, her flirtations with anti-Semitic writing, her revindication of America" (Smith, 1988, p. 33).

3

Against Alain Finkielkraut's *The Undoing of Thought:* Culture, Education and Postmodernism

INTRODUCTION

If an analytic table of contents were drawn up according to objects of veneration and objects of vilification, Alain Finkielkraut's (1988) *The Undoing of Thought* would fall apart neatly at the seams to reveal an obvious and uncompromising division: two sides, the one labelled "Universal," "Absolute," "Reason," "Truth," "Individual" and "Democracy"; the other constructed from a series of terms that constitute opposites — *Volksgeist*, cultures (in the plural), the collective will or unconscious, historical reason, contingency. For Finkielkraut, the first set of privileged terms in this hierarchy represents a process of the historical self-development of humanity leading to the apex of present neoliberal European "civilization," which in the alleged universality of its reason both embodies and attempts to preserve the rationalism of the Enlightenment.

The second set, emphasizing the "local" knowledges and reasons of various particular cultures — of both national and traditional cultures and those of social, economic and ethnic groups within the modern nation state (Raymond Williams) — stand under the combined signs of pluralism and history. The purported decline of the European, universalist, rationalist worldview under the menacing sign of cultural pluralism signifies for Finkielkraut, following his countryman Renan, "The most dangerous explosive of modern times" (Finkielkraut, 1988, p. 43). The terms of this dichotomy can also be described as an attack on the intellectually historical Other — the last past generation of the French left — by a member of the most recent generation of French intellectuals who, together, proclaim the end of one paradigm and the establishment of a new one. The officially designated shift is from poststructuralism to neoliberalism. Rational liberalism is fiercely anti-Nietzschean; its polemical target is both structuralism (Louis

Althusser, Jacques Lacan, Claude Lévi-Strauss) and poststructuralism (Michel Foucault, Jacques Derrida, Jean-François Lyotard, Gilles Deleuze and Félix Guattari). Now that the "philosophy of rebellion" is dead, or at least in its twilight, we can look forward to a renaissance of humanism, liberalism, individualism and democracy. Such is said to be reflected in the new philosophical agenda: "the disappearance of historical teleology," the end of "nihilism, antihumanism, and the critique of identity and the subject" as viable alternatives for French thought; and a return to individualism and humanism, the recovery of human agency, intentionality and consciousness (see Pavel, 1989, p. 17).

This constitutes the generalized intellectual background against which Finkielkraut's *The Undoing of Thought* must be read. At the more specific and popular level, Finkielkraut's attack is against the notion of culture, not as "life with thought" or Enlightenment reason (which is venerated) but as that which embraces everyday life and practice. The first sense is associated with "the higher life," with the separation of history and reason, with universalist values; the second is both local and particularistic. It is *my* culture in the sense that it provides the language, the moral and political traditions that are the historical limits of my being. The collapse of this distinction, this privileged hierarchy, is the cause of our present cultural malaise, and Finkielkraut aims to restore it. He writes: "In effect the term 'culture' now has two meanings. The first asserts the pre-eminence of the life of thought; the second denies this: from everyday gestures to the great creations of the human spirit, is not everything cultural?" (1988, p. 8).

His book, then, is to be considered in heroic terms as the continuation of the struggle of the philosophers of the Enlightenment against German romanticism. It is also to be seen as a violent reaction against the poststructuralist critique of reason, which supposedly has aided and abetted the decline of Enlightenment values. From this latter perspective, at the subliminal level of the text, Finkielkraut's *The Undoing of Thought* represents an escape or liberation from the pedagogical bonds and oppressive tutelage of his teachers — the master thinkers of the 1960s and 1970s — who have been criticized by the emergent generation for the "obscurity of thought and style. . . , their refusal of rational discussion, and their oppression of young scholars, who either had to follow their masters blindly or be excluded from the group" (Pavel, 1989, p. 18).

In these terms, perhaps, one might suggest that it is a family quarrel, peculiar to the highly centralized French cultural milieu and not of much abiding concern elsewhere. But such an interpretation, while tapping psychological motivations, does not adequately grasp the external dimensions of the argument. It does not explain, for instance, the political economy of a text that has arisen to reassert humanism, individualism and individual rights in universal terms at the same historical moment when the new right is on the ascendant, when market-based arrangements conceived in individualist consumer terms have been hailed as the optimal solution for social and cultural life, when techno-science is celebrated as the means of making the transition to the postindustrial society and the ethic of social responsibility has all but vanished from the agendas of Western governments — in short, at a time when a form of neoliberalism provides the best possible conditions under which such a text might flourish. This chapter, following Thomas Pavel (1989), makes some brief remarks on the current intellectual milieu of a recent generation of French thinkers. It then proceeds to outline systematically the structure and content of Finkielkraut's narrative, proposing some criticisms of the position advanced in *The Undoing of Thought* along the way. Specifically, the chapter takes issue with the way Finkielkraut both defines postmodernism and relates it to his understanding of the current cultural crisis of education.

FRENCH NEOLIBERALISM AND THE CURRENT INTELLECTUAL MILIEU

Pavel (1989) begins his account of the recent generation of French intellectuals by observing that the French cultural milieu is notable for its "density," "its powerful alliances" that develop across generations and "its frequent upheavals" in the formation of new cultural consensuses. This is to suggest an explicit model of intergenerational conflict as the motor for intellectual change where paradigm choice is governed as much by the forces of reaction as by intellectual appraisal of what has gone before. Indeed, there is a certain measure of truth in accepting that the poststructuralist writings of Derrida, Foucault, Lyotard and Deleuze were themselves a reaction or rebellion against a particular strand of Hegelianism made popular among the first generation of interpreters (Jean Hyppolite and Alexandre Kojève).

As I suggested in Chapter 1, while the critique of humanism and anthropologism was for Derrida, at the time of writing in the early 1970s, one of the dominant and guiding motifs of current French thought, it was, he thought, more a product of an amalgamation of G.W.F. Hegel, Edmund Husserl and Martin Heidegger with the old metaphysical humanism than a central requestioning of humanism.

In these terms, perhaps, we should not be overly surprised at the negative formation of the younger generation of French intellectuals against their masters. Yet as well as rebellion there is also a detectable and progressive continuity in the thought of the poststructuralist thinkers with the preceeding generation, particularly in terms of a preoccupation with the Hegelian subject — its cultural and historical specification, its displacement, fragmentation and eventual death or rejection.

By way of contrast, there is no continuity, apparent or acknowledged, in the "break" constituted by the new generation, and certainly, if Finkielkraut's *The Undoing of Thought* is considered to be representative of the new orientation, there is not much evidence of analysis or genuine appraisal of poststructuralism.

Pavel reviews the influential French periodical *Le Débat*, its special fiftieth issue (May–August 1988): *"Notre histoire: Matériaux pour servir à l'histoire intellectuelle de la France 1953–1987."* The journal began in 1980 under the general editorship of Pierre Nora with Marcel Gauchet and Krzysztof Pomian as junior partners. In an early contribution, *"Que peuvent les intellectuels"* (1980), Nora provided the warning that *"le règne des penseurs supérieurs touchait à son terme."* In a footnote Pavel lists the names contributing to an issue of *Le Débat* (September 1980) devoted to the intellectual future of France — names, as Pavel comments "that were later to become landmarks of the 1980s: Pascal Bruckner, Alain Finkielkraut, Vincent Descombes, Jean-Luc Marion, Olivier Mongin, Phillippe Raynaud, Pierre Rosanvallon, and Emmanuel Todd" (1989, pp. 18–19). Pavel observes that while their answers ranged widely they "all agree that nihilism, anti-humanism, and the critique of identity and the subject were no longer viable alternatives for French thought" (1989, p. 20).

The central section of *"Notre histoire . . . ,"* entitled *"Mots-Moments,"* Pavel informs us, consists of a detailed chronology expressing key ideas as the spirit of intellectual trends: "It models the epoch from the 1950s to the 1980s as a five-act drama, with Existentialism (1945–56) as the introduction; Alienation (1956–68) as the complication; Structure (1968–72) and Desire and Power (1972–76) as the crisis; and Neo-Liberalism (1976 to the present) as the happy resolution" (1989, p. 20).

French postwar intellectual history is presented, if I am permitted further to summarize Pavel, as the struggle of French culture to free itself from "the shadow of an imperial past" and "the infatuation with Marxism-Leninism." In this scheme of things, Deleuze and Guattari's *Anti-Oedipus* becomes the "twilight of the philosophy of rebellion" and Foucault's theory of power is seen as "a weapon in the last delaying fight against . . . the necessity of making a choice between democracy and totalitarianism" (cited in Pavel, 1989, p. 21). The new intellectual world is "post-ideological" and its inhabitants are "moderate humanists and supporters of democracy." Pavel reports: "The renaissance of liberalism and individualism goes hand and hand with a new sense of the uniqueness of European culture" (1989, p. 22). We are told further that neoliberalism "rejects the hegemony of speculative philosophy, proposing instead a renewed interest in the study of religion, a promotion of the scientific culture and a change of paradigm in the social sciences" (p. 20).

At this point, Pavel engages both the artifice of the drama presented — it could have been conceived differently — and the notion of paradigm, its possible construals, its chronological scope, its "topological properties" and its problematic application to the realm of the social sciences. He indicates that when one is dealing with "the apex of a highly centralized culture such as Paris," the temptation to overstate "short term tremors in intellectual fashion" is greatly increased (Pavel, 1989, p. 20).

To a large degree the proclamation of both the end of the philosophical program initiated by the master thinkers and the beginning of a new one, it appears, is established by intellectual fiat. The irony is that in a so-called postideological age — a phrase that revives the "end of ideology" thesis popular among conservatives in the 1950s and that is pursued with fresh vigor by the likes of Fukuyama in the 1990s — this recommendation for intellectual change seems itself to be transparently ideological. The double irony that vitiates both the new program and Finkielkraut's specific project is that the "reestablishment" of absolute and universal values necessary to ground neoliberalism is apparently achieved not on the basis of transcendental argument but rather on a parochial historical narrative, a re-description of the fate of reason in terms of an account largely internal to French intellectual life.

THE UNDOING OF THOUGHT?

A quick inventory of Finkielkraut's objects of vilification establishes the parameters and chronology of his narrative: Herder, German romanticism and the concept of *Volksgeist* (Part One); UNESCO (United Nations Educational, Scientific, and Cultural Organization), anthropology and the "the philosophy of decolonization" (Part Two); multiculturalism and the human sciences (Part Three); and the contemporary school (Part Four). These contents, titled, respectively, "The Roots of the Human Mind," "Generous Betrayal," "Towards a Multicultural Society" and "We Are the World, We Are the Children," are squeezed between two one-page statements, a sort of prologue ("In the Shadow of a Great Word"), and a final reflection. The latter, entitled "The Zombie and the Fanatic," reads like a cryptic advertisement for the lost values of a forgotten era:

So barbarism has finally taken over culture, in the shadow of which lofty word intolence grows, along with infantilism. When cultural identity does not forcibly lock the individual into his traditional way of life, refusing him access, under pain of high treason, to doubt, irony or reason — that is to say to everything which would help him break free of the collective matrix — then the same effect is achieved by the leisure industry, that creature of the technological age, which reduces the works of the spirit to shoddy goods or, as the Americans say, to entertainment. Intellectual activity gives way to the terrible and mocking encounter between the fanatic and the zombie. (Finkielkraut, 1988, p. 133)

In reconstructive, polemical stories that treat history as a series of fables pointing to moral and epistemological lessons, there are always heroes and villains. In Part One of Finkielkraut's tract, Herder is the villain and Julien Benda the hero. Benda (1969), in his *The Treason of the Intellectuals* denounced the way in which intellectuals of his day were ceasing to uphold the idea of eternal values, devoting themselves instead to the cause of a parochially conceived nationalism and transmuting "culture" into "my culture." This transmutation, upon which the second meaning of culture was rendered, is a legacy of German romanticism. The concept itself originates with Herder in the term *Volksgeist*. Finkielkraut asserts that Herder "drove back the Good, the True and the Beautiful to their local origins, he dislodged the eternal categories from their smug security in heaven and returned them to their earthly place of birth. There was nothing absolute, Herder proclaimed; there were only regional values and contingent principles" (1988, p. 12).

The notion of *Volksgeist*, together with the recognition of religion, language and ethnic origin, provided the conceptual resources to invoke the concept of "nation," which, in the hands of the "revolutionaries" (Joseph de Maistre, Bonald), was to be defined principally by the unity of a culture — a collective historical formation as opposed to the transcendent notion of the aggregration of freely contracting individuals, built on a metaphysics of human nature.

Finkielkraut traces the debate between the revolutionaries (traditionalists) and the *philosophes* (and their republican disciples). He charts the course of this debate through the events of the Franco-Prussian War, the conquest of Alsace-Lorraine and the rise of Pan-Germanism. He writes: "With the triumph of Pan-Germanism, Goethe's educative influence in Germany was wiped out. Culture was reduced to the cult of origins. The *Volksgeist* triumphed, and revealed, to boot, its totalitarian potential" (1988, p. 41).

Alongside these events, Finkielkraut interweaves a narrative on the intellectual fortunes of epistemology. The "German Romantics" and the "French Theocrats" "nevertheless accomplished a veritable epistemological revolution. Their hatred of modernity gave birth to a radically new conception of man. Their nostalgia provoked a mutation in thought which still holds us, broadly speaking, in its sway. Their ferocious reactionaries were also involuntary innovators. In their mania to restore man to his proper place they discovered the unconscious thoughts that work in him, and in so doing they founded the human sciences" (1988, p. 28). We are presented, then, with two starkly contrasting visions of nature, man and culture, which never before had split European opinion to the same extent.

Taking up the story in the next chapter, we are transposed, catapulted, into the mid-twentieth century. The scene is London in November 1945; the event is the establishment of UNESCO. While the thinkers that gathered at the end of World War II to draw up a new agenda for freedom and peace seemed to be adopting the spirit of the Enlightenment — "the intellectual influence of the *philosophes* seemed to hang over the setting up of UNESCO and to dictate to its framers their very terms of reference" (p. 54) — the conception of man that was to furnish the raw materials for the institutional framework began to shift. Finkielkraut maintains, "What had begun as a critique of fanaticism turned into a critique of Enlightenment-style thinking" (p. 55). Abstract humanism, postulating a universal subject in highly individualistic terms, was replaced by an anthropological conception that emphasized concrete and historical modes of existence and their cultural diversity. In particular, Finkielkraut focuses on a text by Lévi-Strauss (*Race et histoire*) prepared for UNESCO in 1951, in which he draws attention to the ethnocentrism implicit in the European view of history as the unilinear progress of a universal reason. Against this view, Lévi-Strauss suggests that the subject matter of anthropology is cultures, in the plural, meaning "particular ways of life" unable to be ranked or put into any sequence of development.

The so-called second death of man is accomplished, according to Finkielkraut, by historians who, following the intellectual fashion set by Lévi-Strauss, sought to stress the variety of the human story, its diversity and discontinuities, instead of inscribing it in a single evolutionary text. By what Finkielkraut calls "this essential *disorientation of history*," historians "pursued the same goal in relation to time as the anthropologists in relation to space" (1988, p. 60). The effect of the study of remote times compounded the undermining of the idea of "European civilization." Finkielkraut puts it as follows: "The emperor suddenly had no clothes. We Europeans of the second half of the twentieth century were, it now transpired, but just another culture, just one more fleeting and perishable human variety" (p. 60).

This state of affairs parodied by Finkielkraut can be resisted only by irony. The undermining was completed, we are told, under Marxist sociology, which disposed of the grand illusion of modern civilization by characterizing it as a set of class and group cultures, not unified but in conflict with the dominant class culture. In this context, he notes how Bourdieu and Passeron define the culture of a group or class as a symbolic system constituted in terms of a selection of meanings that is arbitrary in the sense that it can neither be deduced from any universal principle nor linked by any sort of internal relation to the "nature of things" or "human nature." Finkielkraut complains that in this way sociological theory utilized the same conceptualization that anthropology had employed to explain the relations between the West and non-European peoples.

The philosophy of decolonization re-adopts the romantic idea of culture to speak for the Other rather than one's own culture or for the figural differentiations within one's own culture. Frantz Fanon, in this context, becomes the villain; the most fierce antagonist to the universalizability of the values of European civilization. With Fanon originates the ethnic theory of the nation based on a notion of collective identity, which threatened both individualism and cosmopolitanism. Finkielkraut's historical explanation here approaches a blind partisanship that smacks of a European ethnocentric simplicity. "With monotonous regularity these liberation movements have thrown up oppressive regimes. This is because they have based themselves on the mystical notion of collective fusion rather than on the juridical conception of contract. They have drawn on political romanticism and conceived liberty as a collective attribute rather than as an individual possession" (1988, p. 70). His attack carries through the analysis to a neoliberal understanding of the political language of race. The substitution of the cultural notion of collectivity for an earlier biological conception represents for Finkielkraut simply a return of racism, not its abolition.

One might casually remark here on the propensity of neoliberals (such as Allan Bloom and Richard Rorty) who, having faced the collapse of ahistorical legitimations of liberal society based on universal foundations, wish simply to reassert liberal values in pragmatic and blatantly ethnocentric terms. In this case the glorification of contingent social practices is witnessed in an unconscious slippage indicated in preferred pronouns — we, us, our — that constitutes to my mind a genuine inability to think in terms other than what neoliberals take to be the only possible worldview. It represents a failure of imagination. For that reason this covert ethnocentrism must be accepted and analyzed at the pathological level.

In Finkielkraut's final section of Part Two he points to an alleged reversal in Lévi-Strauss' thinking and in "the double language of UNESCO." Rather than culture depending on race, the reverse is seen to be the case. This discovery, in educational terms, leads from the ethic of self-cultivation to the immersion and re-discovery of one's own culture. Finkielkraut is, of course, protesting against the possibility of substituting a plurality of systems for a closed and universally conceived system — a system that operates within one homogeneous medium of rationality disclosed for us by his chosen heroes of the European Enlightenment. Given this ahistorical and unchanging context, what might appear as progress in understanding on the basis of critical thinking and experience is reduced to the logical function of a set of antinomies.

Part Three becomes the extension of these ethnocentric sentiments under the guise of an argument to attack the notion of "a multi-cultural society." In a situation where, through massive migration, it is now the inhabitants of Europe who are the natives, Finkielkraut maintains, "The fact is that we have to choose. It is contradictory to preach, simultaneously, the virtues of universal communication and the unique, inexplicable character of particular cultures" (1988, p. 93).

"A pedagogy of relativity" is the means by which, he asserts, multi-culturalists intend to overcome the "natural preferences" (not prejudices) of home cultures. Finkielkraut refers to "Proposals for Education in the Future", a report from the Collège de France made to the French President in 1985, and he quotes its first principle: *"The unity of science and the plurality of cultures*. A well-attuned education has to bring together the universalism integral to scientific thinking and the relativism which characterises the human sciences, sensitive as they are to the wide variety of ways of life, understanding and culture" (1988, p. 95).

Rather than countenancing arguments advanced by those, say, within the hermeneutical tradition or the Frankfurt School for a radical separation of the human from the natural sciences, Finkielkraut relies on a clumsy irony, one that smacks of cultural self-righteousness and indignation. Some selected examples follow. Speaking of the human sciences as they are perceived in the report, he suggests:

By collapsing cultivation into culture, they prevent our complacent self-preoccupation and our tendency to construct the world in our own image; at the same time they cure us of our imperialism and tribalism, of our belief that we are the titled bearers of the universal ideal, and of the aggressive tendency to affirm our cultural specificity. (Finkielkraut, 1988, p. 96)

A hundred and fifty years later *the University itself reduces the novel to the level of an achive* and restricts the right to transcend the moment of their birth and place of origin to the works of scince alone. We are warned in the very first words of the Collège de France's report: in science and only in science can man raise himself above the perceptual schema rooted in him by the culture to which he belongs. (Finkielkraut, 1988, p. 97)

To contemplate the possibility of postmodern science would be a complete anathema for Finkielkraut, although such a possibility has been seriously argued by a range of thinkers over the last decade (Lyotard, 1984; Toulmin, 1982). Without responding in argumentative terms to each of these statements, it is clear that Finkielkraut's fear is that culture will be left in pieces. He laments the passing of an age that celebrated French high culture as the universal norm, as guarding the vital ingredients of the French Enlightenment. He laments the corruption of the universalist ideal of high culture and the fact that it is one culture among many. His argument seems to be not that there is something distinct and defining about this culture that is of special note, but that there is something universalist about its nature that ought to supplant and transcend the emphasis on its historical particu-larity. Nowhere is this more strongly expressed than in Finkielkraut's accent on the individual and individuality as a defining characteristic of modern Europe.

The rights of man were established in Europe *against* the widely practised and deeply entrenched system of primogeniture. It was *at the expense of his culture* that the individual European gained, one by one, all his freedoms. Finally, it was, generally speaking, the habit of examining traditions critically which constituted the spiritual foundation of Europe. The anti-imperialist ideology we have learned today has made us forget all this, by persuading us that the individual is nothing more than a cultural phenomenon." (1988, p. 104)

In this gender- and culture-biased passage, Finkielkraut is simultaneously guilty of confusing historical and prescriptive modes of thinking and of romanticizing the notion of the individual. He refrains from serious engagement with historical and philosophical themes surrounding the "death of the subject" as it is explored in the work of Foucault and Derrida. Instead, he wants to celebrate the spirit of the Modern Age and its mythical expression in the (European) nation as comprised of "free and equal individuals." He ignores Derrida's critique of the metaphysics of presence and Foucault's critique of the modes of subjectivity constructed under liberal institutions and practices whereby human beings are made individuals. Nor is there anything here to counter the weight of a corporate capitalism or the bureaucratic state that helped set the wider social parameters within which people are defined as individuals.

It is not, however, until we come to Part Four that the shrillness of Finkielkraut's tone reaches its peak. He has saved himself for a last diatribe, the object of his passionate attack — postmodernism and education. While postmodernists advocate multicultural societies, they do so, we are told, on grounds different from those of the multi-culturalists: where the latter base their case on "the equality of all cultures," the former are alleged to exalt the uncertainties of cultural fluidity over the fixed virtues of cultural rootedness.

Finkielkraut's strategy is largely to ignore the debate about postmodernism that has taken place over the last two decades in order to typify the phenomenon in negative and unproblematic terms. Postmodernism "replace[s] our former exclusive approaches by eclecticism," promotes "a deliberate mingling of styles" and brings together "the most disparate of fads and fashions, and the most contradictory of influences." For Finkielkraut postmodernism is a fragmentary and inauthentic world comprised of culture-tasters and consumer-kings; it is a "raging nihilism" that levels all distinctions in cultures, maintaining, "All cultures are equally legitimate and everything is cultural" (1988, pp. 111–12). "A comic which combines exciting intrigue and some pretty pictures is just as good as a Nabokov novel. What little Lolitas read is as good as *Lolita*. An effective publicity slogan counts for as much as a poem by Apollinaire or Francis Ponge. A rock song is in no way inferior to a melody of Duke Ellington" (p. 113).

Finkielkraut's complaint against postmodernism is that it has blotted out the distinction between culture and entertainment; that it advocates a "new ideal type" — the multicultural individual; that it no longer sees culture as a means of emancipation, or democracy as the access to culture for everybody. This constitutes Finkielkraut's understanding of postmodernism and on this basis he ascribes to education "the present crisis."

The school in the modern sense of that word is a product of the Enlightenment, and it is dying today because the authority of the Enlightenment has been called into question. A gulf has opened between the outlook of society and this institution governed by the strange idea that there is no autonomy without thought, and no thought without hard work on one's own character. . . . School is the last-ditch exception to generalised self-service. . . . The school is modern, but the pupils are post-modern. School aims to form the mind; the pupils have the butterfly minds of young tele-addicts. . . . The pupils translate . . . [the] emancipatory vision into an archaic programme for human subjugation, and, in a single act of rebellion, reject both discipline and teaching, both the master who dominates and the teacher who instructs them. (1988, p. 124)

The "reform" of education has, according to Finkielkraut, resolved the contradiction by making the school postmodern. It has initiated an "education of consumption" based on pandering to the young. It has adjusted methods and curricula to reflect the demands of a youth culture based on rock music, jeans and comics. The postmodern school, driven by hedonism and consumerism, has culminated in the worship of juvenile values. This "general infantilising," this "triumph of babydom over thought" (p. 129) has its deintellectualizing effects not only in education, but also in politics, journalism, art and literature, moral life and religion. Finkielkraut ends his tirade against youth and, indeed, his book with a final excursus entitled "The Zombie and the Fanatic."

The reader initially dumbstruck by this unrelenting attack on all the evils of postmodernism and contemporary schooling in the name of Enlightenment values might wonder at an appropriate response. Could argument and analyses be of any value here? Should we attempt to point to errors of conflation and confusion? Is there any room for empirical evidence of any kind? Do thinking, thought and the possibility of disagreement have roles to play now that the malaise, its diagnosis and its cure, have been so poignantly and so eloquently asserted? On Finkielkraut's totalizing worldview the answers to these questions must be already evident. The theoretical universe is closed to further discussion, analysis or speculation.

CULTURE, POSTMODERNISM AND EDUCATION

Against Finkielkraut's all-embracing perspective I want to venture a few ruminations on the nature and significance of postmodernism and its implications for education and schooling. First, while it is true that postmodernism as it has come to be generally interpreted involves or signals an epochal break both with the modern era and with traditionally modern ways of viewing the world, it is a mistake to identify postmodernism with poststructuralism. This is not to deny that there are relations between the two, only that any simple identification of one with the other is misleading. It is also a mistake to equate postmodernism with postmodernity, or to assert that these terms have their equivalences in terms of simple contrasts with modernism and modernity. To do so is to frame the debate in strictly (and naïvely) modernist terminology that employs an exhaustive binary opposition, privileging one set of terms against the other. Finkielkraut commits all these sins of conflation. To him postmodernism is an unproblematic seamless web incorporating all manner of things: multiculturalism, philosophies of postcolonialism, consumerism, poststructuralism and so on. It follows that Finkielkraut is unable to distinguish ideological positions within the modernist-postmodernist debate (Jameson, 1984) or recognize the way in which a postmodernism of resistance may differ from a postmodernism of reaction (Foster, 1985). Finkielkraut's failure here means that he is prohibited from acknowledging the emancipatory potential of a critical pluralism based on the significance of the new social movements (Young, 1990; Peters, 1991). In related fashion, Finkielkraut deliberately attempts to collapse any distinction between the critical projects of postmodernist theory and postcolonial criticism. As Slemon comments, these projects "have remained more or less separate in their strategies and their foundational assumptions" (1989, p. 4).

Second, postmodernism, considered as an emergent Western cultural phenomenon based on an aesthetic break, is various, displaying a radical plurality of forms. It is not helpful to try to assimilate a postmodernism in architecture, say, with a postmodernism in poetry, or in fiction, in dance or in the visual arts (Trachtenberg, 1985). Indeed, even within each of these activities it does not make sense to suggest that there is a unitary set of assumptions or principles. They make up different language games. There may be overlapping family resemblances of characteristics that happen to be shared by elements within or even among genres, but such resemblances do not constitute nonambiguous or discrete homologies. One would not, for instance, want to treat the novels of John Barth, Donald Barthelme, Robert Coover, Kurt Vonnegut and Thomas Pynchon in the same way, or to suggest that they are of a piece with the novels of Manuel Puig or Carlos Fuentes. Yet it may be possible to argue, as Linda Hutcheon does, following Huyssen, that "postmodern fiction has come to contest the modernist ideology of artistic autonomy, individual expression, and the deliberate separation of art from mass culture and everyday life" (1989, p. 15).

This claim is altogether different from the claims made by Finkielkraut, who assimilates postmodernism to consumerism and mass culture. To conflate these terms and to posit postmodernism as a periodizing concept coming after modernism (as Finkielkraut does) is to ignore the influential interpretation of the postmodern given by Jean-François Lyotard, who argues, "Postmodernism . . . is not modernism at its end but in the nascent state, and this state is constant" (1984, p. 79). Further, as James Collins points out, "The postmodern redefinition of mass culture does not necessitate an open acceptance of all popular texts or the end of 'decidability of effect'" (1987, p. 26). Even Fredric Jameson (1989a, p. 38), who advances a neo-Marxian interpretation of postmodernism as the cultural logic of late capitalism, most recently indicates that a mode of production includes counterforces and new tendencies within itself.

Third, to suggest that "the school is modern" and that "the pupils are postmodern" is to provide a gloss that ignores just about all the important issues. To set up the terms of the debate in this way is both to falsely dichotomize and to trivialize what is at stake. It is a deliberate rhetorical strategy to pit pupils as products of a consumerist mass culture against the school as the guardian of Enlightenment reason. It is to assume that the only answer to the problem is a reform program that returns to the values of the Enlightenment. While it is true that educational theory and practice have always been strongly wedded to the language and assumptions of modernism, it is also true that modernism has exercised a hegemonic and reactionary influence over aspects of the form of schooling. Postmodern criticism in the realm of educational discourse, Henry Giroux argues, is important "because it offers the promise of deterritorializing and redrawing the political, social and cultural boundaries of modernism while simultaneously affirming a politics of racial, gender, and ethnic difference" (1988, p. 6).

In this way postmodern criticism challenges culturally dominant Western models that are underwritten by a foundational epistemology and claim universally valid knowledge, often at the expense of "local," subjugated knowledges. Interestingly, Giroux believes that the project for a critical education does not involve a choice between modernism and postmodernism. In taking this stand he is not alone. Michel Foucault, reading a minor but important text of Kant's, argues that the thread connecting us to the Enlightenment cannot be interpreted in terms of doctrine but, rather, involves a philosophical attitude, "a philosophical ethos that could be described as a permanent critique of our historical era" (1984, p. 42).

Finkielkraut, in a tidy and convenient manner, divides history into the modern and the postmodern, reifying the (French) Enlightenment and refusing to recognize its dark side. The difficulty is that he does not recognize the extent to which the school as a developing institution, historically, has been part of an emerging political anatomy founded on disciplinary power derived from the use of the examination, hierarchical observation, and normalizing judgment as the means of correct training that, together, helped produce docile bodies (Foucault, 1979). Nor is he prepared to recognize the way in which liberal rhetoric concerning the achievement of freedom, equality and democracy through education has, in the twentieth century, served to mask and legitimate the social reproduction of inequalities along the lines of race, gender and class.

Alain Finkielkraut's is a celebration of traditional liberal values. It is a story based on a set of universal values and a certain philosophical and literary canon that defends French (high) culture against both a critique of the Enlightenment, of reason and the Other — other (particularly nonEuropean) cultures and values. To that extent it is very much an expression of its time — an unashamed Eurocentric and ethnocentric reassertion of liberal values at a point in history when Western governments have sought to establish a fully privatized market society. One of the central ironies of the "undoing of thought" is that the very mass consumer society against which Finkielkraut argues is in part an outcome of a set of historical conditions that we call the Enlightenment.

4

Foucault, Discourse and Education: Neoliberal Governmentality

In every society the production of discourse is at once controlled, selected, organised and redistributed by a certain number of procedures whose role is to ward off its powers and dangers, to gain mastery over its chance events, to evade its ponderous, formidable materiality.

— Michel Foucault[1]

Perhaps we could say that while the Renaissance substituted the cult of Man with a capital M for that of God of the Middle Ages, our era is bringing about a revolution of no less importance by effacing all cults, since it is replacing the latest cult, that of Man, with language, a *system* amenable to scientific analysis.

— Julia Kristeva[2]

INTRODUCTION

The condition of postmodernity represents both a break with the foundational philosophies of the Enlightenment and a crisis of its major secular ideologies — classical liberalism and Marxism. Since the dramatic events of 1989 and 1990, the focus of interest in the West has turned outward to the collapse of communism in Eastern Europe. These events have temporarily obscured and overshadowed political and economic developments within liberal-capitalist states. Paradoxically, at just the point when theorists such as Lyotard (1984) are heralding the bankruptcy of the metanarratives (*grand récits*) of the Enlightenment, liberal-capitalist states have witnessed the revival and revitalization of the master narrative of classical economic liberalism in the guise of the so-called new right as a basis for a "minimal" state.

Classical liberalism has been the dominant metanarrative, which, in one form at least, has appealed to reason in the form of an individualism that privileges the rational, knowing subject as the fount of all knowledge, signification, moral authority and action. The particular variant of this metanarrative that informs the economic rationalism of the new right is construed in the classical terms of *Homo economicus*, the assumption that in all of our behavior we act as self-interested individuals. Since the early 1980s the new right has been remarkably successful in advancing a foundationalist and universalist reason — the philosophy of a neoliberal individualism — as the basis for a radical reconstruction of all aspects of society: a change in economic policy favoring supply-side economics and monetarism, a complete restructuring of the public sector and a move away from the traditional welfare state. The form of political reason that has come to dominate the policy agendas of liberal-capitalist governments is Euro-centric in origin and both rationalistic and totalizing in its effects. In the simplest terms, we might say that this form of reason is motivated by an extreme economic rationalism that views the market not only as a superior allocative mechanism for the distribution of scarce public resources but also as a morally superior form of political economy. The central tenet of the theories underlying public sector restructuring, including corporatization and privatization strategies and a concerted attack on principles of the social-democratic state, is a philosophy of individualism that represents a renewal of the main article of faith underlying classical economic liberalism. It asserts that all human behavior is dominated by self-interest. Its major innovation in contemporary terms is to extend this principle to the status of a paradigm for understanding politics itself and, in fact, to understanding all behavior. The economic theory of politics maintains that people should be treated, *tout court*, as rational utility maximizers.

In global terms the new right represents a heightening and renewal of modernism's now dominant metanarrative. With the historical collapse of communism and the apparent popular decline of Marxism, liberalism has become progressively more transparent as the official ideology legitimating advanced multinational capitalism. Under new-right policies of deregulation and privatization, together with a massive state assets sales program, liberal-capitalist states have experienced a growing internationalization of their economies and, concomitantly, the significant influence of multinationals in the economy as key players. At the same time, the new right has advanced and reworked their variant of classical economic liberalism as a totalizing vision of the future. Such a project, for ideological purposes, construes the future in terms of a postindustrial utopian vision based on a faith in science, technology and education as the key sectors that will increase long-term national competitive advantage in the global economy. The new right has harnessed a policy master narrative of individualism to legitimate an extreme form of economic rationalism. This narrative as a legitimating device projects a unity on the future. It is future-oriented although anchored in the past. In a violent act of closure it represents the future in totalizing terms, excluding in the process other possible stories we might inscribe on the future by arguing that there is no alternative.

There is perhaps no better example of the extension of the market to new areas of social life than the field of education. In particular, it is clear that under the principles of neoliberalism education has been discursively restructured according to the logic of the market. Education, on this model, is treated no differently from any other service or commodity. As Norman Fairclough (1992) notes, a major part of this restructuring comprises changes in discourse practices where people find themselves under pressure to engage in new activities that are largely defined by new discourse practices such as marketing, advertising and management. These changes include discursive recodings of both activities and relationships with the result that learners become consumers or clients and courses become packages or products. A more subtle restructuring of the discourse practices of education has occurred in terms of a colonization of education by types of discourse from outside.

Foucault's work provides resources for understanding what I am going to call the *paradox* of the neoliberal state: the paradox is that while neoliberalism can be regarded as a doctrine concerning the self-limiting state, under neoliberal market policies the state has become more powerful. The understanding of this paradox can be fruitfully approached through Foucault's notion of governmentality, where power is understood in its widest sense as the structuring of the possible field of action of others. While neoliberal policies of the privatization of state assets and commercialization of the public sphere have led to a minimal state, or at least to a significant downsizing, the state has retained its institutional power through a new form of individualization where human beings turn themselves into market subjects under the sign of *Homo economicus*. This is the basis for understanding the "government of individuals" in education as a technique or form of power that is promoted through the adoption of market forms.

In the first section of this chapter I introduce Foucault's notion of discourse and its relation to the discursive production of the individual as a basis for an understanding of neoliberal educational policy. Foucault's work can be understood as a critique of the subject and of the liberal metanarrative of the self: an autonomous, rational and full transparent individual self, standing both separate to and logically prior to society, able to make choices in the market in accordance with its desires. In the second section, I investigate the ways in which education has been discursively restructured under the sign of *Homo economicus* as a form of neoliberal governmentality.

FOUCAULT, DISCOURSE, AND THE SUBJECT

Foucault (1983, p. 208) addresses himself to a reformulation of the goal of his work in the Afterword to the book by Dreyfus and Rabinow

(1983) in the year before he died. He indicates that his objective has been "to create a history of the different modes by which, in our culture, human beings are made subjects" and he maintains that his work has dealt with "three modes of objectification which transform human beings into subjects": the modes of inquiry of the discipline-based discourses that objectivized human beings in different and specific ways; the objectivizing of the subject through what he calls "dividing practices" (e.g., mad/sane, sick/healthy) and the way human beings turn themselves into subjects, especially in the realm of sexuality.

These three themes are analyzed in terms of a new economy of power relations that takes forms of resistance against different forms of power as a starting point. Rather than examining the links between the rationalization of society and power from the point of view of its internal rationality, Foucault scrutinizes the relations through the antagonism of strategies. He takes a series of oppositions — dividing practices involving the power of men over women, of parents over children, of medicine over the population at large, of psychiatry over the mentally ill — as a starting point and attempts to define precisely what they have in common. Crucially for Foucault, these are struggles that question the status of the individual; they are struggles, as he says, against "the government of individuals" (1983, p. 212), and their main objective is a technique or form of power. They are struggles against the effects of power that "are linked with knowledge, competence and qualification" (p. 212). Foucault notes two meanings of the word *subject*, suggesting that both meanings indicate a form of power that subjugates and makes subject to. On this basis he argues: "Generally, it can be said that there are three types of struggles; either against forms of domination (ethnic, social, and religious); against forms of exploitation which separate individuals from what they produce; or against that which ties the individual to himself and submits him to others in this way (struggles against subjection, against forms of subjectivity and submission)" (p. 212).

He suggests that while these three kinds of social struggles exist either in isolation or mixed together, the third kind has become more important in the present age, where the state's power is both individualizing and totalizing. This kind of power he investigates historically, in terms of the technique of pastoral power that originated in Christian institutions. The modern state, he argues, constitutes "a modern matrix of individualisation, or a new form of pastoral power" (Foucault, 1983, p. 215). The problem, therefore, is not to liberate us from the state per se but from the type of individualization that is linked to the state through this new form of pastoral power, and to promote new forms of subjectivity that escape the kind of individualization that has been imposed on us. Thus, Foucault focuses on the question of how power is exercised and analyzes the power relationship by focusing on carefully defined institutions where it has taken different forms (based around the school, the family and the justice and economic systems). In this way the exercise of power can be defined in terms of the way in which certain actions may structure the field of other possible actions, and ultimately, this emphasis leads to a focus on government in its widest sense as the structuring of the possible field of action of others. By analyzing power in these terms, Foucault links his analysis of forms of discourse, "the individualisation of discourses," not only with the so-called subject and its pluralist discursive formation but also with traditional themes in political economy and, in particular, with a critique of forms of liberal government (including its most recent neoliberal forms).

Perhaps the most important point that clarifies further Foucault's approach to discourse is his emphasis on the fact that he is a pluralist: the problem that he says he has set for himself is that of the individualization of discourses. In this regard he mentions known and dependable criteria: the isolation of the linguistic systems to which discourses belong and the identity of the subject that holds them together (i.e., the subject of psychiatry, of medicine, of grammar and so forth). To these criteria he adds criteria of *formation*, *transformation* and *correlation*, which permit the description of an *episteme* in terms of its play of specific differences within discursive space. Historical change for Foucault is to be analyzed by reference to different types of transformation in their specificity. Such an approach leads to the establishment of the following schema for studying change, but one that is not to be considered an exhaustive typology.

1. Changes *within* a given discursive formation, including that of deduction or implication, generalization, limitation, by shift between complementary objectives, by passing to the other term of a pair, through permutation of dependencies, exclusion or inclusion. (Foucault's model from which he draws his examples is that of general grammar).

2. Changes that affect discursive formations *themselves*, including the displacement of boundaries, new subject speaking positions, new modes of object-language functioning and new forms of localization and circulation of discourse.

3. Changes that simultaneously affect *several* discursive formations, including the inversions of hierarchies, change in the nature of the directing principle and functional displacements.

Foucault (1991b, p. 59) is concerned with analyzing the play of dependencies between intradiscursive, interdiscursive and extradiscursive levels of discourse in an archeology, which is the description of an archive, that is, "the set of rules which at a given period and for a given society define" the limits and forms of the sayable, of conservation, of memory, of reactivation and appropriation. In line with this approach Foucault's interest was to treat discourse as a monument, to be investigated in terms of its conditions of existence rather than the structural laws of its construction, and to be related "not to a thought, mind or subject which engendered it, but to the practical field in which it is deployed" (p. 61). Thus he returns to the theme of the author and the individual speaking subject, a theme significantly problematized in the structuralism and antihumanism of Lacan's psychoanalytical approach and later, most effectively, by Althusser. Foucault states explicitly at one point:

The question which I ask is not about codes but about events: the law of *existence* of statements, that which rendered them possible — them and none other in their place: the conditions of their singular emergence; their correlation with other previous or simultaneous events, discursive or otherwise. But I try to answer this question without referring to the consciousness, obscure or explicit, of speaking subjects; without referring the facts of discourse to the will — perhaps involuntary — of their authors; without having recourse to that intention of saying which always goes beyond what is actually said; without trying to capture the fugitive unheard subtlety of a word that has no text. (1991b, p. 59)

Elsewhere in the same text he makes it clear that "discoursing subjects form part of the discursive field," adding: "Discourse is not a place into which the subjectivity irrupts; it is a space of differentiated subject-positions and subject-functions" (p. 58).

Foucault's self-imposed task, then, is to challenge and to question the themes of origin, constituent subject and implicit meaning in order "to liberate the discursive field from the historical-transcendental structure which nineteenth-century philosophy imposed upon it" (1991b, p. 62), and he disagrees that progressive politics is necessarily tied to these themes. A progressive politics, on the contrary, is tied to the very questioning of these themes: it is one that "does not make man or consciousness or the subject in general into the universal operator of all transformations" (p. 70). A progressive politics "recognises the historic conditions and the specific rules of a practice" and "sets out to define a practice's possibilities of transformation and the play of dependencies between these transformations" (p. 70).

NEOLIBERALISM, EDUCATION AND THE CRITIQUE OF STATE REASON

Classical liberalism, as Gordon (1991, p. 15) affirms on a Foucaultian interpretation, can be characterized in Kantian terms as a *critique of state reason*. By this he means that liberalism is essentially a political doctrine concerning the limits of the state. In terms of this interpretation of the doctrine, the limits of government are intrinsically related to the limits of state reason, that is, its power to know. The art of government, considered broadly as the administration over a population inhabiting a territory, in its modern sense, depends upon its knowledge of that territory and its inhabitants, made possible by the new sciences of statistics and management (see, e.g., Hacking, 1991). As Gordon remarks: "The finitude of the state's power to act is an immediate consequence of the limitation of its power to know" (1991, p. 16). This interpretation, of course, depends upon a further set of theoretical relations explored by Foucault among forms of reason (rationalities), knowledge and power and upon Foucaultian concepts such as *power/knowledge*. An important part of this interpretation of liberalism assumes the freedom of the individual, because power is defined precisely in relation to the freedom of the individual to act. Gordon provides the following succinct elaboration: "Foucault does seem to have been (at least) intrigued by the properties of liberalism as a form of knowledge calculated to limit power by persuading government of its own incapacity; by the notion of the rule of law as the architecture of a pluralist social space; and by the German neo-liberal's way of conceiving the social market as a game of freedom sustained by government artifice and invention" (p. 47).

The intellectual history of the *problem-space* of liberal government in this view is a history of the acknowledgment and successive interpretation of the unknowability for man or the sovereign of the totality: the economy as a whole or society as a whole. Foucault emphasises the rule of law in liberal thinking as a technical form of government designed to establish conditions of security for which individual liberty is a necessary condition. Such liberty, then, is seen not only as the means to secure the rights of individuals against the abuses of the sovereign but also as "an indispensable element of govern- mental rationality itself" (Foucault, cited in Gordon, 1991, p. 20), because it ensures the participation of the governed in the establish- ment of a system of law that is a necessary precondition for a governed economy. That is, the ideology of individualism, canvassed in concepts such as *Homo economicus*, establishes a system of self-government based upon facilitating forms of natural regulation.

The purpose here is not to rehearse Foucault's novel statement or to revisit Gordon's interpretation of it but to adopt the general perspective (without qualification or discussion) so as to move beyond it in terms of a discussion of the historical revival of the doctrine of the self-limiting state as a basis for understanding present forms of neoliberal govern- mentality within the realm of education. My starting point is to recognize the force of Gordon's criticism and challenge contained in the following remark: "In a nutshell, he [Foucault] suggests that recent neo- liberalism, understood . . . as a novel set of notions about the art of government, is a considerably more original and challenging phenom- enon than the left's critical culture has had the courage to acknowledge, and that its political challenge is one that the left is singularly ill equipped to respond to, the more so since, as Foucault contends, socialism itself does not possess and has never possessed its own distinctive form of government" (1991, p. 6). With this challenge in mind I turn to examining the differences between liberalism and neoliberalism in terms spelled out by Gordon and others following the space for thinking opened up by Foucault's work on governmentality.

Gordon tracks out three versions of neoliberalism that were given some attention by Foucault in his course of lectures at the Collège de France during 1979. He mentions variously the versions of neoliberalism that had taken root postwar in West Germany (*Ordoliberalen*), the United States (the Chicago School) and France. These new forms do not represent an "innocent" return to liberalism's main articles of faith. In other words, the historical revival of liberalism in the present is not simply an exercise in nostalgia, representing a simple and naïve return to past principles. There are major differences between past and present forms of liberalism: neoliberalism, in other words, displays an innovative interpretative strategy in restyling basic principles to accommodate new exigencies. What they have in common, as Burchell claims, "is a question concerning the extent to which competitive, optimising market relations and behaviour can serve as a principle not only for limiting governmental intervention, but also for rationalising government itself" (1993, p. 270).

Gordon attributes to *Ordoliberalen* the capacity to generate new meanings to the "market" considered as a form of governmentality. He emphasizes, for instance, that under this form of neoliberal governmentality, *contra* Hayek, the market is no longer thought of as a natural or spontaneous institution.[3] Rather, the market is seen as an evolving social construct that must be protected and that, therefore, requires a positive institutional and juridical framework for the game of enterprise to function fully. As Burchell clearly indicates, forms of neoliberalism differ from earlier forms of liberalism in that: "they do not regard the market as an already existing quasi-natural reality situated in a kind of economic reserve in a space marked off, secured and supervised by the State. Rather, the market exists, and can only exist, under certain political, legal and institutional conditions that must be actively constructed by government" (1993, pp. 270–71).

Where for early liberalism the limitation of government was tied to the rationality of the free conduct of governed individuals themselves, for neoliberalism, by contrast, "the rational principle for regulating and limiting governmental activity must be determined by reference to *artificially* arranged or contrived forms of the free, *entrepreneurial* and *competitive* conduct of economic-rational individuals" (Burchell, 1993, p. 271). Burchell depicts neoliberalism, following the work of Donzelot, as promoting "an *autonomization* of society through the invention and profileration of new quasi-economic models of action for the independent conduct of its activities," (p. 274) and he clarifies what he means through the example of education under the British Conservative government. It is an example germane to my purposes here and it deserves extensive quotation:

In the area of education, for example, individual schools and other educational establishments are increasingly required to operate according to a kind of competitive "market" logic within an invented system of institutional forms and practices. On the one hand, they still function within a framework set by central government which involves, for example, the direct funding of schools by the State according to a national formula, a compulsory national curriculum with the periodic testing of pupils, government approval of the system and conduct of school management which must conform to a complex body of legislation and ministerial orders, the compulsory publication of individual schools' examination results, and so forth. However, on the other hand individual schools are required to function more and more as independently managed quasi-enterprises in competition with other schools. They are encouraged to strive to acquire a special status or value within the "market" for school services. They have to promote themselves so as to attract more pupils of the right kind so that they can achieve better examination results so that they will continue to attract the right pupils from "parent-consumers" and so that they will obtain increased funding from the State and other private sources." (Burchell, 1993, p. 274)

He concludes by suggesting that "the generalisation of an 'enterprise form' to *all* forms of conduct . . . constitutes the essential characteristic of this style of government: the promotion of an enterprise culture" (Burchell, 1993, p. 275).

For *Ordoliberalen*, as Gordon comments, "the major problem . . . is not the anti-social effects of the economic market, but the anti-competitive effects of society" (1991, p. 42). All three versions of neoliberalism to which Gordon refers are, to a greater or lesser extent, committed to institutionalizing the game of enterprise as a generalized principle for the organization of society as a whole. In all versions this feature is seen to take the form of a kind of individualism that involves fashioning one's life as the enterprise of oneself: the individual becomes, as Gordon notes, "the entrepreneur of himself or herself" (p. 44). This notion is tracked out in terms of the French version's emphasis on the "care of the self," especially in relation to the "right to permanent retraining." It also surfaces in the U.S. version's human capital interpretation of work, where work is construed in terms of two components comprising a genetic endowment and an acquired set of aptitudes produced as a result of private investment in education and the like.

Gordon views the U.S. version as the most radical in that it proposes "a global redescription of the social as a form of the economic." His interpretation is worth quoting at some length:

This operation works by a progressive enlargement of the territory of economic theory by a series of redefinitions of its object, starting out from the neo-classical formula that economics concerns the study of all behaviours involving the allocation of scarce resources to alternative ends. Now it is proposed that economics concerns all purposive conduct entailing strategic choice between alternative paths, means and instruments; or yet more broadly, *all rational conduct* (including rational thought, as a variety of rational conduct); or again, finally, all conduct, rational or irrational, which responds to its environment in a non-random fashion or "recognises reality." (1991, p. 43)

This "progressive enlargement" is based on the behavioral postulate known as *Homo economicus*, that is, the modern rediscovery of the main tenet of classical liberal economics, that people should be treated as rational utility-maximizers in all of their behavior. In other words, individuals are modelled as seeking to further their own interests (defined in terms of measured net wealth positions) in politics as in other aspects of behavior.

On this basis neoliberal governments have argued for a minimal state that has been confined to the determination of individual rights construed in consumerist terms, and for the maximum exposure of all providers to competition or contestability as a means of minimizing monopoly power and maximizing consumer influence on the quality and type of services provided. The application to education is easy to see. Its theoretical underpinnings have not always been made explicit but they clearly issue from a neoliberal perspective, underwriting reforms to educational administration in the so-called move to devolve or delegate responsibility as far as practicable while at the same time increasing powers of local schools and parents as individual consumers of education. Public choice theory thereby results in the "mainstreaming" of education, commodifying knowledge through its core value of individual choice and promoting market-like arrangements that become the basis for enterprise culture, where human beings turn themselves into market individuals.

The notion of enterprise culture, designed for a postindustrialist economy of the 1990s, can be seen in poststructural terms as the creation of a metanarrative (Lyotard, 1984) — a totalizing and unifying story legitimating the prospect of economic growth and development based on the triumvirate of science, technology and education. This master narrative, which projects a national ideological vision, differs from past "stories." It is not based on any attempt to rewrite the past, to redress power imbalances or socioeconomic inequalities. Unlike the social-democratic alternative, it does not adopt the language of equality of opportunity or multiculturalism. Questions of equity and social justice have receded under the economic imperative. This new meta-narrative is based upon a new vision of the future. The language used to sustain this vision is one of "excellence," "innovation, improvement and upgrading," "achieving more with less," "technological literacy," "information and telecommunications revolutions," "international marketing and management," "skills training," "performance," "efficiency" and "enterprise."

The code words enterprise and enterprise culture are the major signifiers of this new discourse. At one and the same time they provide the means for analysis and the prescription for change: education is a key sector in promoting national economic competitive advantage and future national prosperity. In the past there has been too much emphasis on social and cultural objectives and insufficient emphasis on economic goals in education systems. Henceforth we must invest heavily in education as a basis for future economic growth by redesigning the system so that it meets the needs of business and industry. The economic imperative is overriding.

The notion of enterprise culture also captures and updates something of the past popular iconography that surrounded an ideology that motivated U.S. educational reformers in the 1960s during the "sputnik" debate about catching up with the Russians, the "Space Wars" scenario of the 1980s and the more recent Japanese threat to U.S. enterprise. As a metaphor for the discourse of the postindustrial 1990s — in the era of the so-called new world order of the end of the Cold War, arms de-escalation and peace treaties — the focus has shifted away from exploiting fears of imminent destruction in superpower rivalry to the role that the new information, computer and communications technologies (among others) can play in the game of increasing national competitive advantage. The emphasis on possible economic decline in face of international competition and the need to catch up with leading nations occupies center ground.

Increasingly, questions of national economic survival and competition in the world economy have come to be seen under neoliberalism as one of cultural reconstruction. The task of reconstructing culture in terms of enterprise has involved remodelling institutions along commercial lines and encouraging the acquisition and use of enterprising qualities. Thus, and in accordance with this new master discourse, both the welfare state and the education system have been criticized for leading to a "culture of dependency."

If we accept that the notion of enterprise is not confined to business, to be judged purely in terms of short-term monetary gain, then we might want to recognize other kinds of enterprise that will admit of notions of initiative, sustainable practices or simply survival in the crudest sense. If enterprise is to be defined as business, pure and simple, then educators should vigorously resist the notion and its intrusion into education. The notion of enterprise culture can have a number of ideological interpretations, of which some might be enabling for education while others are pernicious. We must begin to sort out the former from the latter.

Education may indeed be the starship of the future. Intelligently conceived, it may become the basis of the so-called new economy, providing the requisite skills, abilities, understanding and attitudes necessary for a postindustrial, information-based society. Yet the notion of enterprise culture, as it has been presented in educational policy discourses, will not enable educators or the business sector to elucidate those models of enterprise that currently service the needs of society and economy by increasing both the level of participation and the welfare of workers through collaborative decision-making and profit-sharing. In other words, enterprise culture, alternatively, could become an agenda for establishing the conditions necessary for a postindustrial democracy. It might identify how such models operate in different areas of the economy, in small and large scale concerns, in new and older industries. Only when educationists and the public more generally can see the benefits of enterprise culture in this way might the notion merit some further serious consideration.

As it is, the notion of enterprise culture has been construed in the narrowest economic sense. It has become part and parcel of a new metanarrative that, in rhetorical terms, presents us with a vision of the future based on a story of the prospect of economic growth. However, while this story allocates education pride-of-place, alongside science and technology, it also reflects the new right's "creative" appropriation of the postindustrial literature. In essence, the discourse can be seen more as a "postindustrialism of reaction" than as one exploring the social-democratic possibilities inherent in postindustrialism.

NOTES

1.   Michel Foucault. (1984). The Order of Discourse. In M. Shapiro, (Ed.), *Language and Politics* (p. 109). Oxford: Blackwell.

2.   Julia Kristeva. (1989). *Language the Unknown: An Initiation into Linguistics*, A. Menke (Trans.), (p. 4). New York: Columbia University Press.

3.   While Hayek has been considered as one of the main sources of inspiration for the so-called new right, he clearly is to be distinguished from the neoliberal position. Hayek emphasizes, in an *antirational* approach, that many of the institutions that characterize society have arisen and function without design: "the spontaneous collaboration of free men often creates things which are the greater than their individual minds can ever fully comprehend" (Hayek, 1949, p. 70). This is Hayek's celebrated conception of "spontaneous order," a reinterpretation of the "invisible hand" hypothesis, which is used to explain and legitimate the market as the paradigm social institution. It is from this basic perspective on what Hayek calls "true individualism" that he derives both his defense of private property and the notion of the minimal state. The general principle of private property is to be understood as the endeavor to encourage people by the pursuit of their own interests to contribute as much as possible to the needs of others. The minimal state is a consequence of the "demand for a strict limitation of all coercive or exclusive power" (p. 16). Hayek effectively summarizes his view of the state thus: "the state, the embodiment of deliberately organized and consciously directed power, ought to be only a small part of the much richer organism which we call 'society,' and . . . the former ought to provide merely a

framework within which free . . . collaboration of men has the maximum of scope" (p. 22). The market, according to Hayek, establishes a workable individualist order because it ensures that the individual's remunerations correspond to the objective results of his or her efforts, and of their value to others. The individual, therefore, must be free to choose and it is "inevitable" that he or she must bear the risk attached to their choice-making because in consequence he or she is rewarded not according to the goodness or badness of their intentions but solely on the basis of the value of the results to others. The preservation of individual freedom, therefore, in Hayek's view, is incompatible with the notion of distributive justice and, in general, with the notion of equality as it has been progressively interpreted over the period of the development of the welfare state. In other words, the notion of individual freedom subscribed to by Hayek and those who follow him is at odds with the twentieth-century notion of social rights, involving the gradual expansion of citizenship, which served as the basis of the development of the welfare state.

5

Architecture of Resistance: Educational Theory, Postmodernism and the "Politics of Space"

Our language can be seen as an ancient city: a maze of little streets and squares, of old and new houses, and of houses with additions from various periods; and this surrounded by a multitude of new boroughs with straight regular streets and uniform houses.

— Ludwig Wittgenstein[1]

The great obsession of the nineteenth century was, as we know, history: with its themes of development and suspension, of crisis and cycle, themes of the ever-accumulating past, with its great preponderance of dead men and the menacing glaciation of the world. The nineteenth century found its essential mythological resources in the second principle of thermodynamics. The present epoch will perhaps be above all the epoch of space. We are in the epoch of simultaneity: we are in the epoch of juxtaposition, the epoch of the near and far, of the side-by-side, of the dispersed. We are at a moment, I believe, when our experience of the world is less that of a long life developing through time than that of a network that connects points and intersects with its own skein.

— Michel Foucault[2]

INTRODUCTION

Educational theory is dominated by considerations of time, by historically oriented theories, by temporal metaphors, by notions of change and progress exemplified, for instance, in "stages of development," whether conceived in terms of individual psychology (e.g., cognition, morality) or of modernization theory. Most of the sociological or anthropological theories that educationalists use as explanatory frameworks or paradigms are variants of European strands of thought that are heavily imbued with nineteenth-century historicist assumptions. In short, "modern" educational theory has all but ignored questions of space, of geography, of architecture. The same criticism can be levelled more broadly at the entire range of disciplines and fields comprising critical social theory.

Paradoxically, structuralism and the broader European formalist movement to which it belonged introduced questions of form, structure and system emphasizing synchronic as opposed to diachronic analyses, but considerations of space in terms of the contingencies of locale, place and site — space in terms of geographic and architectural space — were still far removed from the "universal structures" first mooted by, say, the structuralism of Lévi-Strauss, of Jean Piaget or even of Noam Chomsky. Ironically, even poststructuralism and postmodernism were initially received and interpreted often in terms of a crude historicism. French poststructuralism, in particular, has been interpreted as a reaction against Hegelianism, Hegelian dialectics and philosophy of history. Both poststructuralism and postmodernism have been viewed as periodizing concepts, as movements somehow coming *after* structuralism or modernism in a linear chronological sequence. Jean-François Lyotard (1984) has clearly disputed this chronological interpretation of his hypothesis concerning changes to the status of knowledge in the "postmodern condition." Yet his answer to the question What is postmodernism? — an account he offers in terms of the Kantian sublime, of presenting the unpresentable — concentrates on the dimension of time. In terms of an attack on realism, the postmodern for Lyotard "is not modernism at its end but in its nascent state, and this state is constant" (1984, p. 79). There is, however, an ambiguity in using the notion of the postmodern to refer to both postmodern culture and postindustrial society, because where it may be possible to render postmodern culture in terms of an ethos, style, or attitude that is part of the modern, the sociological concept of the postindustrial seems to imply a periodization. Certainly, the periodizing sociological concept of the postindustrial informs the work of both Alain Touraine and Daniel Bell.

In these conceptions the ruling or dominant accounts are those that concentrate on the dimension of time. The spatial dimension is more or less ignored. In the work of Michel Foucault, space receives the political recognition it deserves. He asserts in an important essay: "Space is fundamental in any form of communal life; space is fundamental in any exercise of power" (1984a, p. 252). These are not empty words, a dramatic rhetorical gesture. Foucault carefully documents the *histories of different institutional spaces*: the clinic, the prison, the school. In *Discipline and Punish: The Birth of the Prison*, for instance, Foucault observes how "disciplinary power" depends upon "a politics of space."

A whole problematic then develops: that of an architecture that is no longer built simply to be seen (as with the ostentation of palaces), or to observe the external space (cf. the geometry of fortresses), but to permit an internal, articulated and detailed control — to render visible those who are inside it; in more general terms, an architecture that would operate to transform individuals: to act on those it shelters, to provide a hold on their conduct, to carry the effects of power right to them, to make it possible to know them, to alter them. (1979, p. 72)

Disciplinary power based on the instruments of observation, judgment and examination are made possible by institutional architecture designed to permit total surveillance: the hospital building is organized as "an instrument of medical action"; the prison is built as a "space of confinement"; the school building is organized as a spatial mechanism for training the individual, for individualization.

This chapter, taking its inspiration from Foucault, is an attempt to overcome the despatialized nature of critical educational theory. In order to achieve this end I review the recent work of critical geographers and critical architects as a prologomenon to suggesting a series of theoretical concerns for a critical theory of education that takes space and the politics of space seriously.

OF GEOGRAPHICAL SPACE: THE POSTMODERNIZATION OF EDUCATION

For the critical geographer Edward Soja, a "despatializing historicism" that "coincided with the second modernization of capitalism and the onset of an age of empire and corporate oligopoly" was so successful in depoliticizing space that "even the possibility of an emancipatory spatial praxis disappeared from view for almost a century" (1989, p. 4). In Soja's view it reemerged as an object of critical social theory only in the late 1960s with "the onset of a crisis-induced fourth modernization" and a consequent restructuring. During this period, Soja argues, the unity of critical theory fragmented around a number of "controversial and confusing terms" — postmodernity, postmodernization, postmodernism — that, in retrospect, "now seem appropriate ways of describing this contemporary . . . restructuring; and of highlighting the reassertion of space that is complexly intertwined with it" (p. 5). He calls for a radical postmodern political program that is spatialized from the outset; a program that is built upon the awareness that space is fundamental in the exercise of power. This reassertion of space ought not to be simply a "metaphorical recomposition"; it ought to involve a critique of historicism and the "deconstruction and reconstitution" of critical theory "at every level of abstraction, including ontology" (p. 7).

Soja's observations on the role of space in critical social theory provide us with a clear global context for educational theory. Education within the context of postmodernization is conceived to play a vital role in terms of both the "new economy," based on so-called knowledge-intensive industries, and social integration. In terms of the main theories focusing on the current transformation of advanced societies — theories of the postindustrial, post-Fordist and postmodern society — education comes to fulfill leading functions. For example, in all three theories education is highlighted in relation to the importance of knowledge: it is conceived as both the production (research) and the reproduction (transmission) of knowledge. Society itself is analyzed in terms of the production, distribution and reproduction of knowledge. In particular, scientific knowledge is often seen as replacing other forms of knowledge, emerging as a new force and sector of production, changing both the power structures (the technocracy debate) and class formations and resulting in new forms of political action based on science and educational policy (Böhme & Stehr, 1986, p. 8).

In most accounts of the postindustrial society, as Boris Frankel (1987, p. 168) notes in a review of what he calls the "postindustrial utopians," education is pictured as being the largest industry in the future, requiring high levels of investment. It is typically seen as being concerned with educational retraining and the expansion of employment opportunities either directly or indirectly. The "utopians" (viz., Alvin Toffler, Ivan Illich, Rudolf Bahro, André Gorz) advocate radical decentralization or "deschooling," with an emphasis on demassified and "prosuming" forms of education. Yoneji Masuda (1990, p. 44), for instance, talks of "knowledge networks" that avoid the restrictions of formal schooling and concentrate on a "personal type" of education and "self-learning," both dependent upon developments in the computerization of society. He mentions also the importance of "knowledge-creative" and "lifetime" education. Frankel's (1987, p. 173) criticism of these kinds of future scenarios focuses upon the educational consequences of free-market forms of decentralization within postindustrial society: a diversity in education promoted only at the cost of the growth of social inequalities between income groups, between urban and rural areas, between different regions. The marketization of education in a demassified and decentralized form, for Frankel, "is a recipe for increased social atomization, isolation and conflict" (p. 173).

Less utopian in orientation, perhaps, are the French theorists Alain Touraine (1974) and Jean-François Lyotard (1984). Touraine remarks in prophetic terms: "The liberal university belongs to the past. The inescapable question now is whether the university will become the locus of integration or of confrontation. In both cases grave dangers may threaten the creation of new knowledge" (1974, p. 13). Touraine, it could be argued, was historically too close to the events of 1968 and too preoccupied with the question of the French university, yet his description of postindustrial society as one where capital accumulation is no longer tied to production per se but more than ever before dependent on the creation of scientific and technical knowledge deserves reiteration. In particular, Touraine's analysis of the nature of new social conflicts and emerging forms of social domination deserve re-statement. Touraine was among the first sociologists to understand the way in which the individual has been pressured to participate not only in terms of work, in terms of production, but also more and more in terms of consumption, and that education must increasingly be seen in terms of a culture of consumption. He also emphasized a form of cultural manipulation where, in terms of social reproduction, education is no longer considered an autonomous public space but rather the major locus for meeting the new postindustrial demands for certain types of advanced industrial skilled labor.

Lyotard's (1984) point of departure in describing the transition in the "most developed societies" to the postindustrial age is also scientific knowledge. He argues that the leading sciences and technologies — cybernetics, telematics, informatics and so on — are all significantly language-based and have transformed the two principal functions of knowledge: research and the transmission of acquired learning. Knowledge is changed within this general context of transformation. Anything in the constituted body of knowledge that is not translatable into quantities of information will be abandoned. Knowledge, in other words, loses its "use-value." It becomes exteriorized with respect to the knower, and the status of the learner and teacher is transformed into a commodity relationship of supplier and user: "Knowledge is and will be produced in order to be sold, it is and will be consumed in order to be valorised in a new production: in both cases, the goal is exchange" (Lyotard, 1984, p. 4).

Already, he argues, knowledge has become the principal force of production, severely altering the composition of the workforce in developed countries. The mercantilization of knowledge will further widen the gap between developed and developing countries. It will disrupt the traditional view that learning falls within the purview of the state and raise new legal and ethical questions for the relationship between the state and information-rich multinational corporations. This is where Lyotard comes closest to addressing traditional questions of political economy. The spatial consequences of both the mercantilization of knowledge and the marketization of education require a critical theory of educational postmodernization that functions as a critique of modernization and development theory. Lyotar's approach has strategic value in allowing us to see the effects of the transformation of knowledge and education on public power and civil institutions. It raises the central problems of the legitimation of knowledge and education in the postmodern condition. He asks political questions concerning the authority of those who decide what is to count as true, scientific and just. In the post-industrial society, where knowledge and power have been revealed as two sides of the same question, the problem of double legitimation necessarily comes to the fore: "In the computer age, the question of knowledge is now more than ever a question of government" (Lyotard, 1984, p. 9). In effect, Lyotard is mapping a complex set of historical and political relations between capitalist techno-science, rationality and the university.

These issues have an intrinsic spatial dimension, which, in part, probably accounts for why geographers have been among the most successful in dealing with them. In general terms, critical geographers have tended to emphasize the context of postmodernity and/or postmodernization as the appropriate space within which to conceptualize and map these issues. Postmodernization is probably best understood, to a large extent, as a continuation of the basic processes of modernization — differentiation (Durkheim), commodification (Marx) and rationalization (Weber) — although this should not imply an endorsement of modernist metanarratives, or totalizing theory. David Harvey (1989, p. 328), as a critical geographer, approaches the modernity-postmodernity distinction from a Marxist viewpoint, arguing that recent transformations are still within the grasp of historical materialism. He hypothesizes that since 1972 we have experienced a "sea-change" in our political and economic practices that is bound up with "time-space compression" in the organization of late capitalism — in particular, the emergence of more flexible modes of capital accumulation, which accounts for the rise of postmodernist cultural forms.

Harvey (1989) devotes a whole section of his *The Condition of Postmodernity* to "the experience of space and time," initially referring to Daniel Bell's assertion that the organization of space has become the primary aesthetic problem of the mid-twentieth century and characterizing modernism in Baudelairean terms. He makes the point that "space" often gets naturalized and, drawing on the work of Henri Lefebvre, he indicates how space is a fundamental source of social power. Spatial practices are never neutral in Harvey's view; they always express some kind of class or social relation and are defined through commodity production. Harvey elaborates the time and space of the Enlightenment project and relates time-space compression to the rise of modernism as a cultural force. In particular, he traces changes in the representation of space with the disappearance of Euclidean and perspective space as systems of reference. The cornerstone of Harvey's thesis is that the so-called postmodern condition is an expression of a new round of time-space compression that has taken place with the transition from Fordism to flexible accumulation.

In this context it is appropriate to mention Manuel Castells' *The Informational City* (1989), which also employs a Marxist approach to the question of the restructuring of capitalism in the 1980s. Castells relates the new model of restructured capitalism to what he calls the "informational mode of development," which, he suggests, can be described in terms of two dimensions, the technological and the organizational. Castells documents the way in which the new informational technologies have been decisive in the implementation of capitalist restructuring by increasing the rate of profit, weighting the accumulation and domination functions of state intervention, and enabling the internationalization of the world economy. He describes the restructuring of capitalism in terms of three fundamental processes. First, the appropriation by capital of a significantly higher share of surplus from the production process is achieved through a fundamental restructuring of the work process and of the labor market. Among important spatial features to be mentioned here is the decentralization of production to regions or countries characterized by lower wages and deregulated business environment. Second, a substantial change in the pattern of state intervention has occurred with a shift from functions of political legitimation and social redistribution to political domination and capital accumulation. This second set of processes involves deregulation and privatization policies, fiscal austerity and a rolling back of the welfare state. Third, there has been an accelerated internationalization of all economic processes, both to increase profitablity and to open up new markets.

The internationalization of capitalism has a clear spatial dimension — the collapsing of time and space, or what Harvey talks of as time-space compression. The neoconservative restructuring of education in Western liberal capitalist states that has occurred and is occurring can be seen in light of both Harvey's and Castells' work. Educational restructuring has been driven by a revival of interest in human capital theory and a renewed policy commitment to investment in human capital. Coupled with the market reform of education, human capital policies in the hands of Western governments have been based on the notion that education is not only a factor of production in its own right but also enhances the information effect, encouraging higher rates of innovation and increasing the productivity of human resources. In terms of the human capital policies promoted by the Organization for Economic Cooperation and Development, for instance, education is seen as "the source of flexibility and responsiveness in relation to technological and social change" (Marginson, 1993, p. 48). Education is restructured as part of the economy. It is no longer viewed as a universal welfare right so much as a form of investment in the development of skills that will enhance global competitiveness. Such investment in human capital assumes perfect competition and a diminution of government subsides: it assumes, in other words, a free market framework for the reform of education. The restructuring process in education shadows workplace reform and reform of the labor market. It has distinct sequential and spatial aspects both nationally and internationally, which can be seen in terms of the emerging division of labor within an informational economy.

OF ARCHITECTURAL SPACE

In an interview with Paul Rabinow conducted in 1982, Michel Foucault comments on his own suggestion that in the eighteenth century there emerged a specific political discourse that reflected upon architecture "as a function of the aims and techniques of the government of societies" (1984a, p. 239). Cities and buildings became spatial models for government rationality, for the exercise of social control and manipulation. The model of the school, for example, as a form of disciplinary architecture demonstrates at an abstract level the relation between educational space and a particular form of disciplinary political rationality that produces an individualized subject.

During the interview Foucault also talks of the epistemological transformations of the seventeenth century in terms of the spatialization of knowledge: in natural history, Linneas' taxonomy involved literally a spatialization of the object of analysis. Drawing on this model one might argue that the late twentieth century involves a new spatialization of knowledge and education based upon the mode of information. The new electronic forms of communication permit an exchange of information that is no longer subject to the traditionally modern constraints of time and space. The spatialization of knowledge and education in the postmodern age is based on the "soft architecture'" of the *network*, which increasingly defines the nature of our institutions and our subjectivities. It is increasingly in terms of computer or communicational networks that we act and define ourselves as subjects.[3] In this section of the chapter, taking my inspiration from Foucault, I examine the importance of architectural spaces, discourse and metaphors for educational theory. I focus specifically on postmodern architecture, on which I will eventually draw as a basis for the consideration of a critical postmodern theory of education.

Historically speaking, as Charles Jencks (1987, pp. 26ff) notes, architecture was the first of the arts to crystallize into a postmodern movement. There had been an intimate and tragic connection between modern architecture and modernization. Where the other arts stood directly opposed to modernization and its effects, to industrialization and (sub)urbanization, to the effects of large-scale development, to the pollution of the environment and the destruction of local culture, architecture had entered into the modern experiment with some enthusiasm. The Modern International Style, based on the acceptance of the principles of Euclidean geometry and the design of universal spaces, went hand-in-hand with large-scale development and the corporate nature of advanced capitalism. By the late 1950s, Jencks maintains, the breakdown of the relationship between modern architecture and modernization became obvious. The rise of the postmodern movement developed in conjunction with a critique of the social failures of modernist housing estates: the dynamiting of the

Pruitt-Igoe estate in St. Louis in 1972 came to symbolize the death of the project of modern architecture.[4]

In these terms it is interesting to contemplate Lyotard's attempt to distinguish one of three debates implied by the notion postmodern by reference to the Italian architect, Victorio Grigotti, who, in Lyotard's words, maintains: "There is no longer any close linkage between the architectural project and socio-historical progress in the realization of human emancipation on the larger scale. Postmodern architecture is condemned to generate a multiplicity of small transformations in the space it inherits, and to give up the project of a last rebuilding of the whole space occupied by humanity" (1989, p. 7).

According to Lyotard, on this account "there is no longer a horizon of universalization." The idea of progress as an elaboration of universal, free and abstract space has disappeared. Heinrich Klotz, it seems, would agree in principle with Lyotard. He identifies a number of characteristics with postmodern architecture that bear directly on this question:

Regionalism has replaced internationalism.

Fictional representation . . . has supplanted geometric abstraction. Postmodernism relies not on the symbolic value of the machine and of construction as defining progress in architecture, but on a *multiplicity of meanings*.

Poetry has supplanted technological utopianism. Postmodernism draws from the world of the imagination rather than from the "brave new world" mentality in which velocity is equated with progress.

Rather than view a building as an autonomous, universally valid geometric form, we can now allow it to be relativized by its historical, regional, and topological conditions, and can appreciate the palpable individuality of the particular solution. Heroism gives way to compromise, to equitable treatment of old and new, and to respect for the given environment.[5] (1988, p. 421)

Among the early critiques of modernism was the revisionist attempt to substitute the notion of place for abstract space, a theoretical move that is currently advocated and has been developed by Kenneth Frampton in terms of critical regionalism. Frampton (1985, p. 20) appropriates the term from Alex Tzonis and Liliane Lefaivre, who warn of its dangers and limitations but nevertheless recommend it as a vehicle for future humanistic architecture. In the past, regionalism has been associated with movements of reform but it has also proved, on occasions, to be a tool of repression. Frampton situates critical regionalism in the position of the *arrière-garde*, that is, "one which distances itself equally from the Enlightenment myth of progress and from a reactionary, unrealistic impulse to return to the architectonic forms of the pre-industrial past" (p. 20). He states: "The fundamental strategy of

Critical Regionalism is to mediate the impact of universal civilization with elements derived indirectly from the peculiarities of a particular place. . . . It may find its governing inspiration in such things as the range and quality of local light, or in a *tectonic* derived from a peculiar structural mode, or in the topography of a given site" (p. 20).

Critical regionalism is a cultural strategy for mediation: it is a practice involving a double mediation, a deconstruction of the spectrum of world culture, on the one hand, and a manifest critique of universal civilization achieved through synthetic contradiction, on the other. Taking his cue from Paul Ricoeur, Frampton sees the paradox as one of becoming modern and yet returning to the sources. The deconstruction is a distancing from the eclecticism of the *fin de siècle*, "which appropriated alien, exotic forms in order to revitalize the expressivity of an enervated society" (1985, p. 21), which I understand also to involve a critical reflection on local cultural sources and resources as a basis for a reaffirmation of forms of collective sprituality. The other part of the double strategy involves a mediation of those universal techniques, which "involves imposing limits on the optimization of industrial and postindustrial technology" (p. 21). The local or regional place-form, both geographically and historically contingent, provides the critical vantage point for resistance to the phenomenon of universal placelessness characteristic of modern architecture and the Inter-national Style. The resistance of the place-form is a notion that Frampton develops by reference to Heidegger's "Building, Dwelling, Thinking," which opposes a concrete, bounded, and particular space/ place linked to ontological considerations of being to the antique abstract concept of space that is intimately connected with Western abstract, "instrumental" reason. The bounded domain anchored in the question of being provides the "absolute precondition" for the built form to resist the imposition of a universal (European) space in the form of the "endless processal flux of the Megalopolis" (p. 25). Frampton develops the notion of the bounded place-form, in its public space, in reference to what Hannah Arendt terms "the space of human appearance" (1958), "since the evolution of legitimate power has always been predicated upon the existence of the 'polis' and upon the comparable units of institutional and physical form" (Frampton, 1985, p. 25).

Critical regionalism is able to enter into a more immediate and direct dialectical relationship with nature than modern architecture, which, through its formal traditions and use of abstract spatial solutions to a universally defined problem of habitation, is mired in "a technocratic gesture which aspires to a condition of absolute *placelessness*" (Frampton, 1985, p. 26). Questions of topography, context, climate, light and tectonic form can be addressed directly and, finally, the "tactile resilience" of the place-form provides an additional strategy for resistance. Critical regionalism, one might say by way of summary, emphasizes the culturally specific, the local, the particular in the built-form — its place — against the metanarrative of modern architecture, with its commitment to universal and abstract space. The place-form of critical regionalism has the resources and potential to resist "the relentless onslaught of global modernization" (p. 29).

In a more recent publication, Frampton (1989) reworks his original thesis, embellishing and explicating it further. In doing so he clarifies his theoretical orientation, which he describes as originating in two lines of German critical thought — one stemming from Hegel and Marx and culminating in Gramsci and the Frankfurt School, the other springing from Nietzsche and Husserl, encompassing phenomenology and existentialism, including the work of both Heidegger and Arendt. This is the basis from which he wishes to build an argument, a discourse of critical architecture, to resist "the current commodification of building, that is, the reduction of buildings to consumable goods" (p. 75). To that end and in opposition, it seems, to both Jencks and Paolo Portoghesi, who is openly disparaging of Habermas' commitment to the incomplete project of modernity, Frampton finds liberative and critical architecture in the "peripheries, rather than in the so-called centres of late capitalist development" (p. 77). He adds:

By critical regionalism I do not mean any kind of specific style, nor of course do I have in mind any form of hypothetical vernacular revival, nor any kind of unreflected so-called spontaneous grass roots culture. Instead, I wish to employ this term in order to evoke a real and hypothetical condition in which a critical culture of architecture is consciously cultivated in a particular place, in express opposition to the cultural domination of hegemonic power. It is, in theory at least, the critical culture, which while it does not reject the thrust of modernisation, nonetheless resists being totally absorbed and consumed by it. (p. 78)

Frampton then proceeds to develop and modify his six points toward a critical architecture as a basis for generating a postmodern expression. I shall not dwell on those points again here, except to say that I am largely in agreement with Frampton's view that an affirmative critical culture is one that provides the resources for an architecture of "place creation" that is both antiphallocentric and anti-Eurocentric. I am also in agreement with Frampton that U.S. postmodernist architecture is, by this standard, reduced to surface images and "oriented towards marketability, social control and towards an optimisation of building production and consumption" (p. 87). Critical regionalism, then, as Demetri Porphyrios points out, is a safeguard "against the cooption of tradition by the strategies of pluralism," because "once tradition and culture are no longer animated by an ethical force, they disintegrate into spurious and vacuous imagery" (1989, p. 90).

Frampton's six points toward an architecture of resistance provides the basis for a reconsideration of the modern built-form of the school, the research institute, the polytechnic and the university; indeed, more generally, for a reconsideration of educational places/spaces even in terms of the postmodern *network*.

THE NETWORKED SPACES OF
SOCIETIES OF CONTROL

Phillip Wexler (1992) has described the successive waves of corporatism in education: the first wave, which led to the commodification and privatization of education through a series of voluntary partnerships between businesses and schools, and the second wave, typified by the "Toyota school," where public institutional mediation between education and economic production disappears entirely and schools are restructured to transparently reflect the demands of a post-Fordist work regime. Wexler argues that the new corporatism recasts the crisis of education as a design problem based on the need for greater flexibility (mirroring flexible accumulation), to be resolved in terms of the *network*: "The reorganization of educational control through the establishment of interlocking networks may increase the centralization of the 'design' function at the same time that the design itself calls for a greater degree of 'innovative,' customized and, above all, 'flexible' social organization and school culture within the controlled network of design" (1992, p. 8).

For Wexler, who is interested in the way the regime of flexible accumulation entails the restructuring and repositioning of student subjectivities, such institutional reorganization of the school integrates a complex new corporatism at the design and control level with a more flexible set of pedagogical practices and, thereby, redefines both school knowledge and student subjectivity. His ethnographic investigations into how students' identities are restructured under the new corporatism are reflected, theoretically, in my concerns for an understanding of the importance of the politics of space. They are also neatly captured at the theoretical level by Gilles Deleuze's (1992) notion of societies of control.

Deleuze (1992) uses the term "societies of control" to denote a set of new forces and processes of free-floating control, which Foucault foresaw as the basis of the immediate future society. Just as disciplinary societies succeeded societies of sovereignty in the eighteenth century to reach their apex in the early twentieth century, so too societies of control have succeeded disciplinary societies, the development of which have accelerated in the postwar period. Disciplinary societies can be distinguished, Deleuze argues in reference to Foucault, by the fact that they initiated "the organization of vast spaces of enclosure. . . . The individual never ceases passing from one closed environment to another, each having its own laws: first, the family; then the school ('you are no longer in your family'); then the barracks ('you are no longer at school'); then the factory; from time to time the hospital; possibly the prison, the preeminent instance of the enclosed environment" (1992, p. 3).

At this point in history, announces Deleuze, we are in a period of generalized crisis in relation to all environments of enclosure. Institutions built on the model of enclosed spaces, the institutions of modernity — school, family, prison, factory, clinic — are finished, despite all efforts to reform them. The closed system, the enclosed space and institutions built on its processes of concentration and distribution are being replaced by the open system based on the control model of the network. As Deleuze comments: "Enclosures are *moulds*, distinct castings, but controls are a *modulation*, like a self-deforming cast that will continuously change from one moment to the other, or like a sieve whose mesh will transmute from point to point" (1992, p. 4).

He illustrates the point by reference to the replacement of the factory by that of the corporation in relation to the matter of salaries. In the factory an equilibrium was struck in terms of the ratio of wages (lowest) to production (highest); in the corporation the process works through a modulation of each salary according to merit.

The factory constituted individuals as a single body to the double advantage of the boss who surveyed each element within the mass and the unions who mobilized a mass resistance; but the corporation constantly presents the brashest rivalry as a healthy form of emulation, an excellent motivational force that opposes individuals against one another and runs through each, dividing each within. The modulating principle of "salary according to merit" has not failed to tempt national education itself. Indeed, just as the corporation replaces the factory, *perpetual training* tends to replace the *school*, and continuous control to replace the examination. Which is the surest way of delivering the school over to the corporation. (Deleuze, 1992:, pp. 4–5)

A distinguishing characteristic of societies of control is the code that functions as a password, controlling the access to information. The two poles of individual and mass that mark disciplinary societies have disappeared. In societies of control, individuals have become "dividuals," a market statistic, part of a sample, an item in a data bank. The distinction between the two societies is revealed in the difference of monetary systems: discipline of the gold standard versus the control of floating rates of exchange based on standard currencies. Here the dominant machine matched with the type of society is the computer, which indicates a different kind of capitalism from the nineteenth century, based on a logic of concentration and the factory as a space of enclosure. Capitalism in the present situation is no longer involved in production, which it has often relegated to the Third World. It is a capitalism of a higher-order production based on selling services. It is consumer oriented, where the operation of markets has become an instrument of control, and control, while short-term and of rapid turnover, is also continuous and without limit. It buys finished products or assembles parts, transforming products rather than specializing in their production. The factory has given way to the corporation and, thus, the underlying logic is not one of concentration, of enclosure; rather, it is a dispersive logic based on the circuit or network. Deleuze argues: "The family, the school, the army, the factory are no longer the distinct analogical spaces that converge towards an owner — state or private power — but coded figures — deformable and transformable — of a single corporation that now has only stockholders" (1992, p. 6).

It is on this basis that Deleuze proclaims the crisis of institutions, of all internal spaces of the closed system characteristic of disciplinary societies. What we are witnessing at this point of transition is "the progressive and dispersed installation of a new system of domination" (1992, p. 7) based upon an open system, where any element within it can be determined at any given instant.

CRITICAL EDUCATIONAL THEORY AND THE POLITICS OF SPACE

This chapter began with a plea for educational theorists to take seriously questions of space. The reassertion of space as an important theoretical consideration for educational theory should be seen, following Edward Soja's work, as, first, a critical questioning of historicism and of the way in which historicist assumptions vitiate educational theory.

Second, there ought to be a careful understanding of how space is fundamental to the exercise of power. This understanding involves, it has been argued, a critical appreciation of the broad historical shifts that are presently occuring in terms of the transformation of advanced societies entailing mutations within the global system of corporate capitalism. In terms of the politics of space, these shifts have been theorized here, following Foucault and Deleuze, as the move from disciplinary societies to societies of control.

Such an analysis is entirely compatible with a range of current debates focusing around terms like "postmodernism," "postmodernity," "postindustrialism" and "'post-Fordism." Indeed, a new spatial awareness might profitably take as its critical object the critique of postmodernization, including the human capital conceptualization of education as the main policy means for effecting the transition to the "new" economy. This geographical appreciation of international space will involve not only the corporatization of education and new decentralized market forms of education but also its spatial effects in terms of social inequalities between different regions and groups. It will also need to concentrate more carefully on the rise of the multinational corporations and their relative positioning vis-à-vis smaller nation-states, particularly in the Third World. Not enough attention has been focused on the spatial effects of the politics of development or of the international disparities systematically generated through the growing internationalization of the world economy.

Third, within the context described above, with an emphasis on the corporatization of education and on decentralized, demassified, marketized forms of education, there is a need to reexamine relations between the state and education. Here greater attention should be focused upon neoliberal self-limiting forms of government within societies of control where the boundaries have been redrawn between the public and the private spheres. Such an emphasis might be aided by the rich and powerful line of research opened up by Michel Foucault's (1991a) work on "governmentality," which emphasizes the way in which the disciplines are governmental forms of reflection, realized as practices and tied to various procedures and techniques that give them effect (see, most recently, Burchell, 1993; Rose, 1993).

Fourth, and perhaps most importantly, there is the need to begin to develop models of understanding and analysis that are motivated by what I have called the politics of space. I can think of no better starting point for this kind of conceptualization than Kenneth Frampton's critical regionalism, which is based on the relinquishment of universal, free and abstract space and the importance of the local and the indigenous, anchored in a specific time and place. Critical regionalism in education theory and practice does not define itself in opposition to new and emergent forms of internationalism, but is sensitive to cultural and historical contexts and recognizes that local culture and traditions provide the normative impulse for networks of resistance to the unthinking onslaught of a global process of modernization.

NOTES

Part of the title "Architecture of Resistance" is taken from the title of a paper by Kenneth Frampton (1985), "Towards a Critical Regionalism: Six Points for an Architecture of Resistance." For a reworking of the original hypothesis see Frampton's (1989) "Some Reflections on Postmodernism and Architecture."

1.   Ludwig Wittgenstein. (1972). *Philosophical Investigations*, G.E.M. Anscombe (Trans.), (p. 8). Oxford: Blackwell.
2.   Michel Foucault. (1986, Spring). Of Other Spaces. *Diacritics*, *16*(1), 22.
3.   Mark Poster (1990), in his *The Mode of Information*, is perhaps the best example of someone who has explored the intersection between the new communicational technologies and poststructuralist theory as a basis for understanding new configurations of the subject. His *Foucault, Marxism and History: Mode of Production versus Mode of Information* (1984) indicates his differences with the paradigm of historical materialism. See also Stephen Pfohl's (1992) *Death at the Parasite Cafe*.

4. Charles Jencks (1987, pp. 27ff) invented the trope of "Death of Modernism/Rise of Postmodernism" by reference to the demolition of the Pruitt-Igoe estate. He indicates that it was a "symbolic fabrication" — even the date was invented — yet almost everyone accepted it as the truth. Postmodernism as a social and architectural movement, Jencks maintains, developed in response to a social need. Its roots are in the "wider social protest against modernization." Jencks (p. 41) postulates five traditions of postmodern classical art, which together can be summarized in terms of the new canons: disharmonious beauty or a fragmented unity; cultural and political pluralism based in a stylistic variety; the celebration of difference, "otherness" and irreducible heterogeneity; urban contextualism, which stipulates that new buildings should fit into and extend the existing city fabric; anthropomorphism, which is not so much a new humanism as a recognition of the metaphor of the body, an integrated organism, as a basis for design and ornamentation; a historical continuum relating the past and present, which accounts for forms of parody, nostalgia, pastiche as well as *anamnesis*; "a return to content," which is open to multiple readings; double-coding established through the use of irony, ambiguity and contradiction; multivalence based on allusions to the past, adjacent references and resonances; reinterpretation of tradition with a displacement of conventions; the development of new rhetorical figures based on paradox, oxymoron, ambiguity, double-coding, and so forth; "return to the absent center" — there is no center but only connections (i.e., the network).

5. I have deleted the numerical listing that Klotz provides in these excerpts that I have chosen to illustrate agreement with Lyotard's interpretation of Grigotti's argument. The other characteristics Klotz mentions are:

The tendency toward fictional representation has led away from the late-modern tendency to view a building exclusively in terms of function, and toward seeing it as a *work of art of building* that belongs to the realm of the illusory.

Postmodernism opposes the sterile faith in the continuous improvement of instruments and construction with *improvisation* and *spontaneity*. Instead of striving for untouchable perfection, it favours the disturbed and the imperfect, which are now seen as signs of life.

Whereas modernism sought to free itself from history and made architecture purely a thing of the present, with postmodernism we have regained *memory*. And rather than exploit history for interesting effects, we can now entrust ourselves to the spirit of irony.

Instead of a dominant style, with its tendency to become dogma, a broad range of vocabularies and stylistic languages exist alongside one another. Postmodernism denies the self-referential inventiveness of the Modern Movement and pays tribute to the pluralism of referential allusions.

Rather than identify architecture with life, postmodernism establishes anew the aesthetic distance from life. Fiction as well as function! (1988, p. 421)

On postmodern architecture see also David Kolb, *Postmodern Sophistications: Philosophy, Architecture and Tradition* (1990), and John Whiteman, Jeffrey Kipnis and Richard Burdett (eds.), *Strategies in Architectural Thinking* (1992). The collection of essays edited by Marco Diani and Catherine Ingraham, *Restructuring Architectural Theory* (1989), provides a good discussion of architectural theory in relation to Jacques Derrida's thought, including essays by Jacques Derrida and Peter Eisenman, alongside an interview with Jean-François Lyotard and a number of critical essays discussing postmodernism, historicism and structuralism/poststructuralism.

6

"After Auschwitz":
Ethics and Education Policy

INTRODUCTION

One could argue that in the present European climate there are omi-
nous signs that the historical self-reflection of the social sciences has
not been at all sufficient to highlight, publicize or help prevent the
contemporary rise of racism. There is disconcerting evidence of the rise
of neo-Nazi sentiments and elements: the attack on foreign migrants
and acquired immune deficiency syndrome victims in Germany and
Austria; the continuing evolution and stability of militant neo-Nazism
in Germany and the current popularity of Strasserism (see, e.g.,
Husbands, 1991); the rise and chequered career of Le Pen and the
National Front in France; the formation, mutation and splitting of
the National Front in Britain; the strengthening of the far right in
Euro-elections following 1989, and the dominance of the so-called new
right in a number of Western countries beyond Europe and, not least,
the horrific and ongoing ethnic cleansing policies in Eastern Europe,
with the spectre of the mass annihilations of people in the villages and
towns of what used to be called Yugoslavia.

These contemporary happenings cannot be viewed as events isolated
in Europe. They cannot be ignored or theorized away. They represent
the inescapable horizon of historical and ethical responsibility within
which social scientists must approach their tasks of knowledge production and policy formulation in the late twentieth century, whether they
be located in Europe or Australasia. They highlight the question: Is
ethics possible, and what forms might it take in cultural postmodernity?

Accounts of the present state of moral discourse claim that (even in
our culture) there is no agreement on a universally accepted framework
for resolving moral claims and little immediate prospect of advancing
toward one. Jean-François Lyotard (1984), the French poststructuralist
philosopher, describes this state of affairs in terms of the crisis of

legitimation of the traditional modernist metanarratives, which served to provide foundations for knowledge, morality and aesthetics and for the cultural institutions based upon them. Lyotard argues that the metanarratives have collapsed: what characterizes cultural postmodernity is an "incredulity towards metanarratives" — an incurable suspicion that all grand, sweeping narratives perform their legitimation functions by masking the will-to-power and excluding the interests of others.

According to this analysis of cultural postmodernity, there are now only different ethical perspectives, which are based on incommensurable premises — a heterogeneity of different moral language-games. Moreover, philosophy is no longer considered the master discipline that can offer foundations; it is, by this account, not a metalanguage into which the claims and demands of competing language-games can be translated and resolved. The resulting pluralism, which is seen as characteristic of cultural postmodernity, has been explained in both Kantian and Weberian terms as an extended differentiation of value spheres, each with its own inner logic. Western culture, it is alleged, has undergone a process of accelerated cultural differentiation, especially since World War II. The liberal myth of a common culture or form of life that functioned to assimilate difference and otherness has split into a seemingly endless proliferation of subcultures and groups. The revitalization of indigenous cultures is seen as an important part of this differentiation process. With a new respect for the integrity of traditional cultures — a respect given only grudgingly under the increasing weight of a moral force deriving historically from philosophies of decolonization — Western liberal states have begun the processes of redressing past grievances and of recognizing languages, epistemologies, aesthetics and ethics different from their own.

The "crisis of reason" and the crisis of foundationalism in general — not only of foundational approaches to knowledge and morality but also of the foundations of our institutions — cannot fail to affect the relations between knowledge and ethics, on the one hand, and policymaking and public institutions, on the other. Indeed, for some commentators the crisis is most clearly exhibited precisely at the point of contact between the social sciences and public policy. Here the frontiers between knowledge, morality and politics have become very fragile as leaders of the new social movements, radical feminists, indigenous cultures, religious leaders, welfare networks and unemployed groups begin to question the totalizing normative framework of the liberal state and challenge culturally dominant values. Indeed, part of the contemporary attraction of neoliberalism as a form of self-limiting government has been the way in which it has applied a series of market techniques to the processes of government itself in order to avoid the combined problems of pressure-group capture and a self-interested bureaucracy.

It is within this general context that I locate my discussion. I have chosen to advertise the theme of this chapter in terms of the highly charged metaphor "after Auschwitz," focusing on the role of the social and human sciences in the development of public policy, particularly in the area of education. The phrase "after Auschwitz" serves to emphasize the critical approach I will be taking to the social sciences in relation to public policy. Following Adorno and Lyotard, I take this metaphor to signal a historical watershed in the critical self-understanding of the social sciences as part of the culture of modernity (see also Bauman, 1989). The first part of the chapter briefly explores the revival of Holocaust memories in recent history, its focus on Auschwitz, and what is known as the "historian's debate"; the second part examines Adorno's and Lyotard's use of this metaphor as one that signals, in emblematic fashion, "an incredulity towards metanarratives" and the third part examines the controversial thesis of the late German social historian, Detlev Peukert, in relation to the history of "social-welfare education" and its contribution to the genesis of the "Final Solution" in the Third Reich. Peukert's work suggests a shift to a paradigm of "biological politics" in the historical understanding of Auschwitz and the imbrication of educational policy in this state of affairs. In the concluding discussion I suggest that Peukert's work and the paradigm of biological politics in understanding Nazi Germany has its parallel in Michel Foucault's twin notions of "governmentality" and "bio-power" as they have been applied to contemporary neoliberal states. Auschwitz, I conclude, constitutes an inescapable horizon for the consideration of the relations of ethics, knowledge and public policy within the continuing process of modernization within neoliberal nation-states.

MEMORIALIZATION OF THE HOLOCAUST

Raul Hilberg (1988), author of the definitive study *The Destruction of the European Jews* (1961), argues that remembering the Holocaust has been an act of revolt. He details the official policy of silence adopted by the Allies and the way both Western and Communist countries continued to obliterate the event. Even the Nuremberg Trials, Hilberg maintains, did not squarely face the fact that Nazis had killed Jews. Against this background of "forgetting" came remembering as an act of revolt first by Israel and then by the United States. After decades of inactivity the United States launched its initial large-scale investigations in 1977, primarily, Hilberg argues, because of the dis-illusionment with the Vietnam War and the consequent search by the younger generation for "old moral certainties." In this context the Holocaust became the "new measuring rod of immorality" and the process of memoralization began in earnest.

The U.S. lead was followed almost a decade later by Canada, which initiated an official inquiry in 1985, and by Australia and Britain, which followed suit in 1986 and 1988, respectively. Where the Americans had indicted war criminals for lying during the immigration and naturalization process (rather than for the crimes they committed), Canada, Australia and Britain went a step further to alter their domestic criminal codes to permit prosecution of war criminals for the crimes they committed. The fact was that after decades of apathy and indifference to the alleged presence of thousands of Nazi war criminals, Western democracies finally began to take some action. The reasons for this turnabout are complex and varied. First, immigration and settlement of displaced persons took place during the Cold War at a point when Western intelligence was desperately seeking means to launch anti-Communist operations. In some instances this involved the active recruitment of pro-Nazi elements (Aarons, 1989, p. xxv). In this fiercely anti-Communist climate collaborators could trade on Cold War fears. By the mid-1980s the Cold War had begun to thaw and by the late 1980s the Communist "threat" no longer existed.

Second, according to Efraim Zuroff (1989, p. 2807), the question of the identity of Nazi war criminals is crucial in the sense that in the immediate aftermath of the war the Allies focused almost exclusively on Nazis of German origin, perceiving the Final Solution as primarily a German-Austrian production. In the American trials, public attention was directed for the first time to the lethal role played by local collaborators. Zuroff notes that almost invariably the war criminals in Australia, Canada and Britain were collaborators of Eastern European origin. Third, the Americans had demonstrated that war criminals could be convicted some considerable time after the crimes had been committed. Fourth, research, documentation and commemoration alongside the role played by the media and a concerted public education campaign brought about the turnaround.

The reversal, almost certainly, was also fueled by a series of political events: the trials of Klaus Barbie and Ivan Demjanjuk, the revelations concerning Kurt Waldheim and the Bitburg incident involving President Reagan. These incidents and the decisions made by Western democracies to alter their domestic law codes were paralleled by an intellectual controversy that erupted in Germany in 1986, known as the *Historikerstreit*, or the "historians' debate." The controversy concerned the conservative attempt to rewrite history and to treat the history of Nazism as just another epsiode of German and European history. Hans Mommsen, the noted German historian, explains: "The call for the history of national socialism to be 'historicized' was a concealed attempt on the part of some of those involved to relativize the crimes of the Nazi regime — which were unique in their sheer scale — and particularly to put them on a par with the crimes of Stalinism" (1991, p. 10).

The conservative leadership of the Federal Republic had staged the ceremony at Bitburg to commemorate the end of World War II. This was a conscious attempt to refashion the German past, to salvage it through the strategy of selective memory highlighting a historical continuity by focusing on anti-Communist sentiments while deaccentuating elements of the fascist past and especially Auschwitz. The ceremony at Bitburg was to provide a symbolic reconciliation between Germany and the United States by burying wartime antagonism between these two powers along with the Nazi crimes. However, this conservative rehabilitation of the German past — a new narrative to legitimize present policies — backfired when it was revealed that 49 members of Hitler's SS were buried at the cemetery at Bitburg.

The incident at Bitburg, which proved a major political embarassment to both Kohl and Reagan, became the sign for a much more heated controversy over conservative attempts to rewrite German history. Ernst Nolte, for example, argued for the normalization or historicization of the Third Reich. Nazism in his view ought to be de-demonized. It should not be treated as an extraordinary, metahistorical event. Nolte (1985) argued for normalization on the grounds that Auschwitz represented nothing new in the history of Europe. He cited the precedents of the annihilation of the Armenians during World War I and Stalin's mass murder of anti-Communists during the 1930s (suggesting a causal connection between the Gulag and Auschwitz). Nolte extended his examination back to the nineteenth century and through to the recent regime of Pol Pot, concluding that the Holocaust is neither unique nor singular but simply one of the series of "annihilation therapies" devised by governments to cope with the ills of the industrial revolution. Charles Maier summarizes the argument and the issues at stake very effectively. "If Auschwitz is admittedly dreadful, but dreadful as only one specimen of genocide . . . then Germany can still aspire to reclaim a national acceptance that no one denies to perpetrators of other massacres, such as Soviet Russia. But if the Final Solution remains non-comparable . . . then the past may never be 'worked through,' the future never normalized and German nationhood may remain forever tainted, like some well forever poisoned" (1988, p. 1).

Jürgen Habermas (1989) became deeply embroiled in the debate. He argued that German historiography was exhibiting "apologetic tendencies." In particular, he accused the conservative historians of attempting to "normalize" or "relativize" the Final Solution as part of a new nationalist and conservative search for a "usable past." In the ensuing debate much of the discussion focused on the singularity of Auschwitz as a historical event, neglecting the critique of neoconservatism offered by Habermas. Conservatives including Michael Stürmer (one-time speech writer for Kohl), Andreas Hillgruber and Ernst Nolte responded to Habermas by questioning his sources and scholarship, thereby ignoring the substantial issues to be debated and attempting to bring the controversy back within the closed circle of professional historians. In his Closing Remarks, Habermas summarized what he thinks has emerged from the debate in terms of the political self-understanding of the Federal Republic. It has, he suggests,

Resulted in the clarification of an alternative. . . . One group has a functionalist understanding of the public use of history; they dispense the slogan, which is formulated in terms of power politics but self-contradictory, of promoting loyalty to NATO and internal cohesion through "national consciousness instead of guilt consciousness." In opposition to this kind of "politics of history," to manipulated historical consciousness in general, the other group advocates enlightenment. (1989, p. 247)

In a further paper, "Historical Consciousness and Post-traditional Identity: The Federal Republic's Orientation to the West," Habermas (1989) makes it clear that the notions of nationalism and national identity he favors are those based on universalist values that are firmly anchored in the heritage of the Enlightenment. Orientation to the political culture of the West is, in Habermas' terms, to be regarded as the greatest intellectual achievement of the postwar period for the Federal Republic. Habermas' appeal to Enlightenment values here links up with his evaluation of postmodernism as a form of neoconservatism (Habermas, 1981a, 1990b) and specifically with questions of postmodern historiography. Charles Maier makes the point clearly. "Jürgen Habermas can be taken as the Federal Republic's pre-eminent spokesman for what might be called the liberal-democratic or social-democratic 'meta-narrative': the conviction that knowledge substantially reflects the real world, is progressive, and can change politics and society" (1988, p. 168).

Yet Maier recognizes that the political agenda of postmodernism need not be reactionary. Indeed, it is exactly his point that revisionist accounts of Auschwitz are *not* examples of postmodern historiography. Rather, they are, in his terms, "products of a diffused postmodern historical sensibility" (1988, p. 170) in a country deprived of postmodern theorists of the stature of the French. The result has been that West German postmodern histories have tended to take the form of "innocent" revivals and have served to draw attention to the way in which "memory" is a socially constitutive act that can be used for certain political purposes (for example, to relativize the Nazi past and make it appear less objectionable or to renarrativize the past to legitimate present policies). Paradoxically, while the German revisionist historians want to normalize the Final Solution, stressing its similarity with other genocides past and present, Theodor Adorno and Jean-François Lyotard emphasize the *singularity* and uniqueness of Auschwitz.

AFTER AUSCHWITZ: ADORNO,
LYOTARD AND MODERNITY

Adorno's position is unmistakable. Nowhere is it more plainly stated than in his *Negative Dialectics* where Adorno argues that culture,

Abhors stench because it stinks — because, as Brecht put it in a magnificent line, its mansion is built of dogshit. Years after that line was written, Auschwitz demonstrated irrefutably that culture has failed. That this could happen in the midst of the traditions of philosophy, of art, and of the enlightening sciences says more than that these traditions and their spirit lacked the power to take hold of men [sic] and work a change in them. There is untruth in those fields themselves, in the autarky that is emphatically claimed for them. All post-Auschwitz culture, including its urgent critique, is garbage. . . Whoever pleads for the maintenance of this radically culpable and shabby culture becomes its accomplice, while the man [sic] who says no to culture is directly furthering the barbarism which our culture showed itself to be. (1973, pp. 355–56)

In this complex statement are the threads that help explain Adorno's philosophy and, to a degree, his motivations: Adorno as a cultural conservative, strongly influenced by considerations of aesthetic high modernism (especially Schönberg and Beckett): Adorno as someone who rediscovers his Jewish origins and Adorno as left Hegelian. When Adorno states that "culture after Auschwitz is garbage," a claim he repeats in various forms — "To write poetry after Auschwitz is barbaric" (*Prisms*, 1981) — he means that (high) culture has lost its power and function to bring about enlightenment. Culture in this sense is the culture of high modernism understood in the German context with the prevailing notion of *Bildung*, with its connotations of educational self-formation as a duty. In a now-famous formulation with Horkheimer, Adorno argued that under capitalism and specifically the "culture industry," culture has finally succumbed to the logic of the production process: the exchange-value has obliterated the original use-value of cultural goods, allowing them to take on secondary or substitute use-values. Accordingly, enlightenment has collapsed into mythology and mythology into enlightenment. On this basis of the transformation of culture under capitalism, individuals are made to conform; subjects are fully integrated.

Adorno came to recognize the full implications of his Jewish heritage only after the full extent of the Holocaust became known. In fact, as Jay notes, Auschwitz became almost an obsession with him, particularly once he had finally returned to his native land in 1953 — to a Germany unwilling to confront and work through its "unmastered past" (1984, p. 19). Jay comments on the significance of the Holocaust for Adorno: "The major lesson Adorno drew from the Holocaust was, in fact, the link between anti-Semitism and totalistic thinking. The Jew, he now came to understand, was regarded as the most stubborn repository of that otherness, difference and non-identity, which twentieth-century totalitarianism had sought to liquidate. 'Auschwitz,' he grimly concluded, 'confirmed the philosopheme of pure identity as death'" (1984, p. 20). Jay adds that Adorno's refusal to spell out a utopian alternative was a result of the Jewish prohibition on picturing God or paradise.

Adorno's status as a left Hegelian is more problematic or, at least, ambivalent. Unquestionably Hegel and dialectics are at the center of things for Adorno, yet at the same time Adorno engages in a critique of Hegel's totalizing reason, playing off Nietzsche against Hegel, a fact that has led commentators to note links between Adorno and the poststructuralists. This ambivalence in relation to Hegel, which leads Adorno to emphasize a determinate negation as general method, can be seen clearly in *Dialectic of Enlightenment*, originally written with Max Horkheimer under the shadow of Auschwitz in 1947 (Horkheimer & Adorno, 1972). In *Dialectic* Horkheimer and Adorno advance the idea that modern science reached its zenith with logical positivism and thereby abandoned any claim to theoretical knowledge in favor of a strict technical utility — instrumental reason — which, stripped of any basis in law or morality, became assimilated to sheer power. In cultural modernity, then, reason has become assimilated to technical power and is therefore unable to address value questions. This is the now famous formulation that takes the form of the critique of instrumental reason. The grim image of Auschwitz here conjures up the ruthless technical efficiency with which the Nazis and their collaborators organized and carried out on such a monumental scale the selection and murder of millions of Jews, Gypsies and others. Science, "murderous science" and, in particular, the genetically-oriented human sciences of anthropology, education and psychiatry were put to the most efficient use under National Socialism in developing the processes of identification, proscription and extermination (Müller-Hill, 1988; Danuta,1990).

The spirit of Nietzsche lurks beneath the surface here not only in the critique of instrumental reason — the will-to-power asserts itself in the form of domination — but also, more generally, in the suspicion directed against ideology-critique itself. The Nietzschean influence and the appropriation of Nietzsche is common to both Adorno and certain French poststructuralist thinkers. Jean-François Lyotard, for example, directly appropriates Adorno for his own purposes of theorizing the postmodern condition. Yet Lyotard (1974) criticizes the underlying notion of the dialectic. He simply does not believe that a political, philosophical or artistic position is to be abandoned because it is "sublated." It is not true, according to Lyotard, that the experience of a position means its inevitable exhaustion and necessary development into another position where it is both conserved and suppressed.

In *The Differend: Phrases in Dispute*, Lyotard analyzes Adorno's use of Auschwitz as a model of a kind of "para-experience" where dialectics is impossible:

The "Auschwitz" model would designate an "experience" of language that brings speculative discourse to a halt. The latter can no longer be pursued "after Auschwitz". Here is a name "within" which speculative thought would not take place. It wouldn't therefore be a name in Hegel's sense, as that figure of memory which assures the permanence of referent and of its senses when spirit has destroyed its signs. It would be a name without a speculative "name", not sublatable into a concept. (1988, p. 88)

Elsewhere, Lyotard picks up on the capacity of proper names to place modern historical and political commentary in abeyance. He writes: "Adorno pointed out that Auschwitz is an abyss in which the philosophical genre of Hegelian speculative discourse seems to disappear, because the name 'Auschwitz' invalidates the presupposition of that genre, namely that all that is real is rational, and that all that is rational is real" (1987, p. 162).

In his more recent writings Lyotard has explicitly adopted Auschwitz as the symbolic end of modernity ("speculative modernity"), defining himself in direct opposition to Habermas: "I would argue that the project of modernity (the realisation of universality) has not been forsaken or forgotten but destroyed, 'liquidated'. There are several modes of destruction, several names which are symbols for them. 'Auschwitz' can be taken as a paradigmatic name for the tragic 'incompletion' of modernity" (1992, p. 30).

This is a claim and theme repeated in various forms. The so-called liquidation of the *project* of modernity symbolized by Auschwitz means, *contra* Kant and Hegel, that universal history does not move inevitably toward the better, that history does not have a universal finality (Lyotard, 1992, p. 62). Following Adorno, Lyotard uses the name "Auschwitz" "to signify just how impoverished recent Western history seems from the point of view of the 'modern' project of the emancipation of humanity" (1992, p.91). After Auschwitz is a phase — a highly charged metaphor — emphasizing a singularity of event, which is symptomatic of a postmodern incredulity toward metanarratives. It symbolizes for Lyotard the confidence the West has invested in the principle of a general progress in humanity, a necessary progress "rooted in the belief that developments made in the arts, technology, knowledge and freedoms would benefit humanity as a whole" (1992, p. 91).

AUSCHWITZ AND SOCIAL-WELFARE EDUCATION

Historians as well as philosophers have been to the forefront in a reinterpretation of Nazism, an area of study where the political and moral stakes are very high. Recently, discussion has moved away from the concept of fascism to a more specific concern for the way in which institutional structures and policy-making within Germany during the period of the Third Reich were infused with a "biological politics." Tim Mason, for instance, comments that there appears to be a new consensus concerning the focus of research on Nazism that revolves around "the broad gamut of Nazi biological politics . . . and on the institutions invented to implement them" (1993, p. 258). The new paradigm of historical understanding views Nazism as an expression of biological politics, and the controversial work of Detlev Peukert as a social historian has provided an insightful and innovative contribution to the establishment of the new paradigm.

Peukert argues that what was new about the Final Solution was "the fact that it resulted from a fatal racist dynamism present within the human and social sciences" (1993, p. 237). He clearly indicates how this dynamism operated qualitatively to ascribe "value" and "nonvalue" in human terms, systematically "culling" and eradicating those deemed without value to the "body" of the nation. "What emerged," he writes, "was an abstract process of selection based on this factitious racist definition of a holistic national entity, and a scheme for a high-technology 'solution' based on cost-benefit analysis" (p. 237).

On the basis of recent research into the development of psychiatry, genetics, eugenics, medicine, social policy, demography and education under the Third Reich, and contemporary accounts of the history of compulsory sterilization, the treatment of "asocial" groups and of foreign workers and the persecution of the Jews and Gypsies, Peukert makes an attempt at an inclusive schematic interpretation of the genesis of Nazi racism. He argues: "The common racist factor in the disciplines and professions of the human and social sciences is the differential assessment and treatment of people according to their 'value', where the criteria of 'value' are derived from a normative and affirmative model of the *Volkskörper* as a collective entity, and biological substratum of 'value' is attributed to the genetic endowment of the individual" (1993, p. 237).

Peukert traces the role played by racist thinking in the history of the human sciences back to the turn of the century, when a scientific approach to the study of human beings and to social problems became a practicable project for the first time. He provides an ideal-typical account of the development of social-scientific discourse in the realms of theory and practice and its relations with the development of social welfare institutions and practices in their combined approach to solve the social question. In much the same way as medicine achieved success in combating epidemic diseases, so psychology and education held out the prospects of the scientific elimination of ignorance and maladjustment. The utopian dream of a Final Solution to social problems seemed only a matter of time. Mass well-being based on the new paradigm of social hygiene and education meant that medicine and social welfare looked not only to the body of the individual but also the collective body of the nation. An emphasis on the health of the body — individually and collectively — was endorsed by the banishment of death as an everyday occurrence, by the demographic transition to the modern mortality pattern characterized by low infant mortality and increased life expectancy. With the process of secularization slowly reaching the masses, the sciences increasingly became the basis for constructions of everyday meanings. Yet, in spite of the idealization of the body, the cult of youth — a virtual identification of modernity with youthfulness — the sciences could not explain death away (as could religion), nor offer eternal life or salvation to the individual.

The answer, Peukert maintains, was to separate out the ephemeral body of the individual as a target of scientific endeavor from the potentially immortal body of the *Volk* or race: "Only the latter — specially, its undying material substratum in the form of the genetic code — can guarantee the undying victory of science itself" (1993, p. 241). This abstract and ideal-typical account is to be found in the writings of actual scientists only in partial and mixed forms, and it is subject to what Peukert calls the trade-cycle of history, such that in periods of scientific growth it finds its fullest expression in the naïve faith in progress while in times of crisis the utopian vision of the *Volkskörper* becomes defined in negative and restrictive terms. Under these conditions, "The central concern now becomes that of identifying, segregating, and disposing of those individuals who are abnormal or sick" (p. 241), and the dramatic shift from mass well-being to mass annihilation takes place.

This schematic understanding advanced by Peukert marks the transition to a paradigm of biological politics. It might be argued that philosophically it stands on the same ground as the *Dialectic of Enlightenment* or Foucault's (1979) *Discipline and Punish*. Nevertheless, one does not have to accept *in toto* Peukert's schema to appreciate his own historical investigations into the field of social-welfare education, which he takes as representative of many others.

On his account the field of social-welfare education arose as a policy response to contradictions within modern industrial society. It focused on youth-service provision and was aimed at rectifying the problems of social deviance. Peukert traces the evolution of the system of social-welfare education in terms of a number of distinct phases. He situates the received problem and its set of desired solutions in the period of German science and social reform progressivism of the 1880s and 1890s. The period of institutionalization (1890–1922) follows, where the goal of state intervention was to secure the right of every child to "mental and physical fitness." Next came the period of routinization and the crisis of confidence during the late 1920s and early 1930s, when, under conditions of financial stringency, educational reformers debated the limits of educability and the limits of education. Within the context

of the general crisis of the welfare state (1928–33), involving retrench-
ment and cost-benefit trade-off, educational programs were cut back in
accordance with the criterion of the value or otherwise of those
receiving the service. The final years of the Weimar Republic saw the
new paradigm of selecting those of value and segregating those of lesser
value displacing the previous paradigm of universality of provision.
Peukert claims,

When the Nazis come to power in 1933, the paradigm of selection and
elimination, already dominant, is made absolute. What is new is not the
paradigm per se, but the fact that its critics are forced into silence. In addition,
through a voluntary preemptive act of obedience, racist terminology is
elevated into the lingua franca of the human sciences and social-welfare
professions. And, as yet another change, one single branch of modern thought,
namely racism, receives supreme state backing and is given even greater scope
to test its theories and put them into practice. (1993, p. 244)

The paradigm of selection and elimination itself, like the earlier
paradigm, comes up against its limits, which leads to a negative
radicalization of the racist utopia focused increasingly upon eradication,
such that, with the outbreak of war, the realization of the Final Solution
becomes complete. Peukert makes it clear that it is

The eugenic, racial-hygiene variant of racism that has provided the key
component parts in the machinery of mass murder: the notion of "nonvalue",
removing ethical status from those affected; the anonymity of the process of
categorisation of the victims in terms of hereditary characteristics (largely
specious in any case); long-standing prior administrative practices involving
institutions of segregation; and, finally, the scientific and technological input
involved in the construction of the apparatus of murder itself. (1993, p. 245)

In the next phase the human and social sciences become engaged in an
all-embracing racial restructuring of social, educational, welfare and
health policy.

Peukert maintains that there was nothing inevitable in the path
that National Socialism followed. He suggests that there were, in fact,
several critical junctures or strategic shifts that were required before
the utopian dream of a scientific victory over the social problem (mass
poverty, ignorance, illness) was transformed into "the mass-destructive
utopia of racist purification of the *Volkskörper* through the 'eradication'
of lives of 'lesser value'" including the shift: from the individual to the
social and national body, from the care for the needy to selection of those
of value and eradication of those of lesser value, from the utilitarian
ideal of the greatest happiness of the greatest number to a cost-benefit
accounting of provision and from "self-indulgent delusions of technological and scientific grandeur to self-reproducing high-technology
mechanisms of annihilation" (1993, p. 246).

AFTER AUSCHWITZ: THE GOVERNMENT OF RESEARCH

A set of interesting and ethically important questions surrounds the positioning of the human and social sciences in Germany after Auschwitz. It was, as Peukert notes, back to normal and business as usual for the vast majority of professionals. A very small group of scientists were prosecuted in the Nuremberg doctors' trial for their involvement in war crimes. But for by far the vast majority of professionals, who continued to hold research and teaching positions within universities, research institutions and government ministries, there was an unproblematic return to the routines of everyday inquiry and a reversion to a pre-crisis mentality. Peukert writes:

Even among those scientists and academics, including some educational reformers, who had preserved their integrity and had been persecuted by the Nazis, coming to terms with the past took place in selective fashion, either because there might be a sense of complicity or because of feelings of impotence. The result, with Nazi sympathizers and persecution victims in the scientific professions alike, was a blocking-off of any systematic analysis of the way in which their professions had been entangled in the history of racism in general and of National Socialism in particular. (1993, pp. 248–49)

The way forward for Peukert is dependent upon restoring an awareness of what actually happened in the past. He suggests that after a quarter of a century of normality, of a restored faith in the progress of the social and human sciences, we are witnessing once again a sense of running up against limits. This impending sense of crisis, he understands, makes it imperative to raise questions about the historical crisis that proceeded the upsurge of Nazi racism. He argues, "A purely factual reconstruction of past events is possible only if, at the same time, we engage in a theoretical debate about options and opportunities within the disciplines and professions of the human and social sciences, past and present" (1993, p. 249).

In West Germany there is, he notes, an increasing skepticism being raised about "the moral categories we bring to bear in our dealings with others, notably those different from ourselves" in face of the rise of neo-Nazi sentiments, the attacks on immigrants and "the continuing survival of a discourse of segregation, untouched by any historical self-consciousness" (Peukert, 1993, p. 249).

On the basis of the foregoing discussion it is possible to argue that this situation — the deep imbrication of the social and human sciences in creating and sustaining the discourse of racism — has nothing to do with present interrelationships between knowledge and policy in neoliberal states. This strategy of argument might wish to preserve the integrity of the social sciences in relation to the state by emphasizing a historical and geographical separation or insularity. On this basis, it might be further argued that present neoliberal policies actually originate in a body of economic and political theory that stresses the limits of government in relation to the market and that the social and human sciences therefore occupy quite a different relationship to the state than they did under state welfarism. Indeed, it could be argued that the problem of how to create a state on the basis of an economic freedom that will secure both the legitimacy and the self-limitation of the state was one that, historically, was thrown up and marked by the very experience of National Socialism. National Socialism, in this view, was not an aberration but rather the inevitable outcome of a series of antiliberal policies that resulted in the exorbitant growth of the state (see Burchell, 1993, p. 270). The argument might conclude that there is therefore no likelihood of history repeating itself, that the social and human sciences under regimes of neoliberalism have a quasi-autonomy that would prevent them from being the ideological handmaiden and policy arm of the all-encompassing state.

Briefly, my response to this move is to invoke and seek to develop the idea of the "government of research" within a framework based on Foucault's notions of governmentality and "bio-power" (see Marshall & Peters, 1995). Let me outline in schematic terms the relevance of the first of these twin Foucaultian notions for the question at hand. First, governmentality refers in Foucault's writings to governmental reason in the widest sense, to "the conduct of conduct," a rational "way of doing things," for acting on the actions of individuals (Foucault, 1988). There is a clear sense of the idea of government in Foucault's later work, which connects and extends his early analysis of power in *Discipline and Punish* (1979), where the disciplines are redescribed as "technologies" of power that presuppose the freedom of those on whom they are exercised and act to affect the way individuals conduct themselves. The notion of government here emphasizes the way in which the disciplines are governmental forms of reflection, realized as practices, that is, tied to various procedures and techniques that give them effect. In later writings, when the notion of governmentality is explicitly introduced, Foucault uses the term in a more specific sense as referring to the domain of the political, a "problematics of rule" (Rose, 1993), which concerns the ordering of the affairs of an established territory and the control of its population. Foucault describes this second sense as a contact point where technologies of domination or power and "techniques of the self" are integrated into institutional structures and practices. Technologies of the self permit individuals to effect or carry out certain operations on their own bodies and souls, so as to reconstruct and transform their selves to attain certain states of wisdom, perfection, purity and even happiness (see Peters & Marshall, 1993, pp. 32–37).

I do not want to defend Foucault's position or to discuss his terminology in any detail. I want simply to demonstrate the way in which his conceptualization opens up a distinctive and rich approach in the analysis of liberalism, particularly in its new forms, in relation to the social and human sciences. In essence, as Burchell (1993, pp. 269ff) comments, Foucault's distinctive approach to the analysis of liberalism consists in analyzing it from the point of view of government reason, as an activity rather than as a theory or as an institution:

For early liberalism, to govern properly involves pegging the principle for rationalizing governmental activity to *the rationality of the free conduct of governed individuals themselves*. That is to say, the rational conduct of government must be intrinsically linked to the *natural*, private interest motivated conduct of free, market *exchanging* individuals because the rationality of these individuals' conduct is, precisely what enables the market to function optimally in accordance with its nature.

By contrast, for neo-liberalism, the rational principle for regulating and limiting government must be determined by reference to *artificially* arranged or contrived forms of the free, *entrepreneurial* and *competitive* conduct of economic-rational individuals. (p. 271)

In terms of this problematics of rule, liberalism can be understood as a form of government reason resting upon the following features as outlined by Rose (1993, p. 290f):

1. Liberalism inaugurates a new relation between government and knowledge.
2. Liberalism depends upon a novel specification of the subjects of rule as active in their own government.
3. Liberal government is inherently bound to the authority of expertise.
4. Liberalism inaugurates a continual questioning of the activity of rule itself.

I do not think that I need to labor the point regarding the intimate connection between government and knowledge within liberalism, or how the former depends on the latter. This situation has been made clear by a variety of scholars. Alvin Gouldner (1971) argued two decades ago that modern social science has always been implicated in a contradictory relationship with the welfare state; that, dependent on a state funding relationship, modern sociology limits its scope of inquiry to reformist strategies. What I think is interesting and productive in the work of those who have sought to develop Foucault's insights is the observation that the potency of neoliberalism derives from the fact that it has managed to turn a series of criticisms of welfare — its cost, its bureaucratic complexity, its degree of centralization, its paternalism — into governmental criticisms, that is, *technical* problems. As Rose comments: "Nowhere is this more so than in relation to expertise, and in reposing the question of the government of expertise in an 'advanced liberal' form. . . . 'Advanced liberal' government entails the adoption of a range of devices that seek to recreate the distance between decisions of formal political institutions and other social actors, and to act upon these actors in new ways, through shaping and utilizing their freedom" (1993, p. 294f).

For Rose, advanced liberal government, therefore, entails a new relation between expertise and politics, such that "the calculative regimes of positive knowledges of human conduct are to be replaced by the calculative regimes of accounting and financial management" (1993, p. 295). Advanced liberal government, according to Rose, also entails a new pluralization of social technologies and a new specification of the subject of government in terms of "the enhancement of the power of the client as customer [which] specifies the subject of rule in new forms" (p. 296).

Finally, a word about "bio-power" in connection with these concerns of government. Foucault (1990) discusses this notion at some length in the first volume of *The History of Sexuality*, where he distinguishes two poles of development: the first, an "anatomo-politics of the human body," which focuses on the optimization of its capacities and its integration into the economic system; the second, focusing on the *species* body — as he says, "the body imbued with the mechanisms of life and serving as the basis of the biological processes: propagation, births and mortality, the level of health, life expectancy and longevity, with all the conditions that can cause these to vary. Their supervision was effected through an entire series of interventions and *regulatory controls, a bio-politics of the population*" (p. 139).

There is more than an uncanny resonance of Foucault's work with Peukert's thesis and the new paradigm of biological politics in recent Third Reich historiography. Indeed, Foucault's genealogy of sexuality and his explanation of how the exercise of power in the late nineteenth century rested upon a "thematics of blood" sheds considerable light on the development of modern racism. He writes:

Racism took shape at this point (racism in its modern, "biologizing", statist form): it was then that a whole politics of settlement (*peuplement*), family, marriage, education, social heirarchization, and property, accompanied by a long series of permanent interventions at the level of the body, conduct, health, and everyday life, received their color and their justification from the mythical concern with protecting the purity of the blood and ensuring the triumph of the race. Nazism was doubtless the most cunning and the most naive (and the former because of the latter) combination of the fantasies of blood and the paroxysms of a disciplinary power. (1990, p. 149)

Bio-power, I would argue, exists in a less obviously statist form under neoliberalism, a form that is essentially commodified, decentralized, and demassified — a form, moreover, that is still actively accomplished, in large part, through the social and human sciences that have become indispensable for present neoliberal forms of government.

By way of conclusion, I have argued that Auschwitz constitutes an inescapable horizon for the consideration of the relations of ethics, knowledge and public policy within the continuing process of modernization within neoliberal nation-states. The lessons of poststructuralism have taught us to detect and respect the *différend* (Lyotard), to pay attention to the individualization of discourses (Foucault), while at the same time to recognize the singularity of the event. To emphasize the singularity of Auschwitz is precisely to avoid the kind of historical generalization that accompanies claims designed to relativize Auschwitz as one more "annihilation therapy." While it may be possible to talk of the paradigm of biological politics in Nazi Germany or bio-power in contemporary neoliberal states and the ways in which the human and social sciences contribute to discourses of racism or, say, human capital — categorizations and normalizations of the educational subject in terms of race and class — these discourses take historically specific forms, just as the discourse of state reason itself has been given historically peculiar interpretations.

The relation between educational policy and ethics cannot be given universal formulation by itself, so to speak, outside history and discourse; it is also a historically specific relation that may take different forms. The relation is a discursive one, the formation of which depends, in part, upon considerations of larger discursive networks — those ideological parameters established by the state and the human and social sciences more generally.

7

Science and Education in the "Information Society"

We are living through a movement from an organic, industrial society to a polymorphous, information system — from all work to all play, a deadly game.

— Donna Haraway[1]

INTRODUCTION

It is a curious feature of the 1990s intellectual climate that notions and theories first realized and developed in the 1960s and 1970s should be recirculated within the general economy of ideas to surface in present policy debates that will have considerable impact upon the future development of advanced industrial economies. The primary example I have in mind is that of "postindustrialism" and its associated or related developments: "the information society" and, most recently, "the Information Superhighway." This is not to argue that these ideas and theories have been recirculated without refinement or reworking. Indeed, in many cases the original notions have become much more sophisticated versions of their earlier predecessors. Some have even been put to empirical test. On the other hand, it is also clearly evident that the original notions emerge as underlying assumptions, which are accepted as given, never problematized or examined with any care.

The idea of postindustrialism was first introduced by Arthur Penty, a guild socialist, as early as 1917 (see Rose, 1991). The notion was revived and used widely by a variety of economists and sociologists from the early 1960s, in an era of optimism when it was thought that there were no limits to growth or to the increasing affluence of the "long boom." In the mid-1970s this optimism and the idea of continuous economic growth on which it depended began to seem both misplaced and naïve. After the oil shocks of the mid-1970s and the bite of worldwide recession, increasingly the mood and discourse shifted to one of crisis, emphasizing doubts about the prospects for continuous economic growth. During this period, when ecological arguments began to find their mark and when governments began to struggle with issues of "deindustrializaton" and economic decline, visions of a postindustrial society appeared both more distant and irresponsible.

Yet during that time new forms of postindustrial theory were being developed, based around the introduction and effects of the new information technologies. They have come to fruition in the late 1980s and 1990s and now dominate contemporary debates. They are, perhaps, more cautious than their 1960s counterparts, but equally optimistic. While they do not see the future unproblematically, they still cling tenaciously to the idea that advanced industrial societies are witnessing a series of interrelated changes as significant as those accompanying the shift from agrarian to industrial society.

The most recent policy documents (e.g., Organization for Economic Cooperation and Development, 1991) emphasize profound changes in information technology use and, in particular, the shift from stand-alone equipment and applications to computer-based networking and new information services. Information networking is seen as providing the basis of new services for the economy and a strategic response to changes in the market environment. In addition, networking is seen as underpinning the trend toward the globalization of all economic activities, as well as having significant implications for both the location and structure of industries and the future international division of labor.

Yet in the 1990s the notion of the information society has lost much of the social, utopian promise it once had. Early theorists (e.g., Masuda, 1981) and national planning visions raised social and political questions concerning the emergence of the information society: the potential for a shift to participatory democracy; new and more extensive forms of welfare; the nature of community; and changes to value and ethical standards. Today the politics surrounding the concept have been submerged as it has been taken up by politicians and policy-makers under the impetus of an economic rationalism. In this new order the older reformist discourse of social democracy, which theorized the state as mediating between the demands of the economy and the needs of civic society, has given way to an economic rationalism that has replaced the coordinating role of the state with that of the market. At the same time this has involved the uncoupling of the economic system from the socio-cultural system. Under a process of structural reform and rationalization, as Pusey comments in the Australian context, formal models have prevailed over practical substance and the economic system has acquired an independence, objectivity and autonomy so much that civic society is seen as a resisting, idealized opponent of "the economy." "Culture and identity dissolve into arbitrary individual choices and, moreover, institutional arbitrariness is no longer a sign of failure but is instead put forward with deadly seriousness as a necessary condition, at the steering level, for the smooth and rational operation of a self-referential system" (1991, p. 21). Science, education and technology have a special place in this new order. Restructured and fully rationalized according to now familiar principles of contestability, flexibility, user-pays and cost-effectiveness, public good science and state education have been commercialized and commodified in the name of increasing national competitive advantage. As Jean-François Lyotard argued in the late 1970s: "Knowledge is and will be produced in order to be sold, it is and will be consumed in order to be valorized in a new production: in both cases, the goal is exchange. Knowledge ceases to be an end in itself, it loses its 'use-value'" (1984, p. 4f).

Within the information society, knowledge and education are hypothesized as the principal forces of production, severely altering the composition of the workforce. Within the context of the transformation wrought by the new information technologies, knowledge becomes an informational commodity indispensable to the economy and the future basis of international competitive advantage. The discourse of economic rationalism, which restructures public good science and recuperates it into the economic system as a leading sector (along with education), recasts the relation between the state and civil society, instituting a break between science as a part of the economic system and culture. Under this view, civic society is seen as an impediment to information-related innovation opportunities, and institutional rigidities are seen in need of regulatory and structural reform.

This chapter examines the notion of the information society with the explicit aim of highlighting the political questions it raises, focusing especially on the neoliberal reformulation of state science and education. The first section of the chapter examines briefly the history of the notion of the information society as it grew out of the debates on postindustrialism. The second section provides an account of post-modern science based upon the work of Stephen Toulmin and others, who signal a "reenchantment" of science or a "return to cosmology" in order to argue the case, on the one hand, against an Enlightenment view of science prevailing in the nineteenth century — at once reductive, mechanistic, unified and based upon a single method — and, on the other hand, for a view of science inextricably bound up with social, political and ethical considerations. The third section extends the emphasis on the political by examining a poststructuralist account of science in the postmodern condition. It draws particularly on the work of Michel Foucault and Joseph Rouse's interpretation of Foucault, as well as Lyotard's *The Postmodern Condition* (1984). The last section briefly considers science and education as *reasons* of state. The general drift of this part of the argument is that under the ideology of economic rationalism, which constructs the future in terms of an overriding economic imperative, state institutions of science and education are no longer regarded as independent spheres. Their purposes have been reduced and they have been encompassed by and put in the service of the economic system. Such a view provides both a source of legitimation and a further rationale for restructuring the state and society to create the necessary conditions for economic growth.

POSTINDUSTRIALISM AND THE HISTORY OF THE INFORMATION SOCIETY

From the outset, the notion of the information society was approached in economic terms, focusing on the changing role of knowledge production within the economy. The first generation of theorists was concerned with the employment effects of the increase in so-called knowledge-producing occupations. Fritz Machlup (1962), for instance, on the basis of crude census data, concludes that employment patterns, in terms of changes to occupational structures in the United States, indicated a strong movement from manual to mental or knowledge-producing labor from 1900 to 1959. He inferred that the United States faced the problem of increasing wage differentials between mental and manual labor or a continuing upward creep of the rate of unemployment. The dilemma, he thought, might be overcome through the reform of education so as to raise the general level of accomplishment.

Others followed Machlup's lead. While revising the calculations, they tended to confirm the general shift from an industrial to an information society, sometimes described as the postindustrial society or the knowledge society (e.g., Parker and Porat, 1975; Porat, 1977). Edwin Parker and Mark Porat (1975), addressing themselves to the questions raised by this economic trend, argued for greater attention to the efficiency of investment in the information sector, concluding that the best chance for productivity gains was in terms of investment in research and development and in education, and they advocated four general areas of policy consideration: national science, education, technology and library.

The second generation of theorists focused on the concept of postindustrial society, emphasizing the centrality of theoretical knowledge as the axis around which new technology, economic growth and the stratification of society will be organized. Daniel Bell (1973) introduces the concept of the postindustrial society in an effort to identify a change in *social structure*, which he describes in terms of three components: a shift from manufacturing to services in the economic sector, the centrality of new science-based industries in technology and the rise of new technical elites and the advent of a new principle of social stratification. He charts the rise of new axial principles that are said to structure institutions in postindustrial society. In particular, he identifies theoretical knowledge as central, replacing private property as the axial institution: information substitutes for capital as the most general operator in the new economy. While the chief economic problem in industrial society was that of capital — the creation of savings and their conversion into investment — in postindustrial society, the chief problem is regarded as the organization of science around the institutions of the university and the research institute. The chief policy issues are the nature and scope of state support for science and higher education, their politicization, and the problems of the organization of work by science teams.

Bell (1973) notes that the axial principle of modern culture, that of the self, is hostile to the functional rationality that dominates the application of knowledge by the technological and administrative estates. Increasingly within postindustrial society, therefore, a disjunction between social structure and and culture appears. Interestingly, writing in the early 1970s under the influence of a postwar Keynesian consensus, Bell comments on the "historical" subordination of the economic function to societal goals, with the corresponding primacy of the political order. This leads him to stress an ideological egalitarianism in the world of work as much as in the citizen's entitlement to a range of basic services and income. Such a view is to be contrasted with the economic rationalism prevailing today, where the economic order has become paramount and the sphere of the state and civil society have become subordinated. Under these conditions traditional concerns for equality of opportunity, social equity and justice have taken second place to the demands of international competition.

Alain Touraine, the French sociologist, published his *La société post-industrielle* in 1969. He was among the first to challenge the assumption that with the shift to new modes of economic organization the traditional notions of class and class conflict would disappear. Writing in the heady days of the late 1960s, Touraine (1974) predicted the rise of the new social movements and their increasing prominence in subinstitutional, ex-parliamentary forms of protest. Reflecting on the new type of society being formed, he christened the changes he observed under the notion of the postindustrial. He also used the terms "technocratic" and "programmed" to indicate the type of power and the nature of production methods, respectively, which are said to prevail. For him, capital accumulation and economic growth are no longer tied to production per se but rather result from a whole complex of social and cultural factors, particularly those involved in the creation of scientific and technological knowledge. This led him to emphasize the way in which the domains of social life, including education, consumption and information, were being increasingly integrated into the realm of production. His focus was the university as the possible locus for integration or confrontation in the future.

The ideas of Bell and Touraine have emerged as prototypes, with some variation, of subsequent debate. On the one side there are those who depict postindustrialism in celebratory terms; on the other side, are those who are more concerned with critique and with the passage to a more emancipatory and sustainable society. For the former group, as Richard Badham maintains, the differences between industrial and postindustrial society are set out in terms of a series of significant contrasts: "between a manufacturing and a service economy; between blue and white collar work; between the dominance of the business corporation and the dominance of the university; between an ideology of growth and an ideology of social welfare and the quality of life; between factory-based class conflict, on the one hand, and the reciprocal antagonism, on the other, of centralised technocrats . . . to the general public" (1986, p. 77).

The former group, along with Bell, includes theorists like Peter Drucker and Alvin Toffler and agencies like the Organization for Economic Cooperation and Development. The latter group, while agreeing with this picture in general terms, sees these developments more as an outgrowth of industrial society than the formation of a genuine postindustrial society that would be associated with increasing decentralization, the demythologization of science and growing popular participation. This alternative is based on an appeal to notions of "convivial" production (Ivan Illich), "selective industrialism" (Theodor Rozak), "intermediate," "alternative" or "appropriate" technology (E. F. Schumacher).

To a large extent this kind of oppositional thinking has remained very much a part of the contemporary debate as it has continued with the third stage of the generation of theory. By third generation I am thinking specifically of Jean-François Lyotard and his seminal work *The Postmodern Condition: A Report on Knowledge* (1984). I have called Lyotard's work both seminal and third generation for a number of reasons. First, to my mind, it represents a significant point in the globalization of the debate — a debate that, second, is specifically philosophical and that brings into focus a number of coalescing themes and previously disparate literatures. While Lyotard's subject matter is the changing status of science and technology in the most highly developed societies of the West, focusing on the control of knowledge and information, his philosophical perspective, influenced strongly by French poststructuralism, enables him to raise afresh the central problems of the legitimation of science and education in the postmodern condition. His analysis has strategic value in allowing us to see the effects of the transformation of knowledge on public power and civil institutions in a way that challenges the dominant conceptions (see Peters, 1995a).

POSTMODERN SCIENCE

There is now little doubt that a symbolic and epistemological break between modern and postmodern science has occurred. It is a break recognized by scholars of different persuasions between a traditional view of science that emphasizes an ahistorical and foundational account of knowledge based on a series of dichotomies such as the theory/observation, fact/value, schema/content distinctions and a view that both stresses the primacy of history for understanding the scientific endeavor and recognizes that the sciences do not constitute a unified logical system but rather ought to be seen as forms of life, communities made up of agreed-upon practices and guided by sets of values. This is to juxtapose a mechanical, reductive and unified science based on a single method against a holistic, organicist and pluralist notion of science, utilizing different methods. It is also to accept a major difference in terms of both the scope of scientific inquiry and the concept of scientific progress. Stephen Toulmin, a Wittgensteinian, argues the case in the following terms:

The emergence of post-modern science has several implications for scientific activity, for our concepts of scientific progress, and therefore, for science policy. One is that the old positivist idea that all the sciences have to be based on a single set of methods is no longer viable. Another is that since the scientist-as-spectator option is no longer open to us, neither is the assumption that science is value-free or that scientists bear no responsibility for the social consequences of their work. Post-modern science must be increasingly bound up with social, political, and ethical considerations. (1985, p. 29)

The Enlightenment view of science that prevailed in the nineteenth century tended to regard science in ahistorical and universal terms. It was seen as being based on a single method, which equated with rationality itself. Science was therefore seen as value-free and quite separate from political or ethical questions. Such a view of science received fresh emphasis and orientation with the formation of the Vienna school and the emergence of the logical empiricists in the 1920s. It was a view known popularly as "logical positivism," which held sway in one form or another until the efforts of a new generation of thinkers — Karl Popper, Thomas Kuhn, Paul Feyerabend, Wilfred Sellars, Stephen Toulmin, Mary Hesse, Richard Rorty and others — began to dismantle it.

Consider, for example, Bruno Latour's (1987, pp. 153–57) account concerning the politics of scientific practice, involving a research scientist and her boss in a leading California laboratory. The scientist sees herself as pursuing pure science — research on a new substance called pandorin — unencumbered by wider social or political concerns. Her boss, the head of the laboratory, by contrast, is involved in political activity most of the time. For instance, during a typical week he negotiates with a major pharmaceutical company over possible patents; he meets with the French Ministry of Health to discuss the opening of a new laboratory; he meets with the National Academy of Science to argue for the recognition of a new scientific subsection; he attends a board meeting of the journal *Endocrinology* to urge that more space be devoted to his area; he visits the local meatworks to talk about a new way of decapitating sheep without damaging the hypothalamus; he attends a curriculum meeting at the university to advocate more molecular biology and computer science; he confers with a visiting scientist about Swedish advances in the instruments used for detecting peptides; and he delivers an address to the Diabetic Association.

Some time later the effects of the boss's decisions, meetings and advocacy begin to impact upon the laboratory scientist. Alan Chalmers recounts the story:

We find that she has been able to employ a new technician, made possible by a grant from the Diabetic Association, and she has two new graduate students, who have entered the field by way of the new courses designed by her boss. Her research has benefitted from the cleaner samples she is receiving from the slaughterhouse and a new, highly sensitive, instrument recently acquired from Sweden which increases her capacity to detect minute traces of pandorin in the brain. Her preliminary results are published in a new section of *Endocrinology*. She is contemplating a position offered to her by the French government involving the setting up of a laboratory in France. (1990, pp. 120–21)

As Chalmers (1990) points out, the laboratory scientist is mistaken in her view that she is engaged in pure science uncontaminated by broader social and political matters. Indeed, the satisfaction of the material conditions necessary for the pursuit of her research is achieved only through the political activity of her boss. Clearly, scientific practice cannot be separated from other practices serving other interests. Further, by extension, it is possible to argue for the social character of all scientific practice. In fact, I take this to be the main argument, with suitable refinements, of both the historicist and sociological turns in contemporary accounts of science, after Thomas Kuhn's (1970) *The Structure of Scientific Revolutions*. In fact, in the Postscript, written in 1969, Kuhn highlights the social character of scientific practice by strongly emphasizing the notion of scientific community — a notion he takes to underlie his earlier work. A scientific community consists of practitioners who have undergone similar educations and professional initiations. These practitioners have absorbed the same technical literature and, while there are competing schools, in general they pursue a set of shared goals. Membership is established through advanced degrees, professional societies, journals read and so on (Kuhn, 1970). The Kuhnian account also has been taken up and elaborated by scholars like Marjorie Grene (1985), who has developed a new philosophy of science in contrast to the old. Her account, which has been called "ecological realism," emphasizes a biological approach to knowing and observing (see Reed, 1992). Both Kuhn and Grene have made their contributions to the understanding of what I will call "postmodern science." There are at least two accounts of postmodern science: one emphasizes the "return to cosmology," the reintegration of science with philosophy; the other functions as a critique of contemporary science, stressing the "bureaucratic rationalization" of science and the way in which science as a reason of state has been put in the service of economic development. Both accounts seek to understand science historically as part of a set of social practices belonging to a culture. Both accounts, making use of this general insight, picture science as a changing enterprise or institution to some extent reflecting changing historical conditions, and to this extent both accounts can be construed as sympathetic to the claims of those who have been excluded from science or suffered as a result of it.

Stephen Toulmin wrote *The Return to Cosmology: Postmodern Science and the Theology of Nature* in 1982. In the third part, Toulmin explicitly addresses the theme of postmodern science as representing a return to cosmology. At one point he writes:

The "modern" world is now a thing of the past. Our own natural science today is no longer "modern" science. Instead . . . it is rapidly engaged in becoming "postmodern" science: the science of the "postmodern" world, of "postnationalist" politics and "postindustrial" society — the world that has not yet discovered how to define itself in terms of what it is, but only in terms of what it has just-now-ceased to be. In due course, the change from modern to postmodern science will evidently be matched by corresponding changes in philosophy and theology also; in particular, the "postmodern" positions and methods that natural scientists are now working out will have implications, also, for a possible reunion of natural science with natural theology. (p. 254)

Toulmin borrows the term "postmodern" from the theologian Frederick Ferré, who devotes his efforts to projecting a new set of values and institutions for a postmodern world. Toulmin's argument is straightforward enough: he argues that science and natural religion separated in the nineteenth and early twentieth centuries as a result of the professionalization of science and its consequent specialization. Under this increasing division of labor, the broader concerns of traditional cosmology disappeared. At the same time the role of the scientist came to be seen as that of a pure spectator, who was expected to report objectively on the world of nature. The spectator view of knowledge carried with it a belief in the "value neutrality" of science such that it was seen as no longer able to throw light on moral, practical and religious questions. In particular, Descartes' celebration of geometry as the model that exemplified the essence of rationality established a heirarchy of knowledge, elevating the sciences that dealt with general phenomena and downgrading those areas of study that dealt with particular events. Further, and perhaps more importantly, "Cartesian dualism made canonical a split in our vision of the world, which had the effect of setting rational thinking humanity over against causal, unthinking nature, and so enthroned the human intellect within a separate world of 'mental substance'" (Toulmin, 1982, p. 238).

Traditional cosmology, before its transition to modern science in the seventeenth century under the influence of Galileo, Kepler, Newton, Bacon and Descartes, performed many and varied functions, at one and the same time practical, theoretical, symbolic and expressive. The return to cosmology that is symbolized in postmodern science seeks to reinsert humanity into the world of nature. Toulmin mentions stoicism of late classical antiquity as the last period in Western history when humanity and nature were thought of as complementary elements within a single scheme or cosmos. He sees green philosophy as a (nonacademic) contemporary counterpart of stoicism, based as it is upon a responsibility to deepen an understanding of the interdependence that binds humanity to nature and combining as it does both scientific and philosophical or ethical elements.

In a later publication Toulmin (1985) emphasizes pluralism and responsibility as hallmarks of postmodern science, where the scientist-as-participant is encouraged to see herself as part of the natural processes she seeks to study. To the extent that scientists recognize their roles as participants, Toulmin argues, they will help to develop a worldview that is less mechanistic, reductionistic and deterministic. Most recently, Toulmin (1990) returns to the seventeenth century to rediscover the the ideal of society as "cosmopolis," a society as rationally ordered as the Newtonian view of nature. Such a view was reflected, for instance, in Hobbes' *Leviathan*, which elaborated a conception of society based on the scientific method as it was then understood. Toulmin reexamines the standard account of modernity and its defects, arguing against foundationalist accounts of knowledge that characterize the appeal to "scientific rationalism." Science that still upholds or legitimates itself by reference to the seventeenth-century view of rationality must be humanized and replaced by a notion of science that both subordinates itself to the needs of citizens and communities and reappropriates the aims and values of practical philosophy implicit in Renaissance humanism.

Other scholars have talked in similar terms to Toulmin: David Bohm (1980, 1985), Rupert Sheldrake (1991), Charles Birch (1988), Ilya Prigogine and Isabelle Stengers (1985), David Griffin (1988), Boadventura de Sousa Santos (1992), Pauline Rosenau (1992), to name some leading figures. Rosenau (1992), for example, develops a conception of "affirmative" postmodernism, which she pits against a "skeptical" postmodernism. The former is the kind of view unpacked by Toulmin and developed further by Griffin as "constructive" or "revisionary" postmodernism, which, he asserts, "involves a new unity of scientific, ethical, aesthetic, and religious institutions. It rejects not science as such but only that scientism in which the data of the modern natural sciences are alone allowed to contribute to the construction of our worldview" (1988, p. x).

Griffin makes an explicit appeal to Toulmin in calling for a "reenchantment of science" based on a postmodern organicism, and both he and Rosenau contrast this view with a skeptical or deconstructive postmodernism inspired by Friedrich Nietzsche, Lugwig Wittgenstein and Martin Heidegger. It is this version that has been developed by French poststructuralist thinkers — Jacques Derrida, Michel Foucault and Jean-François Lyotard, among others. It is a view that focuses on the politics of knowledge and functions mainly as a critique of contemporary Western science as it is practiced in liberal-capitalist societies.

TOWARD A POLITICAL PHILOSOPHY OF SCIENCE

The standard liberal epistemological interpretation of science is based upon the received view of the relationship between knowledge and power. We can summarize this relationship by saying that all interactions between knowledge and power are external, meaning that while power can influence what we believe, considerations of power are completely irrelevant to which of our beliefs are true and what justifies their status as knowledge. In other words, as Joseph Rouse succinctly expresses it: "Knowledge acquires its epistemological status independent of the operations of power" (1987, p. 13). According to this general account, knowledge can be applied in order to achieve power or power may be used to prevent the acquisition of knowledge or knowledge might liberate us from the effects of power, but power cannot contribute constructively to the achievement of knowledge. This standard view rests on three features ascribed to the notion of power: that it is possessed and exercised by specific agents; that it operates on our representations but not on the world represented; and that it is primarily repressive (Rouse, 1987, p. 15). Only the second point needs explanation: our beliefs about the world may be changed or imposed by the exercise of power over us but the exercise of power cannot guarantee the truth of our beliefs nor change how the world is.

The received view of the relations between knowledge and power has been seriously challenged. For instance, pragmatism challenges the claim that power is external to knowledge by arguing that truth is the product of consensus of a scientific community and that there are no identifiable criteria of truth apart from what we arrive at through the practice of inquiry. In this view, if truth criteria themselves are a

product of inquiry, then a consideration of power is integral to epistemology and the traditional epistemological problem of distinguishing true
from false beliefs is transformed into "the political problem of distinguishing free inquiry from inquiry constrained and distorted by the
exercise of power" (Rouse, 1987, p. 19). Such a view has been forcefully
argued for by Jürgen Habermas, the leading representative of Critical
Theory.

Habermas (1971) develops the thesis that all knowledge is political,
by which he means that knowledge is always constituted on the basis of
human interests that have developed in and been shaped by social and
historical circumstances. He classifies three main types of knowledge-
constitutive interests: the technical interest characteristic of the
natural sciences produces instrumental (means-end) knowledge aimed
at prediction and control, the practical interest of the human sciences
produces knowledge governed by the interpretation and understanding
of meaning and the emancipatory interest of the critical social sciences
is premised on the values of freedom and rational autonomy. Further,
the new empiricists (Hilary Putnam, Larry Laudan, Mary Hesse) challenge a range of distinctions that supported the received (liberal)
account of the relation between knowledge and power: fact/value,
theory/practice, pure/applied, scheme/content. They also reject representational or correspondence interpretations of scientific theories. In
their terms, successful theories have nothing to do with the accuracy of
their representations of the world. Successful theories are those that
improve our ability to cope with the world, to control it technically, and
"technical control, the power to intervene in and manipulate natural
events, is not the application of antecedent knowledge but the form
scientific knowledge now predominately takes" (Rouse, 1987, p. 20).

On one very influential account we are now to talk of "power/
knowledge" as an indissoluable unity (Foucault, 1980). Michel Foucault
rethinks the nature of modern power, tracing its development in the
birth of the human sciences and associated liberal institutions of the
clinic, the prison and the school. New mechanisms of modern power go
hand in hand with the birth of the human sciences. Modern power is
productive rather than simply repressive; it is capillary in that it
operates in everyday social practices rather than through beliefs; and it
is both local and continuous. Truth, knowledge and belief are a product
of the "politics of the discursive regime." There is a plurality of incommensurable discursive regimes that succeed each other historically.
Power/knowledge is a discursive regime comprised of a matrix of
practices that defines its own distinctive objects of inquiry, truth
criteria, institutional sanctions and so on. The term "power/knowledge,"
as Nancy Fraser notes, "covers in a single concept everything that falls
under the two distinct Kuhnian concepts of paradigm and disciplinary matrix but, unlike Kuhn, Foucault gives this complex a political

character. Both the use of the term 'power' and, more subtly, that of the term 'regime' convey this political coloration" (1981, p. 274).

Discursive regimes function on the basis of social practices that involve forms of constraint: the valorization of some statement forms over others; "the institutional licensing of some persons as being entitled to offer knowledge-claims and the concomitant exclusion of others; coercive forms of extracting information from and about certain persons and groups of persons; and so on" (Fraser, 1981, p. 274). While Foucault did not apply his insights directly to the natural sciences, others have done so. For example, Joseph Rouse uses Foucault to develop a political philosophy of science. He writes:

Power relations permeate the most ordinary activities in scientific research. Scientific knowledge arises out of these power relations rather than in opposition to them. Knowledge is power, and power knowledge. Knowledge is embedded in our research practices rather than being fully abstractable in representational theories. Theories are to be understood in their uses, not in their static correspondence . . . with the world. Power as it is produced in science is not the possession of particular agents and does not necessarily serve particular interests. Power relations constitute the world in which we find agents and interests. (1987, p. 24)

This kind of view of the relations between knowledge and power also underlies Jean-François Lyotard's account of the postmodern condition. Lyotard's single point of departure in attempting to describe and chart the transition in Western societies to the postindustrial age is scientific knowledge. He argues that the leading sciences and technologies — cybernetics, telematics, informatics and the growth of computer languages — are all significantly language-based, and together they have transformed the two principal functions of knowledge: research and the transmission of acquired learning.

Knowledge is changed or redefined within this context of general transformation. Anything in the constituted body of knowledge that is not translatable into quantities of information will be abandoned. Knowledge, in other words, loses its "use-value." The technical transformation wrought by a continued miniaturization and commercialization of knowledge machines will further change the way in which learning is acquired and classified. Knowledge is exteriorized with respect to the knower, and the status of the learner and the teacher is transformed into a commodity relationship of supplier and user. As Lyotard argues: "Knowledge is and will be produced in order to be sold, it is and will be consumed in order to be valorized in a new production: in both cases, the goal is exchange" (1984, p. 4). Already knowledge has become the principal force of production, altering the structure and composition of the work force in the most developed countries.

The commodification of knowledge widens still further the gap between developed and developing countries. It disrupts the traditional view that learning falls under the state's responsibility and raises new ethico-political questions concerning the relationship between the state and information-rich transnational corporations. This scenario, Lyotard admits, is not original or even necessarily true, but it does have *strategic value* in allowing us to see the effects of the transformation of knowledge on public power and civil institutions, and it raises afresh the central problem of legitimation. Who decides what is true or what is to be regarded as scientific, as belonging to the discourse of a scientific community? In postmodern society, where knowledge and power are to be regarded as simply two sides of the same question, the problem of legitimation of knowledge necessarily comes to the fore. The question of knowledge is now more than ever a question of government (Lyotard, 1984, p. 9).

SCIENCE AND EDUCATION AS REASONS OF STATE

Science has become a reason of state. More closely linked than ever before to the modern notion of development with its connotations of progress, competition and nationalism, science and education as reasons of state have been subjected to a new rationalization designed to optimize its contribution to the system's performance. Science, as Lyotard (1984) argues, has increasingly fallen under the sway of another game, that of technology. The game of technology, as opposed to science, whose goal is truth, follows the principle of optimal performance (maximizing output, minimizing input). Its goal or criterion is efficiency rather than truth or justice.

That science has become a reason of state tied to the politics of national development is not necessarily a recent phenomenon: the relation of science to development was cemented during and immediately after World War II, playing a focal role in the politics of the Cold War. Arguably, modern science was conceived of as a reason of state: certainly Francis Bacon conceived of science as power over both nature and humanity in the service of the king. Increasingly since World War II, science, education and technology have been recognized as playing fundamental and determining roles in relation to socioeconomic development. A number of factors have reinforced and highlighted this recognition: the relation between new forms of multidisciplinary basic science and emerging generic technologies (e.g., electronics, information and communications, advanced materials and biotechnology); the role of these generic technologies in driving a new Kondratiev "long wave" of economic development; the consequent need for countries to fund future-oriented programs of basic mission-oriented or strategic research and the changed external "boundary conditions" under which the scientific research system must now operate, because science has entered a "steady state" (Ziman, 1994) where demands for public accountability and "value-for-money" necessarily imply greater selectivity in the allocation of funds and more systematic approaches to planning.

In liberal-capitalist states since the mid-1980s we have witnessed the adoption of corporatization, deregulation and privatization strategies as part of a deliberate political project, involving a massive restructuring of the core and peripheral public sector. These changes have originated in a marked shift of political philosophy that postulates a society in which free individuals maximize their own interests in the marketplace according to agreed rules of conduct, and thereby also maximize the use of information and resources to the benefit of the community as a whole .

In this view, information and the transfer of knowledge is at the very heart of the market mechanism. There is an emphasis on the competitive marketplace as a superb cultural adaptation to facilitate the acquisition and communication of knowledge rather than on the technology itself. The marketplace is seen as the essence of the free society, because allegedly it provides an objective system for adjudicating between winners and losers; that there will be winners and losers is a fact that must be accepted as a consequence of establishing a free society. The role of government is limited on this conception: to establishing clear rules of conduct; to ensuring that information is freely available; to providing, by way of taxation, certain common goods and services which would not otherwise be provided and to supervising socially undesirable practices.

In terms of the two key informational services — research and education — the state must be careful to avoid threats posed to a free economic order through unwarranted intervention. In these areas, as in the provision of welfare services, the state must avoid the domination of delivery systems so as not to distort the free flow of information or to compromise the ethic of individual responsibility. The pursuit of education must be unhindered by statist interventions to secure particular outcomes for particular groups in the interests of equality of opportunity. The provision of welfare services by the state ought to be reduced to minimalist proportions — to a safety net — so as not to distort the functioning of the market order nor lessen the imperative of responsibility for one's welfare.

State income redistribution and the pursuit of social justice, state enterprise and state collaboration with trade unions, on this account, are seen as areas of governmental irresponsibility that suppress the information available to individuals. The results of policies based on this neoliberal philosophy are clearly evident in historically high levels of unemployment that is both structurally entrenched and deeply segmented along lines of class, race and gender.

To a large extent the underlying principles that have served as a basis for the restructuring of science and education policy reflect what

Christopher Hood (1990) and others have called New Public Management (NPM). NPM is characterized by a shift: from policy development to management; from aggregation to disaggregation in public service organization (disaggregated budgets, internal markets and rivalry); from planning and public service welfarism to a stress on cost-cutting and labor discipline; from process to output controls and accountability mechanisms (performance measurement); from permanent public bureau production to term contracts and private sector delivery (Hood & Jackson, 1991, p. 178). NPM combines "new institutional economics" (public choice theory, principal-agency theory, and transaction cost theory) built around ideas of contestability, user choice, transparency and incentive structures, with elements of the fashionable "corporate culture" doctrines of the 1980s. It represents a development of the scientific management of Taylor and has become a vehicle for new-right ideology, emphasizing an avoidance of direct state management and a corresponding favoring of marketlike arrangements for the allocation of scarce public resources. Further, Hood (1991, p. 3) notes that NPM is associated with attempts to slow down or reverse government growth in terms of public spending and staffing; the shift toward privatization and quasi-privatization and away from core government institutions; and the development of automation, particularly in information technology and in the production and distribution of public services.

Clearly, science policy restructuring has occurred in line with a new philosophy of administration, the principles of which reflect a political ideology. Science, accordingly, will come to be practiced within a particular set of ideological parameters. Can the practice of science be separated from questions concerning the funding of public good science? Can the practice of science be separated from the policy context that articulates strategic goals concerning the overall direction of research, emphasizing its contribution to economic performance, particularly research in economic sectors that already have a competitive advantage or can add value? Will the practice of science in the future take place independently of national priority research themes? The answers to these questions, in my view, are quite plain.

In many liberal-capitalist countries where state policy has effectively given up on the possibility of equalizing the imbalance between the supply and demand sides of the labor market and where neoliberal reforms of the public sector remove traditional means appropriate to pursuing a policy of full employment, the problem of structural unemployment, with all its long-term social costs, seems likely to increase. In these circumstances, the prospects elaborated by utopian postindustrial thinkers who emphasize the job creation possibilities of the new information technologies, the growth of the "electronic cottage" (Alvin Toffler), the employment potential of the tertiary sector, or even the strategy of formalizing the informal sector through new forms of self-employment require the most careful scrutiny.

An evaluation of the information society thesis must come to terms with the technological determinism underlying most versions. In such accounts technology is presented in unproblematic terms as somehow being autonomous, having a life of its own, and driving the modernization process. This kind of view, together with the significance it attaches to a unilinear notion of progress, has greatly restricted imagination in the policy process. Not only does it obscure questions of power in selecting the form and direction of technology and its relations to issues of national growth but it also prevents reflection on the need for making choices. It also serves to discourage public participation in debate over the criteria that ought to be used in making public choices.

Technologically deterministic postindustrial theories postulating the existence of the new economy proceed from simplifying assumptions about the role of the new information technologies in driving economic development and the demand for new skills. They generally interpret these developments as a neutral, natural and inevitable outcome of market logic. Such determinism is part of the wider discourse of development, which has taken different forms. The theory of linear progress that underlies modernization in the West has been criticized recently for being falsely represented as universalist, ahistorical and teleological on the basis of an ethnocentric Western development paradigm. According to so-called convergence theory, all industrial societies are becoming increasingly alike in structural terms. Yet various authors have pointed out the way in which Japan and the newly industrializing countries seem to be developing models quite different from the Euro-American one (see, e.g., Sugimoto, 1990).

The assumption of a uniform modernization process based on one paradigm would seem to be a great mistake if it were to be carried into the debate on postindustrial futures. It would be a mistake in the sense of homogenizing possibilities for particular futures that, nationally, must take into account not only the growing internationalization of the world economy but local conditions and preferred options. It would seem to be a mistake even on empirical grounds in that even among countries like the United States, Germany and Sweden there are quite different postindustrial trajectories to be recognized (Esping-Andersen, 1990). As Sugimoto (1990, p. 59) maintains, one solution is to postulate multi-linear (or polycentric) models of social change, which might recognize differences within the Euro-American mode of modernization as well as other modes entirely (Japanese, newly industrializing countries). Such an approach might also militate against the views of international policy agencies, which often proceed on what might be called an undifferentiated development model based on the Euro-American paradigm, which is assumed to be homogeneous.

NOTES

Chapter 7 is based on material revised from two papers: Michael Peters, 1993, "Employment Futures and the Politics of the Information Society in New Zealand" in Richard Harker and Paul Spoonley (eds.), *Science and Technology: Policy Issues for the 1990s* (pp. 49-68). Wellington: Ministry of Research, Science and Technology & Educational Research and Development Centre, and Michael Peters, "Postmodern Science in Aotearoa? Conservation, Cosmology and Critique," a paper originally presented as a seminar at the Department of Conservation, Wellington, December 5, 1992, and published locally in Eleanor Rimoldi (ed.) 1993, Research Unit for Maori Education Research, Research Monograph Series.

1.   D. Haraway. (1990). Manifesto for Cyborgs. In L. Nicholson (Ed.), *Feminism / Postmodernism*. New York: Routledge.

8

Vattimo, Postmodernity and the Transparent Society

INTRODUCTION

It is clearly possible to talk of contemporary Italian thought in terms of the debate on "postmodernism." In the field of architecture, for instance, the work of Paolo Portoghesi and Victorio Grigotti (among others) establishes a distinctive Italian contribution to the international discussion. For Portoghesi (1982), drawing on the work of Jean-François Lyotard (1984), the postmodern is a "rupture" with modernism rather than a simple change of direction or a label for converging tendencies. The incredulity of the *grand récits*, which has precipitated a crisis of theoretical legitimation, has also, according to Portoghesi, challenged the fundamental principles of architectural modernity. Drawing not uncritically on the new electronic technology that modulates the move to postindustrial society, Portoghesi talks in optimistic terms, of a return to historic forms and compositional systems as a way of establishing an *architecture of communication* premised on the restitution of the role of the subject to the community of its users. Grigotti, for his part, in the words of Lyotard believes: "There is no longer any close linkage between the architectural project and socio-historical progress in the realization of human emancipation on the larger scale. Postmodern architecture is condemned to generate a multiplicity of small transformations in the space it inherits, and to give up the project of a last rebuilding of the whole space occupied by humanity" (1989, p. 7).

Expressed in these terms, it is clear that both Portoghesi and Grigotti tend to side with Lyotard against Habermas. Indeed, as Portoghesi (1982) has commented, the true "new conservatives" — a reference to Habermas' (1981a) polemic against French poststructuralism[1] — are not those who return to artistic traditions to counter the effects of modernization, but those who pose as the guardians of modernity at any cost.

In the English-speaking world, the recent novels and philosophical works of Umberto Eco are well known, as are the novels of Italo Calvino, who has been christened a "postmodernist" by John Barth. Calvino's (1989) collection of essays, *The Literature Machine* (originally delivered as lectures as early as 1966), clearly demonstrates a highly original voice in the understanding of literature — its relations with philosophy and science, its narrative functions, its political uses. It is a voice that is both historically aware and sensitive to contemporary theoretical developments, to the work of the "Tel Quel" group and to Roland Barthes in particular (see, for instance, the symposium on Calvino, *Italian Quarterly*, 1989).

Eco, in conversation with Stefano Rosso (1991, p. 242), agrees with those who consider the postmodern as a spiritual rather than a chronological category — a *Kunstwollen* (a Will-to-Art), a stylistic device, and even a worldview. He maintains that the postmodern response to the past consists in recognizing that the past must be "revisited ironically, in a way which is not innocent" (p. 243), and proceeds to discuss his own work *Ie nome della rosa* (*The Name of the Rose*) in exactly those terms. He equates structure with openess and invokes the model of the labyrinth as a basis for textual conjecture: the classical labyrinth (Ariadne's thread), which has an entrance, a center and an exit; the mannerist labyrinth, a root-like structure with many dead ends but only one exit and the network called the rhizome (after Deleuze and Guattari), which has "no centre, no periphery, and no exit" (Eco, 1989, p. 248).

At one point discussing the notion of the postmodern, Eco links up his comments with the Italian debate over the "crisis of reason" and Gianni Vattimo's notion of "weak" or "soft" thought (*pensiero debole*).[2] He writes: "People spoke too long of a praxis founded on reason (*Vernunft*) as if there were only one 'reason'. They discovered that there was not one 'reason,' and (in Italy, for example) people began to talk about the crisis of reason (here in America they probably talk instead about epistemological anarchism à la Feyerabend). In any case, there is a crisis of reason if we are referring to the reason of Descartes, Hegel, and Marx" (1989, p. 244).

Rosso (1990) represents the concerns of Vattimo on the "crisis of reason" in Italy as "above all a reaction against the dominant Crocean philosophy and, more generally, against 'idealistic historical reason'" (p. 80). Rosso writes: "The late 'renaissance' of Heideggerian and Nietzschean studies, the dissemination of French poststructuralism, the renewal of interest in the culture of Vienna of the first decades of our century and in some themes of the Frankfurt School, all coincide in contemporary Italy with the crisis of Marxist historicism, which had been a kind of common ground for most Italian thinkers in the fifties and sixties, prior to the pervasive diffusion of structuralism" (p. 80).

This crisis of reason, which Rosso describes as both fashionable and somewhat inflated, was emblematic of the collection of essays edited by A. Gargani (1979) with that very title, *Crisi della ragione*, where all contributors begin with an understanding of the crisis of classical reason, to which they oppose a "plurality of reasons," including Heidegger's "destruction" of Western metaphysics, and post-Wittgensteinian analytic philosophy.[3] Gianni Vattimo still sees a residue of foundationalism in these projects and "points to hermeneutics as the only non-metaphysical way of reflecting on the relationship between language and being and the problem of what lies 'beyond language'" (Rosso, 1990, pp. 81–82). Vattimo's work, steeped in interpretations of Heidegger and Nietzsche, is constructed at the intersection between hermeneutics, nihilism and postmodernity. It is against this background that Vattimo's most recent contribution, *The Transparent Society* (1992), should be read. This chapter, first, discusses Vattimo's notion of the "end of history" as a preliminary, in the second half of the chapter, to examining the significance of *The Transparent Society* .

VATTIMO'S "THE END OF (HI)STORY"

Vattimo's (1991) essay "The End of (Hi)story," is concerned with the interpretation of postmodernity as the end of history and the problems of legitimation raised by such a definition, focusing particularly on the possibility of rationally founded critique. He begins by pointing out that if the notion postmodernity has any meaning at all, it has to be in terms of the description the end of history. Both Lyotard (1984) and Habermas (1981a) agree on this characterization. Jean-François Lyotard, for his part, maintains that the *metarécits* — those legitimating grand narratives of modernity — have dissolved. More properly, postmodernity is characterized by "an incredulity towards metanarratives" that served to legitimate science by appeals to "the dialectics of the Spirit, the hermeneutics of meaning, the emancipation of the rational or working subject, or the creation of wealth" (Lyotard, 1984, p. xxiii). Habermas, according to Vattimo, accepts this definition of postmodernity but simply disagrees that we are presently in that condition. By taking on the task of defending the "project of modernity," Habermas is committing himself not only to the historical project of the *emancipation* of mankind and consequently to the prospect and renewal of a particular metanarrative that implies a possible rational course of history but also to the possibility of a rationally founded critique based upon it. Where for Lyotard the metanarratives have been decisively confuted by major events of our time,[4] for Habermas these events represent nondefinitive defeats of the project of the Enlightenment.

Reflecting on these positions, Vattimo maintains that if the metanarratives have been dissolved (as he, indeed, thinks they have), then what is finished is not only certain views of history but history itself:

> If the *metarécits* that made it possible for us to think of history as a unitary course have been confuted, as Lyotard assumes, history itself has become impossible. To imagine that history, as a course of events, keeps going no matter what we feel about the *metarécits* we used to believe in would amount to assuming that the specific *metarécit* that conceives of history as an objective course of events has not been dissolved; or, in other words, that the course of history, as a unitary and continuous course of events, is not "simply" a *metarécit* but a true description of the very reality of history. Now, this is exactly what the *metarécits* used to claim and exactly what the postmodern consciousness does not believe any more. (1991, p. 134)

In addition to Lyotard's "extravagant" thesis, Vattimo also adduces the work of Hayden White on the rhetorical nature of historiographic strategies used to reconstruct the past, and he approvingly refers to Nietzsche's critique of *Historismus* and Benjamin's *Theses on the Philosophy of History* to establish the idea that "history as a unitary course has . . . become inconceivable (and impossible)." "We have," he says "entered that condition that already A. Gehlen had called *post-histoire*'" (1991, p. 134).

The problem that Vattimo identifies in Lyotard's thesis is that "The dissolution of the *metarécits* is itself a (paradoxial) kind of *metarécit*" (1991, p. 135). He expands the criticism by arguing that the decisive events that Lyotard suggests, confute the metanarratives possess that capacity only by virtue that they, themselves, are part of the framework of another legitimating *metarécit*. In other words, Lyotard "still uses a procedure of *historical* legitimation in arguing that the *metarécits* have been dissolved" (p. 135). This is not a trivial objection that points to self-inconsistency, and its acceptance does not entail the rejection of Lyotard's position. Indeed, it is only by recognizing the paradoxical nature of the problem that Habermas' criticisms can be met and the problem of legitimation solved. Vattimo's point is that Lyotard, unlike his "eminent predecessors" Nietzsche or Heidegger, pays too little attention to the paradox in which he is caught.

Vattimo wants us to dwell on the paradox, to meditate productively on the paradox, rethinking it in terms of the Heideggerian concepts of *Andenken* and *Verwindung*. To do so, Vattimo maintains, will clearly show the way in which metaphysics as the philosophy of first principles cannot simply be regarded as something that we can leave behind, a kind of error that we can easily rid ourselves of. This is the case not because of deeply ingrained psychological or cultural habits or even because of the impossibility of inventing a nonmetaphysical language. It is because of a more radical reason: "metaphysics cannot simply be overcome because to overcome it would mean to perpetuate its methods and structures" (Vattimo, 1991, p. 136). For Vattimo, following Nietzsche and Heidegger, there can be no "overcoming" of metaphysics, no clear break with modernity, because the concept of overcoming belongs to the metaphysical system which characterizes modernity.

The only way to step out of metaphysics is by *Verwindung*, a concept with a cluster of meanings ranging from "distortion" and "resignation" to "healing." Postmodernity, thus, has a relation of *Verwindung* to modernity in the sense that we can step out of metaphysics only by accepting it with resignation as a sort of illness. But to view things in this way, to treat the metaphysical system as a whole, as a tradition, and to recollect (*Andenken*) its turning points, to attempt an "archeological" retrieval of the tradition, is a distortion of its purpose, which has always been oriented through the pursuit of logical truth to a knowledge of the principles of reality. It is a distortion because to view the tradition in this way is to disregard the authoritative character of the pursuit of logical truth and its claims to knowledge while at the same time recognizing it as the primary concern of the tradition, most strongly developed in the instrumental reason of twentieth-century technology.

To retrieve metaphysics by recollecting its turning points is to return to the question of Being. As Vattimo writes: "What remains un-thought in metaphysical tradition is the *Ereignis* character of Being, Being as an event and not as a stable structure like Plato's *ontos on*. What the recollection achieves is the discovery of this 'eventual' character of Being: metaphysics appears to Heidegger as the 'series' of the epochs in which Being has opened itself in the form of different *archai*, each one claiming to be a stable (metaphysical) structure while it was 'just' an 'epochal' openness, a sort of *épistème* in Foucault's sense" (1991, p. 137).

Being, in Heidegger's terms, thus, cannot be grasped as presence, a stable and ultimate structure. Above all it is not a new foundation. Being, as Vattimo explains "is not, but 'happens' . . . and can only be 'thought' of in the form of recollection, as something that is always already gone" (1991, p. 137). This style of thought as recollection is therefore a *Verwindung* of the search for the foundations that characterize traditional metaphysics. Postmetaphysical thought as recollection, which corresponds to Being conceived of in terms of event, displays a kindred spirit with postmodern sensibilities; with "the tendencies towards a free — even arbitrary — revival of the forms of the past" in architecture and literature, where past forms and styles are evoked not as part of a foundational motivation to understand the present but as "a repertory of rhetoric *exempla*" (p. 138).

Verwindung and *Andenken* help us to solve the problems of legitimation of postmodernity, because they unmask the still metaphysical character of postmodernist theories, which, like Lyotard's, argue the case by appealing to what has *happened*, by appealing to a particular interpretation of a course of events. This is the argument put forcefully by Vattimo:

If we simply assume, as an indisputable fact, that the events of our time have completely dissolved and liquidated the *metarécits* of metaphysics, we really remain, as Habermas says, without the slightest possibility of a rational critique of the present. On the contrary, if we recognize that, as Heidegger suggests, the end of history belongs to the history of Being, we will still have a criterion — be it paradoxical — for rational arguing and for historical options. (1991, p. 139)

To be sure, such a view involves a *metarécit*, the *metarécit* of the history of Being — but this *metarécit*, contrary to Lyotard and Habermas, "is recognized as having the sole meaning of the progressive . . . dissolution of all the *metarécits* — that is, of the dissolution of Being as a stable structure in favour of Being as an event" (Vattimo, 1991, p. 139). The notions of *Verwindung* and *Andenken* provide us with the negative criteria "to engage actively in the de(con)struction of all the metaphysical residues that still are alive in our philosophy, psychology, ethics, culture in general" (p. 141).[5]

THE TRANSPARENT SOCIETY

It is in *The Transparent Society* that Vattimo builds upon his thesis of the end of history to link the birth of postmodern society with the decisive role that mass media plays in the transition. He states clearly in the opening pages: "According to the hypothesis I am putting forward, modernity ends when — for a number of reasons — it no longer seems possible to regard history as unilinear" (1992, p. 3). History as both the progessive realization of emancipation and the perfection of the human ideal has become problematic precisely because of its evolutionary or developmental assumptions that picture the West in terms of the process of modernization as the apex of civilization to date. The ideological character of the idea of unilinear history was exposed through the radical critiques mounted in the nineteenth and twentieth centuries. Vattimo, in particular, refers to Walter Benjamin's "Theses on the Philosophy of History" to show how such a view is an interest-based representation of the past and, therefore, inherently political. Vattimo writes: "There is no single history, only images of the past projected from different points of view. It is illusory to think that there exists a supreme or comprehensive viewpoint capable of unifying all others" (1992, p. 3).

But then if there is a crisis in the idea of history it is a double crisis, because to challenge such a view is also to render problematic the idea of progress on which it relies: "if human events do not make up a uni-linear continuum, then one cannot regard them as proceeding towards an end, realizing a rational program of improvement, education and emancipation" (Vattimo, 1992, p. 3). The challenge to both the idea of history and that of progress takes place not only internally as a critique of assumptions underlying nineteenth-century historicism but also at the level of political practice in terms of the Third World rebellion against European colonization and imperialism.

The dissolution of modernity is, then, to be considered in part a reflection of the crisis of European colonialism and imperialism. It is also, strategically and perhaps more importantly, a result of the advent of the "society of communication." Vattimo lays down his major thesis in the following terms: "What I am proposing is: (a) that the mass media play a decisive role in the birth of a postmodern society; (b) that they do not make this postmodern society more 'transparent,' but more complex, even chaotic; and finally (c) that it is in precisely this relative 'chaos' that our hopes for emancipation lie" (1992, p. 4).

In making these claims Vattimo is self-consciously putting himself in opposition to the prevailing thesis in Critical Theory, based, in particular, upon the work of Adorno and Horkheimer (1972), who, in *Dialectic of Enlightenment*, take a very pessimistic view of the role of the mass media and the society of mass consumption. To Horkheimer and Adorno, the same logic of commodification manifest in production replicates itself in the sphere of consumption. The culture industry, including the mass media, succumbs to the market and cultural values are produced in order to be sold: the goal is the same — original use-values are reduced to a common set of exchange-values. The Marxian commodification thesis, first formulated by Horkheimer and Adorno in the realm of culture, has been taken up more recently by the French sociologist Jean Baudrillard (1970), who, in drawing on a semiotics, argues that consumption is based upon the active manipulation of signs. In Baudrillard's (1983) more recent work, the endless circulation of signs eventually effaces the distinction between the image and reality. Thus, as Linda Hutcheon observes, the mass media, according to Baudrillard, "have neutralized reality by stages: First they *reflected* it; then they *masked* and perverted it; next they had to *mask its absence*; and finally they produced instead the *simulacrum* of the real, the destruction of meaning and of all relation to reality" (1989, p. 33).

The dominant view in Critical Theory, from Horkheimer and Adorno, to Lefebvre through to Baudrillard, has been a pessimistic view echoing the Orwellian idea of "Big Brother."

It is explicitly against this "received" view that Vattimo defines his position. To him the mass media have been largely responsible for the dissolution of the "grand narratives." In spite of the power of capital, its concentration in the new telecommunications monopolies, the mass media has, in Vattimo's view, led to a veritable explosion and proliferation of different world views. Within the "information market" all manner of groups, cultures and subcultures have been able to secure a "voice," and this pluralization of different cultural voices has spelled the end of the unilinear view of history and of the idea of progress that underlies it. Such a pluralization renders impossible the conception of any single reality, objectively given once and for all. In late modernity there exists, in a truly Nietzschean manner, only multiple perspectives, conflicting and intersecting images and interpretations, which constitute the only reality there is.

In terms of the emancipatory ideal of the transparent society, the media are considered to be the window of an objective and knowable reality. The media, "modelled on lucid self-consciousness, on the perfect knowledge of one who knows how things stand (compare Hegel's Absolute Spirit or Marx's conception of man freed from ideology), is [sic] replaced by an ideal of emancipation based on oscillation, plurality and, ultimately, on the erosion of the very 'principle of reality'" (Vattimo, 1992, p. 7).

The transparent society is the organic counterpart to the trans-parent model of consciousness underlying a subject-centered reason, a tradition that begins with the laying down of the foundations of modern philosophy by Descartes and Kant. The ideal of perfect self-con-sciousness at the societal level becomes the standard against which the mass-media society is contrasted, especially in Hegelian and Marxist accounts: the market or the bureaucracy prevent the proper realization of the model, leading to the perversion of the ideal of emancipation or genuine freedom of information.

Under the alternative model proposed by Vattimo, following both Nietzsche and Heidegger, emancipation at this historical conjuncture lies precisely in a "loss of reality": it lies in the plurality and complexity of voices and consists in *disorientation*, which is at the same time a liberation of dialect, of local differences and rationalities, each with its own distinct grammar and syntax. As Vattimo notes: "With the demise of the idea of a central rationality of history, the world of generalized communication explodes like a multiplicity of 'local' rationalities — ethnic, sexual, religious, cultural or aesthetic minorities — that finally speak up for themselves. They are no longer repressed and cowed into silence by the idea of a single true form of humanity that must be realized irrespective of particularity and individual finitude, transience and contingency" (1992, p. 9).

Freedom in this pluralistic world is experienced as "a continual oscillation between belonging and disorientation" (Vattimo, 1992, p. 10): it is always problematic, never guaranteed and "remains a possibility still to be recognized and taken up" (p. 10). Such oscillation, as Nietzsche and Heidegger have indicated, is more in keeping with the notion of being as an "event," as an outcome of dialogue and inter-pretation, than as a stable structure, fixed once and for all; and the postmodern world, increasingly dominated by the mass media, offers the possibility of redefining the experience of oscillation as "an opportunity of a new way of being (finally, perhaps) human" (p. 11).

Vattimo champions and explores these themes further in relation to a number of selected topics: the relation of the human sciences to the society of communication; the rediscovery of myth and how the world is "fabled" by the media; the problem of art in a society of generalized communication; the shift from utopia to heterotopia; the dissolution of metaphysics; an ethics of communication — to name some of them. I shall concentrate on the first of these topics, because the discussion will serve to highlight aspects of Vattimo's thesis in relation to the transparent society, although all the remaining chapters deserve extended discussion and analysis.

The chapter "The Human Sciences and the Society of Communication" provides Vattimo with the subject matter for recasting the importance of the human sciences in their organic relation with the society of communication and for criticizing further the ideal of self-transparency within the tradition of the program of Enlightenment emancipation. The starting point is the reciprocal determination of the human sciences and the constitution of modern society as the society of communication: "the human sciences both follow from and promote the development of the society of generalized communication" (Vattimo, 1992, p. 13). The centrality of information — its circulation and intensification — is not merely one aspect of modernization so much as its central process. Technology is now more oriented toward the development of information and the construction of society as "images" rather than toward the mechanical domination of nature under the sway of the natural sciences. Information technologies provide both the actual and potential direction for the cybernetic development of the system as a whole. One might say that they provide a crucial determinant of the process of postmodernization, defining the contemporaneity — the exchange of information in real time — of the postmodern world. As such they run up against and displace the utopian notion of self-transparency that both informed the social ideals of modernity and defined the very essence of the Enlightenment.

Vattimo traces how the ideal of self-transparency is and has been conceived to constitute the substance, end and method of the human sciences in relation to the program of emancipation. The general demand for freedom is modelled on the promise and realization of the full self-transparency of reason in the public domain. Such a view, which is widespread in critical social theory, explains both the commitment of thinkers like Jürgen Habermas and Karl Otto Apel to the "incomplete project of modernity" and their attempt to realize such a project by recourse to a Kantian ethics developed at the level of discourse in terms of the depth hermeneutic of psychoanalysis. It is at the level of discourse that validity claims inherent in ordinary talk can be discursively redeemed. In the "ideal speech situation" or the "community of unlimited communication," the ideal of the perfect transparency of knowledge prevails, based on the universalization of reciprocal rights and responsibilities and proceeding without coercion or domination through the force of pure argumentation. As Vattimo notes, this romantic ideal predominates in contemporary theories of communication: "The society of unrestricted communication in which the community of logical socialism [Peirce] is realized is a transparent society. It manages radically to reduce motives for conflict, precisely by eliminating obstacles and opacity via a process modelled loosely on a certain ideal of psychoanalysis" (1992, p. 20).

The problem for Vattimo is that the prospect of the normative ideal of self-transparency, when measured against the present situation, runs aground empirically. The fact is, Vattimo argues, that the intensification of social communication and the concomitant development of the human sciences simply do not lead to a growth in the self-transparency of society. Indeed, just at the point historically when the ideal of self-transparency becomes technically possible based upon contemporary developments around new informational and communicational technologies, the ideal itself is revealed to be one of domination rather than emancipation; one, that is to say, based on the viewpoint of a central subject that attempts to reduce the multiplicity of events, and of centers of history — "of places where information is gathered, unified and transmitted" (p. 22) — into a single perspective of universal history. The nature of the ideal is thus revealed as ultimately ideological.

In Vattimo's terms, the society of the human sciences and generalized communication has moved toward "the fabling of the world" rather than toward self-transparency: "The images of the world we receive from the media and the human sciences, albeit on different levels, are not simply different interpretations of a 'reality' that is 'given' regardless, but rather constitute the very objectivity of the world" (1992, pp. 24–25).

Such a characterization of the human sciences is justified in terms of the "hermeneutic turn" and the "return" to the notion of narrative evidenced in the current historical and sociological interest in rhetorical and narratological models. It is, I would say, also further evidenced in discourse as a central concept within contemporary social and cultural theory. Meanings are not found or given as in the representational view of language; they are actively constituted through discourse. Discourse thus tends to both historicize and politicize the study of language, displacing the emphasis on formal and abstract systems with an accent on the historical specificity of what is said and what remains unsaid at particular places and times. This view of discourse is far removed from Habermas' ideal of a universal norm of communication action that is said to be immanent in speech itself and that allegedly enables participants to arrive at consensus without distortion or external restraint. It is a view in stark contrast to Habermas' modernist, universalist vision of a "noise-free," fully transparent sphere of communication. Rather, it accords more closely with the view of language and discourse developed by the French poststructuralists, who repudiate the dream of a universal language to investigate the inherent differences and opacities and who believe that consensus can be established only on the basis of acts of exclusion.

Symbolic systems are to be distinguished from myth insofar as they are "historical" and, therefore, display a critical and self-reflexive distance. Vattimo writes: "If we cannot pretend (any longer?) to unveil the lies of ideology and strike an ultimate stable foundation, we can still emphasize the plurality of 'tales' and put it to use in freeing ourselves from both the inflexibility of monological tales and the dogmatic systems of myth" (1992, p. 26).

Vattimo maintains that if the metanarratives have been dissolved, then what is finished is not only certain views of history but history itself. He criticizes Lyotard for appealing to the way things are, to a certain set of facts, which, he suggests, is paradoxical, and he recommends the adoption of the metanarrative of the history of Being as the way out of the paradox. His critique of the "transparent society" is, in effect, an application of this argument: it is a debunking of a metanarrative based on the transparency of reason in terms of a central ahistorical and universal subject and its relation to the realization of freedom. While the ideal of self-tranparency is clearly a normative conception that has, indeed, been the motivating force for theories of communication in critical social science, the opposing notion of opacity or chaos, which Vattimo assumes to be justified by the contemporary situation, seems equally a normative conception.

A number of questions intrude at this point: How far is the conception reached by Vattimo legitimated historically by a program that issues from his Heideggerian reading of the "end of metaphysics"? To what extent is Vattimo's "plurality of voices" an empirical question? He seems to suggest that it is, when he plots the history of the contemporary world as the history of the present society of generalized communication, driven by developments in information technology. How else, for instance, are we to regard the following claim? "If we measure the present situation against the prospect of the normative ideal of self-transparency, we are faced with a series of paradoxical facts. . . . In general, the intense development of the human sciences and the intensification of social communication do not seem to produce a growth in self-transparency of society. Indeed, they seem to have the opposite effect" (Vattimo, 1992, p. 22).

If this constitutes an empirical claim, as Vattimo clearly thinks it does, where is the evidence, and how might we verify or falsify such a claim, except by reference to the theory in terms of which the claim is advanced? And is this theory a theory emerging out of a program that takes seriously the history of Being? In other words, if Vattimo's view is irreducibly tied to the Heideggerian thesis, to what extent does this enter the picture in an a priori fashion? What role do historical facts really play here? In terms of the history of Being, is it possible any longer to embrace the subject-object distinction upon which the recognition of facts depends? These are not esoteric questions. They bear centrally on questions of theory evaluation and, ultimately, on questions of power — an issue, it might be argued, that Vattimo deftly side-steps.

At one point Vattimo writes: "Of course, one could object that having a voice does not correspond to true political emancipation — economic power is still held by capital. This may be so: I won't pursue the issue here" (1992, pp. 5–6). The problem is that in terms of contemporary theories of communication the issue has been pursued fiercely by a number of scholars, both of neo-Marxist and postmodernist persuasion, and in a way that bears fundmentally on both the issue of power and its relation to plural cultural forms.

Leaving aside the question as regards "other cultural universes" to which Vattimo refers and concentrating for the moment on the question of internal differentiation, which is seen to be a feature of the West in the postmodern condition, it is a matter of the utmost importance to understand whether this pluralization is genuinely a reflection of difference that grants a voice to emergent new social formations previously denied the means of representing their concerns or whether this pluralization is more simply an epiphenomenon.

Given the internationalization of the world economy based on the "informational mode of development" (Castells, 1989), where multinationals now vie with nation-states, especially in the strategic area of telecommunications, the question of power becomes paramount. It might be argued, accordingly, that the same processes of rationalization (Weber), commodification (Marx), and differentiation (Durkheim) that were seen to be the driving forces of modernization in traditional accounts continue to exercise their influence in the present context, promoting a new international division of labor in the global informational economy and thereby structurally disadvantaging Third World countries. Certainly, at the very least, such a view indicates that neo-Marxist approaches provide a basis for recognizing that the restructuring of late capitalism in the informational economy represents also a form of neoimperialism for developing countries. This is not to say that neo-Marxist approaches are without problems, theoretically speaking. It is unclear whether Marxism, for instance, can divest itself of its nineteenth-century assumptions of historicism and still retain its explanatory power. Vattimo has not only done us the service of articulating a philosophy of difference, which at the closure of Western metaphysics demonstrates the inadequacy of the ideal of the "transparent society" and the way it grounds the tradition of critical thought in its approach to mass media, but also has yet to address and come to terms with the question of power in the society of generalized communication.

NOTES

1. As I have explained in the Introduction, Habermas (1981a, p. 13) is the self-styled defender of what he calls the "project of modernity," which he traces back to Kant and Weber, against the "antimodern sentiments" of a variety of postmodernist thinkers. He attributes the term "postmodernity" in this early paper to the French current of though, the tradition, as he says, "running from Bataille to Derrida by way of Foucault" (p. 13), and he compares the critique of reason of these French philosphers to the *Young Conservatives* of the Weimar Republic. For Habermas' more recent reevaluation of postmodernity and poststructuralism see his *The Philosophical Discourse of Modernity* (1990b).

2. Indeed, Eco's (1989) correspondence with Stefano Rosso on postmodernism predates the publication of Vattimo's and Rovatti's (1983) *Il Pensiero Debole (Weak Thought)*, an edited collection of essays to which Eco contributed. For a bibliographic note on Italian postmodernism in terms of the crisis of reason, postmodernism and weak thought, see Rosso (1990, pp. 90–93).

3. See the recent collection of essays on Italian postmodernism edited by Dino Cervigni (1991) in *Annali d'Italianistica*, including the fine essay, "Postmodern Chronicles," by Peter Carravetta. See also Antonio Negri's essay "Postmodern," in his *The Politics of Subversion*, where he interprets postmodernism as "the mystified ideology of the new collectivities, or rather, as a primitive but effective allusion to the scientific determination of new subjects which in the Marxian phase of real subsumption (or more simply, in the phase of general circulation and communication) are being formed" (1989, p. 206).

4. Vattimo summarizes Lyotard's claims thus: "the *metarécit* of the rationality of what is (Hegel) has been confuted by Auschwitz; the *metarécit* of the socialist revolution, by Stalin and his gulags; the *metarécit* of the free-market economy, by the recurrent crisis in capitalist societies; and the *metarécit* of democracy, by May 1968" (1991, p. 132).

5. Vattimo's (1988, p. 1) *The End of Modernity* (originally published as *La fine della modernità* in 1985) is "a study of the relationship that links the conclusions reached by Nietzsche and Heidegger in their respective works . . . to more recent discourses on the end of the modern era and on postmodernity." As Jon Snyder (1988) notes in his introduction to the English translation of that work, Vattimo studied with Hans-Georg Gadamer and Karl Löwith at the University of Heidelberg after the war, focusing on hermeneutics and ontology and specializing in the work of Heidegger, Schleiermacher and Nietzsche. In regard to the present chapter see especially Chapter 10, "Nihilism and the Post-modern in Philosophy," of *The End of Modernity*; see also Vattimo's "Nietzsche and Heidegger," where he analyzes the relationship between Nietzsche and Heidegger and concludes, *"The overcoming of metaphysics is not the overturning of the metaphysical oblivion of being: it is this very oblivion (nihilism) taken to its extreme consequences"* (1986, p. 28).

9

Cybernetics, Cyberspace and the University: Herman Hesse's *The Glass Bead Game* and the Dream of a Universal Language

This chapter is dedicated to the memory of
Bill Readings

These rules, the sign language and the grammar of the Game, constitute a kind of highly developed secret language drawing upon several sciences and arts, but especially mathematics and music (and/or musicology), and capable of expressing and establishing interrelationships between the content and conclusions of nearly all scholarly disciplines.The Glass Bead Game is thus a mode of playing with the total contents and values of our culture; it plays with them as, say, in the great age of the arts a painter might have played with the colors on his palette. All the insights, noble thoughts, and works of art that the human race has produced in its creative eras, all that subsequent periods of scholarly study have reduced to concepts and converted into intellectual property — on all this immense body of intellectual values the Glass Bead Game player plays like an organist on an organ.

— Hermann Hesse[1]

INTRODUCTION: THE UNIVERSITY IN LATE MODERNITY

What is at stake between the defenders of the "project of modernity" and those who claim postmodernity as a new and distinctive aesthetic, ethos or attitude, if not the dream of a universal language? With the "linguistic turn" in twentieth-century culture, philosophy reasserted itself as the master discipline, *the* metalanguage, into which all claims and counterclaims could be translated. Philosophy assumed the status of a master language, both innocent and universal, which allegedly could provide the means by which disagreements might be rationally discussed and resolved. An innocent master language is one that is, in today's cybernetic terms, noiseless or fully transparent: it conforms to Jürgen Habermas' (1984, 1987b) ideal of a fully rational, dialogical society modelled on everyday communicational processes where so-called validity claims immanent in ordinary conversation can be redeemed at the level of discourse through the force of pure argumentation alone.

The dream of a universal language and conceptions of the subject based upon it have been called into question by Jean-François Lyotard's (1984, 1987) critique of modernity, which he places within the context of the crisis of legitimation of Enlightenment metanarratives. To Lyotard, Habermas' conception represents the latest, perhaps last, attempt at building a systematic and totalizing philosophy; one which, while based upon the emancipatory vision of a universal and transparent communicational society, paradoxically turns out to be both terroristic and exclusory. While Habermas and the defenders of the project of modernity dream of a universal language based upon the telos of unforced consensus, Lyotard and those today who regard metanarratives with some suspicion or incredulity want to repudiate such a dream, arguing that difference and dissensus are principles at the very heart of language and that, therefore, we should learn both to detect the differend (a cognitive task) and to respect it (an ethical obligation).

The application of such arguments and ideals to the modern institution of the university is clear. For one side of the debate the dream of a universal language promises the possibility of reestablishing some part of the classical idea of the university; for the other it masks a will to knowledge by the dominant culture and a totalizing discourse that excludes all Others and in the process sounds the death-knell of the promise of a genuine democratic institution. Habermas (1987a) wants to recall the classical idea of the university as held by Schelling, Humboldt and Schleiermacher and to examine contemporary variants of its renewal in order to inquire whether there are any remnants of the classical idea sufficient to found an integrated self-understanding of the modern university. Given the demise of epistemologically-centered philosophy on which both the speculative unity of the sciences and the university institution was based, he wants to inquire whether there is some remnant of this classical idea that still might serve as a unifying force to found the university institution in the late modern context. He finds such a remnant in the notion of learning processes, which echoes his notion of the communicational society and reflects his desire to preserve the emancipatory impulse behind the Enlightenment through a project aimed at relinking modern culture with an everyday praxis. The university in these terms is seen to play a vital role in reconstituting an organic sociocultural unity, valorizing the life-world and cultivating institutions out of it that set limits to the purely functional and instrumental imperatives of the economic system. If modernity has failed, according to Habermas, it has failed by allowing the splintering of a totality of life or the unity of experience into a "pluralization of diverging universes of discourses," which has shattered the naïve consensus. He places his hope for universal freedom in a reconstituted public sphere based upon the evolving communicative practices of a revitalized bourgeois print culture, which, historically speaking, happened to be at once largely white, heterosexual and male.

Lyotard's (1984, pp. 72–73) response is to seek clarification of the kind of unity sought by Habermas. He asks: Is it a kind of Hegelian-inspired organic whole, or rather a Kantian recognition of the need to navigate between the different discourses of cognition, ethics and politics? The first he says does not challenge the notion of a dialectically totalizing experience; the second can take place only under the restraints imposed by postmodernity on the thought of the Enlightenment and, in particular, on the unity of language — of the subject and of history.

For Lyotard (1984), the traditional legitimating metanarrative of the speculative unity of knowledge and its humanist emancipatory potential have allegedly fallen away to reveal knowledge and power as two sides of the same question. The institution of the modern university, based on the traditional disciplines and unified through the force of philosophy, is nearing its end. In the postmodern era the leading sciences and technologies — cybernetics, telematics, informatics and computer science — have transformed the principal functions of the university. These *language-based* sciences and technologies, which together define the instrumentality of the dominant technoscientific system, have altered both research and learning. Anything in the constituted body of knowledge not translatable into a computer language will be abandoned, and the status of the learner and teacher is transformed into a commodity relationship of supplier and user. The traditional distinction between science and technology, in other words, has collapsed, and now it is possible to represent this new interdisciplinarity motivated by language developments only as the historical convergence and progression of the conglomerate technoscience. In these very stark terms it is no longer possible to talk of the enterprise of science separate from its institutional sites and networks of power. It is no longer possible to talk of science in transcendental or ahistorical terms, divorced from institutional sites or from the wider policy context. Simply stated, science has become the major force of production, a movement in the circulation of capital.

Jacques Derrida concurs: "One can no longer distinguish between technology on the one hand and theory, science and rationality on the other. The term techno-science has to be accepted" (1983, p. 12). Within postmodernity it is no longer possible to distinguish the principle of reason from the idea of technology. The Kantian distinction between the technical and the architectonic has been surpassed in historical terms. What is more, the military and the state can invest in any sort of research at all, for now control and censorship are exercised more directly through limiting the means or "regulating the support for production, transmission and diffusion" (p. 13). In addition, external forces are intervening within the university. Presses, foundations, private institutions, think-tanks and the mass media intrude in the politics of the university in a characteristically novel way. Derrida suggests that the concept of informatization is the "most general operator here which integrates the basic to the oriented, the purely rational to the technical" (1983, p. 14). Derrida's Heideggerian reading arrives at similar themes concerning the threats currently facing the university as does Lyotard. While their starting points differ (as do their sources of inspiration), their conclusions coalesce. While Derrida does not explicitly tie his analysis to the postindustrial society or, indeed, to the postmodern con-dition, as Lyotard does, the implicit signs are obvious: the separate accounts converge in a rendering of the concept of technoscience, its historical effects on the principle of reason and the dangers it repre-sents for the future of the university.

The distinction between the technical and the architectonic has collapsed and science and technology have become integrated into the conglomerate technoscience as part of the historical development and outgrowth of a universalist, rationalist philosophy. It represents a new totalizing impulse unified not only in the imperative to conform to the optimal efficiency of the system but also in the cultural terms of developing a society based on a common digital code symbolized variously as the information society or, more broadly, as cyberspace culture. The neoconservative functionalist policy perspective teaches us that the values of optimal performance and efficiency, which have been given a greater impetus through the new information technologies, are the necessary ones to guide the process of societal modernization.

When it comes to university policy both Habermas and Lyotard find common enemies in the new instrumentality governing the system, represented by the combination of neoconservativism, general systems theory and cybernetics. Together they take arms against the kind of system rationality espoused by Niklaus Luhmann, who, it seems, is satisfied with a functional operationality as the basis for a free society. Habermas, for his part, has alluded to the way in which a neocon-servative, functionalist interpretation currently dominates the realm of educational policy-making in the West. He complains that in terms of this view, "universities present themselves as part of a system requiring less and less normative integration in the heads of professors and students the more it becomes self-regulating via systemic mechanisms and the more it orients itself to the environments of the economy and the planning administration" (1987a, p. 7). He describes how, during the period of greatest educational expansion in the Federal Republic (the 1960s through to the early 1970s), oppositional ideologies grew up focusing on the same false premise "that the issue was whether to renew or retain the idea of the university" (p. 6). This dispute, he maintains, enabled neoconservatives to point to the way in which "the general patterns of societal modernization have also determined university developments" (p. 6) and also gave them the opportunity to emphasize the need for a greater functional specialization of the university within a more differentiated scientific system. From this perspective the traditional normative autonomy of the university could only be seen as a hindrance, and yet at the same time anniversaries provided the convenient ceremonial occasions on which "to cloak the university's systemic autonomy by rhetorically affirming an earlier tradition" (p. 7). Habermas suggests that "thus veiled, the flows of information between now functionally autonomous subsystems (for example, between the universities and the economic-military-administrative complex), can be all the more discreetly co-ordinated" (1987a, p. 7).

Against this background of contemporary theory I shall argue that the dream of a universal language that characterizes modernity ultimately aspires to the ideal elaborated by Hermann Hesse in his metaphor of the Glass Bead Game: an ultra-aesthetic language-game played by master scholars that involves all branches of knowledge and values, and is capable of reproducing the entire intellectual content of the universe. Hesse sets his futuristic utopian novel in the pedagogical province of Castalia in the year 2400, at a time after the decline and degeneration of Western culture, which "had been in the air . . . from the time of Nietzsche" (Hesse, 1970, p. 24) and had subsequently experienced a cultural and spiritual restoration, culminating in the development of the Game.

I can think of no better metaphor with all its allusive qualities, its pedagogical possibilities and cultural prophecies than *The Glass Bead Game* to investigate the place of the university in the cultural history of symbolic logic, cybernetics and perhaps even a European formalism, which underlie the present incipient development of the "mode of information" to employ Mark Poster's (1990) characterization, or "the Information Superhighway," to use Al Gore's populist term, or, more simply, "cyberspace," to use a more critical term coined by William Gibson (1984).[2] We might also think of the emerging structures of the Internet and the World Wide Web as its most recent embodiments. I will treat these developments as aspects of late modernity, and I will understand the broader theorizations of postmodernity in a Lyotardian manner as modulations within modernity in the same way that we talk about a major and a minor key or thematic variations in music.

I have chosen Hesse's *The Glass Bead Game*, first, because the central symbolism of the Game squarely relates to the modernist dream of a universal language — a noninstrumental form of symbolic exchange, guided by the telos of consensus and oriented to the unity of mind and purpose. In this sense Hesse's Game is much closer to Habermas' ideal speech community and the given, stable, bourgeois subject than to Lyotard's conception of the differend and multiple, hybrid, cultural subject positions. Second, as the "novel of education" it not only belongs to the tradition of the German *Bildungsroman* (perhaps the last), but it also engages that tradition in a self-reflexive manner. It is no accident that the ethos of the German educational tradition historically defined by the *Bildungsroman* informs Habermas' conception of a humanist pedagogy and the ideal of the liberal university based on the stability of the universal subject of communication — the hero of knowledge — and the rational consensus of like minds.

The tradition of Hesse's *Bildungsroman* — its philosophical underpinnings in a German idealism based on self-formation of the unified subject — provides a cultural lens through which to understand historically Habermas' commitment to one form of communicative practice as representing the promise and the best hope of completing the Enlightenment project of emancipation. The trouble is that while the culture of the white, heterosexual, male bourgeoisie may have instituted a form of communication practice that was important historically in the development of a certain kind of freedom, autonomy and individuality — and hence of a certain kind of democracy — this, in itself, does not constitute sufficient reason for generalizing the experience of a highly specific cultural form as a universal basis for freedom, nor does it provide good grounds for assuming in an age of mass telecommunications that the future will ape the past.

FROM THE GLASS BEAD GAME TO CYBERSPACE

Let me for a moment dwell upon the extraordinary generative and allusive qualities of the Glass Bead Game itself as described by Hesse's narrator in his "General Introduction to Its History for the Layman," because there are many resonances with what has come to be called cyberspace, and it has a kind of analytic power that enables us to appreciate the differences between the two metaphors. The Game is a highly developed universal language based upon a musico-mathematical logic; it represents an "eternal idea" expressed in various ways by Pythagoras, by the Hellenistic Gnostics, by the ancient Chinese and by the Arabian-Moorish cultures. Hesse mentions its prehistory in terms of scholasticism and humanism, leading to "the academies of mathematicians of the seventeenth and eighteenth centuries and on to the Romantic philosophies and the runes of Novalis's hallucinatory visions" (1970, p. 16). Clearly, the abacus — the paradigm calculating device — and the *I Ching* were conscious prototypes for Hesse,[3] as was chess, that paragon of reason. Other models for the Game mentioned include various musical instruments — it is described at one point as a kind of gigantic organ with stops and pedals — and it is strongly associated with forms of musical composition (the Bach fugue, the concerto movement). More mundanely, the history of the Game is said to be related to crossword puzzles and card games. Its Eastern origins are based, in part, upon the Chinese ideogram and its mystical nature is said to derive from the science of alchemy. The Game, in something resembling its final form, we are told, originated simultaneously in England and Germany as a kind of memory or training exercise used by musicians and musicologists working in the new seminaries for musical theory. "The inventor," says the narrator, was "Bastian Perrot of Calw, a rather clever, sociable, and humane musicologist, [who] used glass beads instead of letters, numerals, notes or other graphic symbols" (Hesse, 1970, p. 31). Once taken over by mathematicians some two to three decades later, the Game was developed to a higher degree of flexibility with a greater capacity for sublimation and self-consciousness. It was developed to a point where "it was capable of expressing mathematical processes by special symbols and abbreviations" (p. 32); and it was applied subsequently to classical philology, to logic, to the visual arts and to architecture. Yet "what it lacked in those days was the capacity for universality, for rising above the disciplines" (pp. 36–37). Scholars, each according to the rules of their own disciplines, developed their own special languages using the Game, but the development of its capacity for synthesis and universality had to wait another five hundred years — not a technical or formal obstacle but rather a *moral* one. As Hesse's narrator explains: "Some dreamed of a new alphabet, a new language of symbols through which they could formulate and exchange their new intellectual experiences" (p. 36). "Such a language, like the ancient Chinese script, should be able to express complex matters graphically," and a Swiss musicologist from Basel (Joculator Basiliensis), applying himself to the problem, invented the principles of a new language so that it became possible "to reduce mathematics and music to a common denominator" (p. 37). The Game of games, thus, came to its present spiritual status and pinnacle of development, taking over the role of both art and speculative philosophy as a new world language, through which players could harmoniously express previously opposing sets of values in a kind of divine unity: law and freedom, individual and community. We are told at one point: "The symbols and formulas of the Glass Bead Game combined structurally, musically, and philosophically within the framework of a universal language, were nourished by all the sciences and arts, and strove in play to achieve perfection, pure being, the fullness of reality" (p. 40).

What we have in Hesse's notion of the Game is a cybernetic conception of self and society: an analysis based upon a finite set of mathematico-musical rules, which define the Platonic universe of eternal ideas. It is *the* universal language game, reducing all disciplines to a common denominator. It is a game that only certain gifted individuals can master, and these individuals, morally transformed in the process, come to represent a suprapersonal aesthetic and cultural ideal. The Game has a history of development, of technological improvement and refinement. It is the highest symbol of the tendency toward

universality and the synthesis of science and the arts. To see the Game
as a machine or solely as a machine is to ignore essential aspects of its
symbolism, and, yet, unmistakably, it prefigures characteristics of the
modern computer —a feature pointed out almost a generation ago by
Theodore Ziolkowski (1965, pp. 289, 291) who associated the Game with
symbolic logic and regarded it as an "appropriate symbol" for an age of
IBM machines (cited by Antosik 1992, p. 44, n.35). Stanley Antosik
(1992:35) goes considerably further to talk of "utopian machines,"
comparing Leibniz's Universal Characteristic and Hesse's Glass Bead
Game, to suggest that "both bear striking similarities to the modern
computer." Leibniz, whom Norbert Wiener regarded as the patron saint
of cybernetics, is cited by Hesse's narrator as one of the precursors of the
Game. Antosik makes the comparison between the "utopian machines"
of Leibniz and Hesse in the following terms: "Both conceptions hinge on
a universal symbolic logic that could serve in the world of computers as
a universal algorithm, and the countless programs derived from this
ideal algorithm would be able to analyze and synthesize knowledge
within any discipline, along with the connections and analogies among
disciplines" (1992, p. 38).

The notion of the game as a metaphor for language, philosophy and
Antosik notes structural parallels between these utopian machines
and the modern computer, mentioning the equivalents of memory, the
external database and the central processing unit, and he concludes
that "Hesse's machine might appear superior to Leibniz's by displaying
some features that resemble an ideal analog computer rather than a
digital one" (1992, p. 39). Both modern Platonists, Leibniz and Hesse
prefigure the development of artificial intelligence. Their utopian
machines based upon symbolic logic and an ideographic system of signs
ultimately represents the Platonic Form of Mind. The greatest single
difference between the two conceptions is that the Glass Bead Game,
while universal in its scope, is not designed to discover new knowledge:
the Game merely preserves and manipulates the best of the past —
ideas, images, values, sounds — an eternal past, which for Hesse
refutes rather than confirms the idea of progress (pp. 40, 42).

The notion of the game as a metaphor for language, philosophy and
culture is also used by both Wittgenstein and Saussure. Where
Wittgenstein emphasizes the diversity of language games, of games in
the plural, Hesse speaks of one game only — the Glass Bead Game —
which at its zenith possesses a massive integrative power with the
capacity to wield a total cultural synthesis — East/West, science/art,
being/becoming, art/technology, technology/religion; a oneness at the
same time both profoundly spiritual and intellectual. Hesse writes in
this regard: This same eternal idea, which for us has been embodied in
the Glass Bead Game, has underlain every movement of Mind toward
the ideal goal of a *universitas litterarum*, every Platonic academy, every
league of an intellectual elite, every *rapprochement* between the exact

and the more liberal disciplines, every effort toward reconciliation between science and art or science and religion (p. 16).

For Hesse, the Glass Bead Game represents the high point of two contradictory lines of intellectual development in European culture since the end of the Middle Ages: the struggle for liberation of Reason against all forms of authority, especially that of the Church, and the search for a new means "to confer legitimacy on this freedom, for a new and sufficient authority arising out of Reason itself" (p. 19). Significantly, he sets his story against the background of a European cultural decline around the time of the 1930s, thematically echoing both Nietzsche and Spengler.[4] Hesse calls that time "the age of Feuilleton." It is, of course, roughly the time when Hesse was engaged with writing the novel or major portions of it,[5] contemporaneous with the rise of National Socialism.

While Hesse's metaphor of the Glass Bead Game presages the modern development of cyberspace, it does not surpass the stability and transparency of the bourgeois humanistic subject nor question the relation of language to the subject. It remains within the tradition of the "apprenticeship novel" based on the model of the white, heterosexual, male individual of unique and exceptional character who is committed to the inner life and the path of spiritual realization in the transition from disciple to master. However, Hesse's dream of a universal language, by emphasizing an integrative power capable of realigning alphabetic, graphic and sound components into a single common denominator, possesses a family resemblance with the kinds of claim recently made by Richard Lanham (1993) or George Landow and Paul Delany (1993) on behalf of cyberspace and the new forms of electronically mediated communication for a greater synthetic unity of the humanities as a basis for a multidisciplinary university curriculum.

BILDUNGSROMAN, CASTALIA AND THE UNIVERSITY

By having the narrator proclaim his Castalian beliefs as a "modern," Hesse is not only deliberately engaging the genre of *Bildungsroman* in a self-reflexive way, he is also engaging its early German forms as a novel of educational self-formation that depicts the linear, progressive and unproblematic development of a single hero in terms both individualist and humanist. In the words of Bakhtin, contemplating the problem of the *Bildungsroman* in general, Hesse's novel presents "the image of *man in the process of becoming*" (1986, p. 19), recasting the theme of self-identity in the changing complex of time and space represented, for example, in the posthumous writings, the three fictional lives or biographies (which are part of Castalian training) and the clear dissociation from earlier forms of biography. The narrator says at one point, for instance: "We moderns are not interested in a hero's pathology or family history, nor his drives, his digestion, and how he sleeps. . . . For us, a man is a hero . . . only if his nature and his education have rendered him able to let his individuality be almost perfectly absorbed in its heirarchic function without at the same time forfeiting the vigorous, fresh, admirable impetus which make for the savor and worth of the individual" (p. 13).

Here, perhaps, Hesse also comes close to a cybernetic conception of self and the way in which a canon defines us as a network of tastes, habits and dispositions. One critic, Martin Swales, has noted that Hesse's narrator "writes from a position in which the manifestations of individuality are to be regretted as some kind of pre-Castalian aberration"; that "our narrator is bitterly critical of the bourgeois convention of storytelling because it implies a cult of *individual* selfhood" (1978, pp. 130–31). Certainly, the narrator speaks of the "obliteration of individuality" and the "integration of the individual into the heirarchy of educators and scholars" (p. 10). The figure of the sage or the ideal of Socratic ethics, emphasizing the suprapersonal, is seen as the most appropriate model (p. 12). The submersion of self in the scholarly community is the essential principle guiding the underlying pedagogical ideology of Castalia. And yet, as Swales points out, "History itself becomes a source of constant pedagogical debate in the novel," and it is "one of the deepest ironies of the book that the narrator, in spite of himself, chronicles the life of a man whose intractable individuality and historical self-assertion transcends Castalian ideology and is potentially the source of the province's regeneration" (pp. 133, 136). It is interesting that in recent works devoted to the study of the *Bildungsroman* — for instance Martin Swales (1978), Michael Beddow (1982), Randolph Shaffner (1984) and even M. M. Bakhtin (1986) — only Swales devotes any attention at all to Hesse. It is clear that *The Glass Bead Game* is not only indebted to the *Bildungsroman* tradition but that Hesse experiments with its conventions in playful and innovative ways.[6] Swales (p. 145) regards Hesse's work as an immanent critique of that tradition. He suggests that the work wrestles with questions of teleology, pitting a Castalian tendency toward universality against Castalia's own specific history and that of its protagonist. Swales maintains that "The theme of history [is] intimately bound up with its own historicity as a literary text" (p. 142) for its narrative argument is not only tied inescapably to a chronological structure but also reflects the author's intellectual self-examination following the collapse of the Third Reich.

The Glass Bead Game, nevertheless, remains within the tradition of the *Bildungsroman* and tied to the central category of *Bildung*, of the organic self-formation of the individual striving for aesthetic and spiritual completeness through the transformative power of art. In so doing it remains faithful to a tradition, with the unmistakable imprints of Goethe, Schiller and Humboldt, that defines the ethos underlying both the German Enlightenment and the modern German educational ideal. It is an ideal sketched by Kant in terms of the process that releases us from the status of immaturity. Enlightenment is that moment when we come of age in the use of reason, when there is no longer the need to subject ourselves to forms of traditional authority. Clearly, it is an ideal that dominates the modern *épistème*, privileging the universal subject as the foundation of all knowledge and signification and confirming the humanist notion of a fully rational, autonomous and responsible self.

The Order of Castalia is the pedagogical institutionalization of the Game that emerges in the twenty-first century. Unlike its cyberspace counterpart, or at least recent claims made for its radical democratizing potential and the prospect of a reconstituted virtual public sphere (Lanham, 1993; Rhinegold, 1994; Poster, 1994), the Order is at once élite, male, hierarchical and highly disciplined: it represents a kind of hybrid of the seminary and the university. The Order, at its height, exists as a network throughout Europe and the rest of the world, with each country and small town having its own branch and Game Commission. Only those talented boys who have been suitably trained for ten years in élite schools and inculcated with the virtues of poverty and celibacy are deemed ready to become members and finally to enter the Spiritual Kingdom. Only then are they ready to play the Game either individually or in groups, one day, perhaps, to take part in one of the ceremonial public Games supervised by the *Magister Ludi* — the Master of the Game. Each Game Commission is responsible for its Game Archives, and together the Commissions constitute an international Academy charged with preserving the purity of the Game's symbolic language.

In a clear sense Hesse's dream of a universal language presupposes a universal subject described in relation to that language as master of the Game. As an ideal it is exclusively male and élitist, equating maleness with the abstract self-mastery of a set of logical rules that essentializes one set of Euro-centric values and one subject position proclaimimg its cultural dominance. As an ideal it presupposes a hierarchical pedagogical relationship of disciple to master, where the master subjects the disciple to certain kinds of tests and initiations in a process of tutelage. As an ideal it privileges the intellect over the body, thus ignoring questions of sexuality and sexual orientation. The Game itself, in its synthetic power, reduces all languages and cultures to a common denominator homogenizing cultural difference and erasing the differend of subject positions.

These criticisms of Hesse's ideal bear a striking resemblance to the kind of criticisms raised against Habermas' position by the French post-structuralists. As Mark Poster explains: "The issue dividing Habermas and the French poststructuralists is the relation of language to the subject in an era of electronically mediated communication" (1992, p. 573). Habermas, defending the Enlightenment impulse of the project of modernity, merely substitutes the practice of communicating subjects for the autonomous individual and thereby "reduces cultural or symbolic interaction to communicative rationality. . . . As transcendent, universal attributes of speech, communicative rationality requires no cultural change, no reconfiguration of the subject, no restructuring of language. . . . The problem raised by Lyotard and others is not to find a defense of rationality but to enable cultural difference, what the Enlightenment theorized as 'Other', to emerge against the performativity or rationality of the system" (1992, p. 573). Poster (1992) suggests that there is a convergence between poststructuralist attempts to subvert the Enlightenment paradigm of the subject by theorizing the ways in which the subject is reconfigured in electronically mediated communication, on the one hand, and "critique of white male culture from positions outside of it on the other hand" (p. 573).

Yet, even given these criticisms, if we accept Hesse's reflections upon and playfulness with the conventions of the *Bildungsroman* as a set of innovative strategies limited by specific cultural and historical factors, if we accept his engagement with a literary tradition in a local sense without attempting to legislate for other canons or traditions or to universalize its experience, structure and contents, then I think we are left with a portable or transferable heuristic for cultural study.

THE UNIVERSITY IN CYBERSPACE: CYBERNETIC CONTROL OR NETWORKS OF RESISTANCE?

One might seek to draw a limited analogy between the the Glass Bead Game and the Internet at its present stage of development in the late twentieth century with its common communications protocol, Transmission Control Protocol/Internet Protocol, which provides a common language for interoperation between networks that use a variety of local protocols. The three-level hierarchy of local area networks, regional and backbone networks might be said to correspond to the Game Commissions, and the volunteer committees who set the technical standards for interoperability might be seen to constitute the equivalence of an international Academy.

In terms of this limited analogy one might want to establish an argument that links the cultural institution of the Game with cybernetics and with the idea of the university in cyberspace. I should say that I am not using the term "cybernetics" in its scientific sense as the comparative study of automatic control systems formed by the nervous system and the brain, and by mechanical-electrical or electronic communications systems. Nevertheless, I do not doubt its more scientific application to social systems, and certainly scholars have applied cybernetic theory to an understanding of the functioning of human organizations. Indeed, given the way in which new economic imperatives have translated into higher education policy with the prioritizing of science and technology, and the concomitant advent of information technologies with their rapid spread and institutionalization through networks of all kinds, it is clear that such symbiotic developments, interfacing with each other, fall within the original definition of cybernetics as it was first proposed by Norbert Wiener in his now classic work *Cybernetics* (1948). It is evident that there is a strict isomorphism between so-called goal-seeking machines and living organisms, operating at the level of systems, where information — its iterative feedback cycles — is seen as the core concept for considering the effectiveness of an organization. *Prima facie*, I think a case could be made for considering a university system and its national forms as clear instances of organizational cybernetics, in the technical sense of a set of communicational control systems, designed and controlled through a network of financial sanctions and rewards, which interacts with the market environment (see Peters, 1994). I am not concerned here to make the case for a scientific application of the term. Rather, I want to steal back the original meaning of the term to do some philosophical and political work.

The original meaning of the term is, of course, Greek *kybernetes*, translated as "steersman." In its Latin form we have "gubernator" whence we get our English word "governor." Thus, cybernetics, in the metaphorical sense in which I am using it, becomes "the *governing* of systems" or, more simply, "the government *of* or *by* systems." I was therefore not surprised to learn that Plato, in the *Clitophon*, says, "The cybernetics of men, as you, Socrates, often call politics" or that, predating the U.S. mathematician Wiener's use, the French physicist André Ampère first used the concept cybernetics in writing about the science of government in the early 19th century. In this metaphorical usage the term "cybernetics" captures something of the logic and discourse of economic rationalization as it has been carried out by neoliberal governments in the West since the mid-1980s. It captures the kind of objections raised by both Lyotard and Habermas, although on different grounds, against systems theory and its policy application to universities. It captures also a genealogy of cybernetics as a rationalist epistemology, *par excellence*, "structured by the quest for a cybernetic modelling of human intelligence capable to eliminate uncertainty" (Porush, 1994, p. 4) — an epistemology built on the work of von Neumann, Turing, Wiener and Shannon, which, as Porush maintains, produced the atomic bomb and shaped the culture of the Cold War. It coagluates with the present high profile of cognitive science with its emphasis on artificial intelligence, computer analogies of the brain, the study of neural networks, connectionism in general and even current conceptions of self-directed learning. It also strongly resonates with Baudrillard's (1983) third order of simulation — a neocapitalist cybernetic order intent on total systems control — where the self is defined in terms of information flows, a terminal within multiple networks.

Yet this totalizing and forbidding vision must be pitted against its existing countercultural practices. The existence of a common alphabet does not dictate the canon or the kinds of literature yet to be written.[7] Cyberspace, by contrast, is really a speculative term rehabilitated from the genre of critical science fiction ("cyberpunk") and, particularly, William Gibson's (1984) *Neuromancer*. Gibson's term both prophesies and names the absence of a certain space, because the kind of inhabitable, three-dimensional space he names does not yet exist; however, it has become part of the social imaginary. In other words, it has a metaphorical and allegorical presence but nevertheless functions to name a certain kind of social and cultural space that it is at the same time willing or insinuating itself into being and into knowledge, if I can use a Nietzschean expression. What space does it name and how is that space important for the idea and the institution of the university? In what ways does cyberspace reconfigure the subject and what are the political implications of these new configurations?

I suppose it names the space of the Internet, the network of networks; it names Al Gore's conception of the Information Superhighway. I admit a preference for Gibson's term over the engineering metaphors of the Clinton administration, because cyberspace functions implicitly as a critique of the engineering obsession with what Mark Poster (1990) has called the "efficiency of information," rather than the "reconfiguration of communications exchange." Cyberspace names the hypertextual virtual reality of the World Wide Web. It names the space of a complete textual environment based upon text-based computing, giving rise to notions of the "virtual text" and "virtual author." This is where it comes close to the question of the university with a focus on new kinds of writing and reading practices.

This is to say, in short, that electronic text-processing, as Paul Delany and George Landow claim, "marks the next major shift in text-based information technology after the printed book" (1993, p. 6), a shift based on the common denominator of the digital code. Delany and Landow (pp. 12ff) indicate some of the fundamental features of text-based computing that they believe will shape the emergent world of digitized and networked information, and thereby by implication the place of the university in cyberspace. They focus upon the features of dematerialization, manipulability, and the emergence of new discourse forms. Electronic text exists only as a piece of code that can be transmitted in a different medium and reconstituted at its varied points of arrival. We all know the advances that word-processing makes to cutting, copying and editing the text. These advances have been further supplemented through online database searches and hypertext and hypermedia concordances that produce new forms of interlinked multimedia textuality. Networked text distribution upsets the gatekeeping hierarchies of written texts surrounding the printing and publishing industries in ways that disturb both the market and traditional modes of regulation of the text.

Not surprisingly, these developments have led literary and humanist scholars to talk of the remarkable convergence between poststructuralism and the new communications technologies. George Landow, for instance, speaks of a paradigm shift taking place in the writings of Jacques Derrida and Theodore Nelson, of Roland Barthes and Andries van Dam, arguing that "we must abandon conceptual systems founded upon ideas of center, margin, heirarchy, and linearity and replace them with ones of mulitlinearity, nodes, links, and networks" (1992, p. 2). Jay David Bolter, explaining hypertextuality in terms of poststructuralist notions of the open text, remarks, "what is unnatural in print becomes natural in the electronic medium and will soon no longer need saying at all, because it can be shown" (1991, p. 6). He suggests that the computer is restructuring our economy of writing, changing the cultural status of writing and publishing, and altering both the relationship of the author to the text and of the author and text to the reader. Yet for him the "networking of culture" does not lead to a totalizing synthetic cultural unity but only to a network of interest groups where hierarchical structures of control and interpretation have broken down. Paul Delany and George Landow (1993) use poststructuralist theory to explain some of the fundamental features of text-based computing, and Richard Lanham suggests that "poststructuralism and the common digital code seem part of the same event" (1993, p. xi). He remarks on what he calls the extraordinary convergence of democracy, technology and the university curriculum. Gianni Vattimo (1992), in *The Transparent Society*, builds upon his thesis of the "end of history" to link the birth of postmodern society with the decisive role that mass media play in the transition. Modernity ends, Vattimo maintains, when it no longer seems possible to regard history as unilinear. The dissolution of modernity is a result of the "society of communication," yet for Vattimo mass media do not make society more transparent but more complex, and even chaotic, and it is in this relative chaos and complexity that our future hopes for emancipation lie.

The dispersal of the text escapes the demand by print culture for texts of standard size and format. The ease of replication, transmission, modification and manipulability not only raises new legal and political problems of intellectual property, copyright and plagiarism but questions the continuing role of the traditional library as a central university institution. One commentator, Andrew Odlyzko, indicates that advances in technology will drastically affect the library, that institution central to print-based culture and to the modern university. He predicts that technology will solve the librarian's problem — the crisis in publishing created by increasing prices and increasing scholarly output — and will eliminate most of their jobs, for "most functions of traditional libraries are connected to the notion that information is preserved on pieces of paper that are bulky and expensive" (1994, pp. 24–25). His argument is that the paradigm of the print-based library is no longer appropriate, especially in a worldwide information system where scholarly information is made available for free. The function of the print-based library has been usurped, and it is not just the library, which lies at the heart of the modern university, that is problematized by these developments, but the university itself, or at least the university as a campus space centered around a library.

To be provocative one might say that the postmodern university or the university in postmodernity will come to exist solely in cyberspace with no need for large installations, campus buildings, libraries, lecture theaters. No need, perhaps, for large multicampus metropolitan universities. In the short term, each individual multicampus university may become functionally wired through the benefits of information technologies, and universities in turn wired more effectively as a truly unified system of information flows and exchanges. In the intermediate term — possibly 20 years hence — they may be outmoded and the concept of a university or even a national university system (in the longer term) may become simply another anachronism.

The first virtual or online university has already been assembled. Joseph Wang (an astrophysicist at the University of Texas at Austin) has conceived and set up the Globewide Network Academy, an online university with no physical site. Courses are open to anyone who has access to Internet. Globewide Network Academy completed its first online course in August 1994, and it aims to become a fully accredited university offering degrees to its participating students.

In a similar vein, Roy Ascott (1994), director of the Centre for Advanced Inquiry into the Interactive Arts, proposes the creation of a Planetary Collegium, which he describes as

A non-hierarchical, non-linear, and intrinsically interactive learning organism; integrating people and ideas in electronic space throughout the world, combining cognition and connectivity. What better creative instrument could serve our unfolding telematic culture? This would be a global community in which each member has more or less equal power and authority in access to knowledge and in the means of its configuration and distribution; a community concerned with art and the advancement of learning through collaborative inquiry and shared experience. (p. v)

The Planetary Collegium serves "as the paradigm of the 21st century Interversity" and cannot be implemented top down. Rather, as Ascott indicates, "It is emerging, bottom up from the infinity of interactions within the Net, an emergence which is chaotic, informal, even random" (p. v). This conception opens up new spaces for the contemplation of the concept of a discipline, for the production of new hybrid discourses and for reassessing the relation of language and comunication to the question of the subject.

NOTES

This chapter is based on a seminar originally presented to the research group convened by Bill Readings around a project entitled "L'Université et la culture: la crise identitaire d'une institution," based on the Departments of Comparative Literature and English at l'Université de Montréal on Friday, December 9, 1994. Tragically, Bill Readings died in a Chicago plane crash on October 31, 1994. I thank members of the research group for their personal kindnesses to me and for their constructive comments on this chapter. I also acknowledge the helpful comments of Jean-Claude Guédon, co-editor with Bill Readings of the e-journal *Surfaces*, and Thierry Bardini of the Department of Communication.

1.   Hermann Hesse. (1970). *The Glass Bead Game (Magister Ludi)*, Richard and Clara Winston, (Trans.) (pp. 14–15). London: Jonathan Cape. Originally published as *Das Glasperlenspiel*, Zurich, Verlag, 1943.

2.   Theses terms and their cognates have a genealogy with and a strong family resemblance to a host of other terms, as I have tried to demonstrate throughout this book: the postindustrial society (Alain Touraine, Daniel Bell), the knowledge society (Peter Drucker), the service class society (Ralf Dahrendorf), the personal service society (Paul Halmos), the technetronic era (Zbigniew Brzezinski), the postscarcity society (Herman Kahn), the postbourgeois society (George Lichtheim), the society of the spectacle (Guy Debord), the bureaucratic society of controlled consumption (Henri Lefebvre), postcivilization (Kenneth Boulding); perhaps also, post minimalism (Pincus-Witten), postperformance (Denis Oppenheim), postmodernismo (Frederico De Onis), Post-Modern (Arnold Toynbee), POSTmodernISM (Ihab Hassan), the postmodern condition (Jean François Lyotard); and, no doubt, postlogical positivism (Mary Hesse) and post-Kantianism (Richard Rorty); as well as postcolonialism, poststructuralism and the like.

3.   Hesse visited Richard Wilhelm, the translator of the *I Ching*, in November 1926, only one year before he first thought about his magnum opus, and he claimed that Wilhelm's translation had given him a "spiritual" answer to his crisis born of the tendency to attempt to relate to different sides of the same question at the same time (Freedman, 1978, p. 350). See also Goldgar (1966–67), who discusses the structure of the Game and the novel in terms of its correspondences with the Japanese game of Go.

4.   Nietzsche along with Goethe was Hesse's favorite author and as a youth he decorated his room with his portraits (Freedman, 1978, p. 68). Hesse was later to write an essay called "Zarathustra's Return" and was clearly influenced by Nietzsche's concepts of cyclicity and polarity. Norton confirms that Hesse demonstrated an enthusiasm for Spengler's *The Decline of the West*, which "very probably influenced Hesse's predictions of European collapse and rebirth" (1973, p. 35).

5.   See Remys (1983, pp. 1–3) for an account of the complicated genesis of *The Glass Bead Game*: Hesse, it appears, first entertained the idea of the novel as early as 1927; by 1931 he had outlined five biographies, parts of which figure in the novel; by 1934 he had completed the introduction. The poems were written between 1932 and 1941; the chapters of Knecht's life were written between 1938 and 1942 and the entire novel was completed on April 29, 1942.

6.   Swales notes, for instance, that the name of Hesse's hero, "Knecht (servant) is a quizzical echo of that of Goethe's hero, Meister (master), and Knecht becomes

Master of the Bead Game. Moreover, the Castalian province clearly recalls the 'Pedagogical Province' of *Wilhelm Meister's Travels*" (1978, pp. 139–40).

    7.   I am indebted to Jean-Claude Guédon for this metaphor.

10

Monoculturalism, Multiculturalism and Democracy: The Politics of Difference or Recognition?

The standards and values, the underlying epistemology of general education linked American norms and values back to a European past and projected it, in turn onto a global stage with a solon, like FDR, or an atomic Pericles, like JFK, as their embodiments. It is not surprising that, while the subject of this education is the nation, its object is the world. This last great agent of this Western projection is "America" — but not just any America. It is an America that takes over and, at the same time, is tied to European ideals — an America that fuses an evolutionary ideal of progress with foundational norms of Beauty and Truth. It is the product of a tense and highly problematic modernist fusion of technological progressivism and neoclassicism.

— Michael Geyer[1]

INTRODUCTION

The debate over monoculturalism and multiculturalism is not new, although these terms have taken on a distinctive and peculiar hue of meaning in the later twentieth century. Their effective history was intermingled from the start with the political, social and economic conditions that led to the development of the modern nation-state, with the history of European racism, white supremacism and colonization. Their prehistory is tied up with the perceptions of the first European explorers and missionaries who "discovered" the New World and the worldview and cultural heritage of the European settlers who followed. The early statement of the ensuing debate is recorded in eighteenth-century European parliamentary and public debates over first contact with indigenous peoples, the civilizing mission of the West, problems of land purchase and the appropriate means of colonial government.

The oppositional force of multiculturalism as an idea received part of its historical impetus first from local indigenous struggles; from the concept of "negritude" and the combined influence of philosophies of decolonization of, for example, Frantz Fanon and Aimé Césaire and from Marxist theories of imperialism. Multiculturalism received one of its early official global statements with the setting up of the United Nations Educational, Scientific, and Cultural Organization in 1945. Later, in 1951, Claude Lévi-Strauss, in a text prepared for the United Nations Educational, Scientific, and Cultural Organization, drew attention to the ethnocentrism implicit in the European view of history as the unilinear progress of a universal reason to suggest that cultures, meaning particular ways of life, are unable to be ranked or put into any sequence of development.

In critical moments of cultural reconstruction the multiculturalism/ monoculturalism doublet have regularly resurfaced. In the United States a particular version of the debate has resurfaced as a debate over the reform of university curricula. As Michael Geyer explains, the debate on multiculturalism, having nearly vanished from academic agendas, reentered U.S. universities from two very different sources.

The civil rights movement was undoubtedly the single most important force, combining political, social, and cultural components and shaping all other popular mobilizations for presentation and participation. The other opening was much more limited and precarious, an intellectual rather than a social force. It came with the massive incursion of French thought particularly in the humanities. Post-structuralism may have been a marginal affair in its European origins, but it entered American universities as privileged European knowledge. The two sides rarely mixed, but their efforts converged in one respect. Both facilitated, each in its own way, a recovery of submerged knowledge, a working through of the repressed. Together they have moulded the basic issues of a contemporary politics of representation that is at the core of the debate on multiculturalism. (1993, p. 513)

Geyer may be astray in his assessment of the influence of poststructuralism within Europe and of the intellectual and political linkages between multiculturalism, the structuralist anthropology of, say, Lévi-Strauss and Maurice Godelier and later French poststructuralists, but he is certainly correct in identifying both the twin sources of a contemporary politics of representation and the politically most volatile public space for their development — U.S. higher education. He is also correct, to my mind, to argue that multiculturalism and monoculturalism are "neither politically nor intellectually unequivocal positions" (1993, p. 514) — both may be associated with compensatory or transformatory strategies — and to attempt to disentangle the positions from which to argue identity politics.

While the position of cultural conservatives supporting a form of monoculturalism is perhaps easy enough to distinguish, although politically complex in terms of its sites of cultural production, the position of some liberals who argue from universalist grounds and construe the debate to reform university curricula as one between "essentialists" on one side and "deconstructionists" on the other is too simplistic and in need of active interpretation. So too, the positions of multiculturalism, especially in relation to what has been variously termed "postmodernism," "poststructuralism" or "deconstructionism" require careful interpretation. While postmodernism and multiculturalism are politically similar and, perhaps, even interdependent in certain ways, sharing a rejection of Enlightenment master narratives based upon universalist claims, Mark Poster (1992, p. 577) has pointed out that the relationship between the two should be seen as a "troubled alliance," troubled to the precise extent that either position can extricate itself from the norms of Enlightenment politics.

This chapter begins the task of disentangling these positions. First, it provides some background to the recent emergence of cultural conservatism and the attack on multiculturalism and poststructuralism within U.S. higher education. Second, it examines a new liberal alliance brought together under the umbrella of Amy Gutmann's (1994) edited collection, *Multiculturalism: Examining the Politics of Recognition*, based on the work of Charles Taylor, Jürgen Habermas and others. Finally, I argue for what Cornel West (1990) has called the "new cultural politics of difference" and, following Poster (1992), I briefly examine the nature of the troubled alliance between multiculturalism and poststructuralism.

THE EMERGENCE OF CULTURAL CONSERVATISM

Most people are aware of the general shift to the right that took place in global politics during the 1980s, the emergence of the new right and a set of policies based upon neoliberal principles expressing, on the one hand, the failure of big government and, on the other hand, a commitment to free-market solutions. In the field of higher education, as in other policy realms, this has meant a transparent alignment of the system to reflect the needs of the economy. Accordingly, we have experienced the introduction of new forms of corporate managerialism with an emphasis on clear accountability structures, delegated authority, and corporate planning; and the introduction of user-charges for most forms of higher education, together with a greater emphasis on student loans schemes. Under neoliberalism education is conceived more as a private investment good accruing to an individual over his or her lifetime earnings rather than a universal welfare entitlement or public good.

Alongside a recognition of these policies, most people have become aware of the extent to which higher education has become one of the most highly politicized issues of the 1990s. One manifestation of this is the debate over "political correctness,"[2] which seemed to take over the popular imagination with ease. It was a debate that started and is best epitomized by John Searle's (1990) "The Storm over the University," which appeared in the *New York Review of Books*, and Richard Bernstein's (1990) "The Rising Hegemony of the Politically Correct," published in the *New York Times*. The statements and sentiments of Searle and Bernstein were contemporaneous with a wave of popular conservatism that began, perhaps, with the publication of Lynne V. Cheney's first report as the Chairman of the National Endowment for the Humanities, *The Humanities and the American Promise* (1987), and included a series of books, now well known, attacking the liberal nature of higher education and demonizing liberals and radicals who wished to reform university curricula: among them, E. D. Hirsch's (1987) *Cultural Literacy*, Allan Bloom's (1987) *The Closing of the American Mind*, Roger Kimball's (1990) *Tenured Radicals*, and Dinesh D'Souza's (1991) *Illiberal Education*.

Cheney's stance, encapsulating the general tenor of criticism and the primary issue at stake, is given in a talk he gave to a meeting of the American Council of Learned Societies in 1988:

When I become most concerned about the state of the humanities in our colleges and universities is not when I see theories and ideas fiercely competing, but when I see them neatly converging, when I see feminist criticism, Marxism, various forms of poststructuralism, and other approaches all coming to bear on one concept and threatening to displace it. I think specifically of the concept of Western civilization, which has come under pressure on many fronts, political as well as theoretical. Attacked for being elitist, sexist, racist, and Eurocentric, this central and sustaining idea of our education system and our intellectual heritage is being declared unworthy of study. (cited in Messer-Davidow, 1993, p. 41)

While witness to a set of policy changes that threatened to change the basic mission of the university — constituting threats to both institutional autonomy and academic freedom — and a new wave of popular conservatism, few people on the left understood in the 1980s the extent to which either Cheney's statement was taken from "an already crafted conservative political discourse" or the right had "manufactured the attack on liberalized higher education by means of a massive right-wing apparatus dedicated to making radical cultural change" (Messer-Davidow, 1993, pp. 41, 43). The right had become a formidable force during the intervening decades dating from the mid-1950s by wielding a coalition of conservative strains. During these same years the right had also greatly and deliberately enlarged its infrastructure. Ellen Messer-Davidow provides a detailed account of the establishment of right-wing "foundations, think-tanks, media, training institutes and legal centers" that in the 1980s "began to focus their resources on cultural change" (1993, p. 44).

Foremost among these developments was the project called "cultural conservatism," developed by Paul Weyrich, president of the Free

Congress Foundation, and his associated group of conservatives. The project of cultural conservatism, which Messer-Davidow remarks "was to be the template for a new American politics" (1993, p. 45), recognized that politics based on culture rather than economics was to be dominant in the twenty-first century. The project sought to cast off the negative public image of the new right and to define in positive terms what it stood for against the forces of the left. The primary element of self-definition was considered to be the concern to actively conserve traditional Western culture on the grounds that traditional Western values are *functional* values, that is, deemed to be functionally true. The agenda to reform culture became an agenda to reform those institutions responsible for transmitting Western culture.

Through an articulated system of think-tanks, foundations, media, legal centers, training centers, and grass-roots organizations, the right has manufactured an attack on the liberalized nature of U.S. higher education: an attack on academic feminism, an attack on academic theory[3] and an attack on multiculturalism, which has been the broadest, Messer-Davidow suggests, because "the opening of the curriculum to previously excluded races and cultures overlaps with other efforts in the academy and society that conservatives oppose" (1993, p. 42), such as affirmative action and African-American and gay activism.

What often goes unnoticed in conservative arguments is the extent to which monoculturalism in U.S. higher education is itself a cultural construct fabricated in the twentieth century. As Michael Geyer explains:

To be sure, monocultural higher education is rooted, in some way, in Renaissance humanism, Enlightenment classicism, and the imperial sciences of man and space — all of which have come under intense scrutiny. But nothing really is quite that old in American higher education. Monoculturalism in American higher education is a thoroughly twentieth-century construct. Moreover, it was not passed on, properly speaking, by European descendants as a *tradition*; the founding generation exhibited a violent hostility to said tradition(s) as well as to taxes, both together jeaptardizing European-style higher education, and later generations of immigrants were by and large not the kind of people to pass on university education. Instead, these successive waves of "colonists" adopted, took over, appropriated, and preserved selectively (that is, "cultivated") European thought as American culture. (1993, p. 502).

Geyer (1993) argues that an examination of the place, the subject and the goal of a monocultural general education reveals the conditional, public and political nature of U.S. higher education. The merger between general and higher education, he suggests, is crucial to the success of the U.S. university as an institution — a feature that distinguishes U.S. from continental European universities, whose institutional autonomy is related more narrowly to an unequivocal mission involving the production of knowledge. The broader role of U.S. universities provided an "institutional space for meritocratic mediation" (p. 505) between the corporation and the state, and the formation of a canon of learning that emerged on the basis of pragmatic grounds, congealed in the 1930s and 1940s, to be reformed in the 1960s. The resulting monocultural canon, open to variation, represented a fusion of national culture and universal values, ideal for a Fordist age. The success of this monocultural ideal, Geyer states, was

Closely tied to the emerging role of the United States as a hegemonic power. This is expressed ideologically in the common pronouncement that the United States unified the West, completed the course of Western development, and set global standards of civilization in fierce rivalry with the Soviet Union. . . . General education became the normative knowledge of a rapidly expanding new middle class and its masculine civic culture. It is high culture for an Atlanticist age. (1993, p. 509)

Geyer suggests that, given this monocultural construction, it is pointless to debate whether higher education is meant to reproduce or criticize culture. Rather, "the question is *now*, after a long period of growth lasting roughly from the 1920s to the 1970s, whether *we*, today, should reproduce the academic culture of the past half century in the image we make of it, return to an even older one or the image we make of that, or take up again the labors of cultivation and, thus, produce a very American moment as opposed to an oxymoronic 'American tradition'" (1993, p. 503). In short, this is, he suggests, the very question that is at the basis of current debates about higher education.

A NEW LIBERAL ALLIANCE?

A new liberal alliance is in the process of formation. It is epitomized by the work of Amy Gutmann (1994) who, taking to heart a sermon from Charles Taylor on the "politics of recognition," fused together with Jürgen Habermas' phenomenological analysis of struggles within the "democratic constitutional state," mounts an attack upon both deconstructionists and essentialists in the multicultural "storm over the university" (Searle, 1990) in order to make room for a liberal education. It is a polemical battle and one that Gutmann has harnessed for moral purposes and out of respect for what she considers to be fundamental liberal democratic values. The edited collection to which I refer, origi- nally entitled *Multiculturalism: Examining the Politics of Recognition*, was first conceived to mark the inauguration of the University Center for Human Values at Princeton University, of which Gutmann is director. It is an important book and one which has grown in reputation and size since the original centerpiece essay by the well-known and respected Canadian philosopher, Charles Taylor, was first published in

1992. Subsequently, the collection underwent translation in Italian, French and German. The German edition includes an extended essay by Habermas on the struggles for recognition in the democratic constitutional state. The expanded English edition, published in 1994, includes Taylor's original essay alongside Habermas' account, together with a further essay by K. Anthony Appiah, who is professor of Afro-American Studies and Philosophy at Harvard University, and a series of commentaries on Taylor's reflections by Susan Wolf, Steven C. Rockefeller and Michael Walzer. These essays, taken together with Amy Gutmann's introduction, carry an undeniable authority and establish a kind of middle ground. Of course, it does more than that: it establishes a political interpretation of the term "multiculturalism" based upon the tradition of liberal democracy. In one sense, given the people involved, it serves and will serve for some time as the standard-bearer of the liberal interpretation of multiculturalism. Accordingly, it deserves the closest intellectual scrutiny.

To a large extent, Taylor's essay can be seen as a "communitarian" response to the question of multiculturalism, inspired, in part, by his own recent philosophical work based on tracing the sources of the moral self (1990) within the Western cultural tradition and based, in part, upon his experience as a Canadian facing the prospect of Quebec separatism. In a rich historical essay Taylor examines two changes, which, together, he suggests, "have made the modern preoccupation with identity and recognition inevitable" (1994, p. 26). The first change took place, he argues, when the notion of dignity was substituted for that of honor, ushering in a politics of recognition; the second emerges at the end of the eighteenth century with "the subjective turn" of modern culture and the development of the notion of authenticity, which he traces to the influence of Jean-Jacques Rousseau and Herder. The second change, in particular, modifies and intensifies recognition as the universalist and egalitarian basis for democracy through *individualizing* identity, that is, according a kind of moral importance of our own inner natures. Together, both changes have the combined force to displace and undermine social hierarchies and socially derived identification, which was the basis of traditional society.

I have no difficulty with this historical account. I do not doubt Taylor's scholarship or the general conclusion he arrives at as part of the historical story. What I do not think Taylor emphasizes strongly enough is the contingency of these developments. He seems to be wedded to a thesis concerning the historical inevitability of the emerging interrelationship between notions of dignity and authenticity; and he passes quickly and without adequate justification from the historical story to an apparently neutral and universal description concerning the definition of identity, as though the historical story somehow warrants a philosophical conclusion: "We define our identity *always* in dialogue" (Taylor, 1994, p. 33, emphasis added).[4]

Taylor maintains that the move from honor to dignity issued forth into a "politics of universalism" emphasizing the equalization of rights and that the ideal of authenticity gave rise to a politics of difference — the demand for recognition of the unique identity of particular individuals or cultural groups — which, he suggests, is also established on the basis of a universalist potential, "The potential for forming and defining one's own identity, as an individual, and also as a culture" (1994, p. 42). The latter is said to grow organically out of the former but the two modes of politics come into conflict in that the "politics of equal dignity" insists that we treat people in a difference-blind fashion, whereas the "politics of difference" claims that universal difference-blind principles are, in fact, a set of particular, culture-bound norms (and theories), representing the present apogee of one contemporary dominant cultural formation.

Faced with such conflict between apparently competing universalist principles — a conflict that Taylor examines and elucidates by reference to the case of Quebec separatism — Taylor forsakes procedural liberalism for an equivocal communitarian liberalism based on the presumption of the value of all cultures, what Michael Walzer (1994) redescribes, more simply, as "Liberalism 1" and "Liberalism 2."[5] I say equivocal because it is not clear that Taylor wants to accept the full force of his own radical conclusion. He pictures these two views as incompatible and *universalist* views of liberal society, indicating that "The rigidities of procedural liberalism may rapidly become impractical in tomorrow's world" (1994, p. 61), where "all societies are becoming increasingly multicultural" (p. 63). He even acknowledges the work of Frantz Fanon as critical in the attempt by subjugated peoples to escape a kind of internal colonization and recognizes that a greater place ought to be made in universities and schools "for women and for people of non-European races and cultures,"[6] but he cannot bring himself to accept other than a presumption in favor of equal respect for cultures and is not sure whether this presumption can be validly construed as a right.

Taylor's essay is a courageous statement of his beliefs and both stimulating and penetrating in terms of its insights, but it also is equivocal and idealist in attempting to find a compromise between two uncompromising sets of ideals. He says at one point, and almost as a parting remark: "There must be something midway between the inauthenticity and homogenizing demand for recognition of equal worth, on the one hand, and the self-immurement within ethnocentric standards, on the other" (1994, p. 72).

Taylor does not sufficiently explain how two accounts and sets of principles, both purportedly universalist and true, can come into conflict. Does this imply an internal inconsistency at the heart of the liberal tradition? On the one hand, he approvingly recounts the subjectivist and Romantic turn of modern culture in the explication of the emergence of the modern notion of identity, while, on the other hand, refusing to seriously countenance its contemporary philosophical forms. His casual and off-hand references to "neo-Nietzscheans" (for example, "subjectivist, half-baked neo-Nietzschean theories," [1994, p. 70]) does him no credit and mars his argument. (He mentions Foucault and Derrida only once, without reference to specific texts and in entirely derogatory terms.) This represents a crude denial of the very "dialogical" grounds for the question of identity that he attempts to assert on the basis of an authentic, multicultural, liberal communitarianism.[7]

Part of his conceptual troubles, I believe, is that he attempts to account for the conflict between two modes of political thinking and demands in terms entirely internal to the history of the liberal tradition. While I have no difficulty agreeing with him in terms of the account he presents of the "politics of dignity," encompassing the demand for equal rights and the emergence of various forms of European and American individualism, it seems to me that the politics of difference clearly originates from outside the liberal tradition and that its development can neither be explained internally to an account of that tradition not contained by it. The politics of difference surely comes into being historically not primarily *as a result* of progressive thought within the liberal tradition but rather *as a reaction* against its (ethnocentric) claims to universalism, and this cultural challenge is what contemporary liberalism seeks to accommodate theoretically. In other words, these struggles originating at the peripheries of liberal culture and its societies, and historically tied to local indigenous movements of opposition against the ethos of assimilation, have forced the question of their recognition and the issue of cultural rights to center stage as an act of political will. It is largely their *struggles* that have forced these issues into statutes.

THE NEW CULTURAL POLITICS OF DIFFERENCE

I have argued elsewhere that the project to reform liberalism and the project of radical democracy based on a notion of community, whether defined in universal or historical contingent terms, have been unsuccessful precisely to the extent that they have ignored the poststructuralist critique of subject-centered reason and the historical importance of the new social movements (see Peters, 1995b). Both liberals and communitarians, I argued, following Iris Young (1992) and others, are tied into a basic opposition characteristic of the binary logic of modernism: they each privilege one term or concept that the other seeks to deny. The former, committed to an ideology of individualism, privileges the individual in universal and ahistorical terms as the ultimate unit of analysis. I argued that both Kantian and market liberals share an emphasis on rationality as the exclusive predicate of individual actors but, where Kantian liberals provide a procedural interpretation of Kant's concept of autonomy and his notion of the categorical imperative to emphasize formal rights, market liberals draw on the behavioral postulate of *Homo economicus*, arguing that people should be treated as "rational utility-maximizers" in all of their behavior.

Further, I argued that communitarians, by contrast, claim that liberal theory is excessively individualistic and, historically and culturally, not sufficiently sensitive. Liberal theory, on this account, misunderstands claims to rights. Rights are not to be treated as transcendent principles but rather as historical and contingent features of liberal communities. Communitarians deny methodological individualism, arguing that rationality can be predicated also of institutions and political cultures. In this view, the political community is not merely an aggregate of individuals but rather constitutive of what it is to be a human being. We are what and who we are by virtue of our membership in a community of shared values and meanings. Communitarians, while more historically sensitive, are wedded to a notion of community that is privileged over and against the notion of the individual in an appeal to an organic unity.

I have also maintained that there is an intimate relation between the postmodern critique of reason and the rise of the new social movements (see Peters, 1991). I interpret the growth of what Habermas (1981) has called "new social movements," by which he means sub-institutional, extraparliamentary forms of protest originating in the 1960s and developing thereafter, as the historical means by which Marxism as the master discourse of liberation has been stripped of its overtly rationalistic and scientistic elements that it inherited from the Enlightenment.

Marxism taught us the valuable lesson that we make history but under conditions that are not of our own choosing. This was the first moment of the critique of the subject. While Marxism championed the collective subject in terms of the priority of class, equally it insisted that the subject was always inserted into existing social practices and that groups and individuals can never be the sole origin or authors of those practices. As Stuart Hall remarks in this regard: "That is a profound historical decentering in terms of social practice" (1991, p. 43). Many of the incipient social movements — those based around the philosophy of decolonization and feminism — drew their inspiration from the Marxist critique, sometimes combined with the Freudian critique, which also disturbed the stable language of identity by emphasizing the importance of unconscious processes in the formation of the self.

The old identity politics of the social movements of the 1960s introduced some theoretical refinements, splitting and questioning the priority of class as the leading collective subject whose goal was emancipation. There was greater recognition, in particular, of race and gender as specifying in a nonreductive way lines of oppression. In an important sense these social categories depended, in their early stages, on essentialist readings: it marked them out in contrast to the other dominant modernist readings of political identity — those of class and of nation. Where the notion of class permanently broke apart the idea of a homogeneous collective unity of nation, those of race and gender led to a greater understanding of an internal social differentiation. Yet these social movements still subscribed to the old logic of identity as stable and homogeneous categories, which, as Hall remarks, "could be spoken about almost as if they were singular actors in their own right but which, indeed, placed, positioned, stabilized, and allowed us to understand and read, almost as a code, the imperatives of the individual self: the great collective social identities of class, of race, of nation, of gender, and of the West" (1991, p. 14).

The poststructuralist critique of the subject and of reason was instrumental in unsettling the modernist discourse of identity, in taking the process several stages further. It problematized the category of the individual as the last vestige of a rationalistic liberalism that has privileged the Cogito — the self-identical and fully transparent thinking subject, the origin and ground of action — as *the* universal subject against which all irrational others are defined. It carried out this critique in a way that problematized not only the unity of the subject but also that of any group, which, on the basis of an alleged shared experience, may have been thought of as an organic unity or singular actor.

Cornel West offers the characterization of what he calls the "new cultural politics of difference" in the following terms:

Distinctive features of the new cultural politics of difference are to trash the monolithic and homogenous in the name of diversity, multiplicity and heterogeneity; to reject the abstract, general and universal in light of the concrete, specific, and particular; and to historicize, contextualize and pluralize by highlighting the contingent, provisional, variable, tentative, shifting and changing. . . . What makes them novel — along with the cultural politics they produce — is how and what constitutes difference, the weight and gravity which is given in representation, and the way in which highlighting issues like exterminism, empire, class, race, gender, sexual orientation, age, nation, nature, and religion at this historical moment acknowledges some discontinuity and disruption from previous forms of cultural critique. (1990, p. 19)

In postmodern critical theory, which, to some degree, underwrites the new politics of identity, the subject is no longer seen as a unitary, rational ego — as it has been historically produced and self-reproduced under the combined influence of the liberal human sciences; rather, it is seen as occupying different subject-positions within discursive practices that are produced by the power/knowledge relations of particular discourses. As such the subject exists in-process, only as a partial, and sometimes nonrational voice occupying multiple sites or positions which might themselves be contradictory. As Stuart Hall comments:

The great collective social identities have not disappeared. Their purchase and efficacy in the real world that we all occupy is ever present. But the fact is that none of them is, any longer, in either the social, historical or epistemological place where they were in our conceptualizations of the world in the recent past. They cannot any longer be thought in the same homogenous form. We are as attentive to their inner differences, their inner contradictions, their segmentations and their fragmentations as we are to their already-completed homogeneity, their unity and so on. They are not already-produced stabilities and totalities in the world. They do not operate like totalities. If they have a relationship to our identities, cultural and individual, they do not any longer have that suturing, structuring, or stabilizing force, so that we can know what we are simply by adding up the sum of our positions in relation to them. They do not give us the code of identity as I think they did in the past. (1991, p. 15)

What I have come to accept only recently, under the force of feminist arguments, is the critique of community. The notion of community has been appealed to in order to sanction some very dubious practices. I am thinking here of the notion of community as advanced by neoconservatives to reconstruct and venerate cultural traditions — a modern one culture, one nation interpretation common to attempts such as Allan Bloom's *The Closing of the American Mind* or Alain Finkielkraut's *La Défaite de la Pensée*. The notion of community here is central to the ideal of assimilation at the heart of liberal ideology: it expresses the vision of a common national culture in which all individuals, freed from their ethnic origins, their tribal histories, and their traditional cultural beliefs, can participate in a modern democratic society. In this view, cultural pluralism and ethnic diversity are seen as a threat to the demands of modern society because such pluralism promotes the idea of group identity, group loyalties and group rights. It is, therefore, not surprising that modern liberal discourse in its conception of citizenship has systematically excluded groups historically defined as Other. It has effectively pursued this end by promoting an idea of civic community that is both homogeneous and monocultural. Such a view of civic community that originates in a shared order of being as the foundation of *one* group with a bounded and coherent identity is, as Yeatman states, completely at odds with the "contemporary politics of voice and representation" (1992, p. 3).

The communitarian critique of liberalism has taught us to be suspicious of the universalist and rationalist pretensions underlying an individualism that both abstracts the individual from their social and cultural contexts and disregards the role of social relationships in constituting the nature and identity of people. It has also helped us to realize that the individuals of neoliberalism, posited as rational utility maximizers and theorized to form communities based fundamentally on competition, covertly screen out different cultural and gender values. Yet at the same time communitarian philosophy, in substituting one universalist notion for another, privileges unity over difference, the social self over the individual self. This republican discourse sets up a vision of a substantive civic community based on the regulative ideal of a participatory and dialogical reason that is, however, monocultural and intolerant of a plurality of differences. The communitarian ideal postulates a public that comes into being through reason, a rational consensus that assimilates substantive cultural differences and denies the heterogeneity of social life (Yeatman, 1992).

Not only is the communitarian ideal intolerant of cultural differences, it also often disregards gender-related problems. It is clear that traditional communities have been highly oppressive for women, ascribing them subservient roles on the basis of a primitive division of labor. It is easy, in face of the individualization and privatization of society, to falsely romanticize the notion of community, not recognizing the way in which arguments based on its appeal can be undesirably utopian and politically problematic. For instance, as Young (1990, 1992) argues, alienation and violence are as much a function of face-to-face relationships as they are of mediated social relations. Contemporary studies of rape and child abuse make this point very strongly.

The starting point for a politics of difference is the combined critique of liberalism and republicanism, of individualism and community, to show that all homogeneous constructions of individual or community identity are, in fact, historical and contingent constructions that depend on deliberate and systematic exclusions. Social groups conceived in these terms are therefore noninterrelational and mutually exclusive. A politics of difference, by contrast, unfreezes fixed and essential identities. It treats difference as variation rather than exclusive opposition. It sees identities as both relational and contextual, often a matter of political choice. To this extent, a politics of difference understands that the identity of the subject is constructed at the point of intersection of a multiplicity of subject-positions "between which there exists no a priori or necessary relation and whose articulation is the result of hegemonic practices" (Mouffe, 1988, p. 35).

Marxism and Freudianism led to a profound decentering of the subject as the fount of all reason, signification and action. Both individuals and groups are always inserted in existing social practices and can never be the sole origin or authors of those practices. The social movements of the 1960s and 1970s established some refinements, questioning the priority of class as the leading collective emancipatory subject. There was a greater recognition of ethnicity and gender as specifying, in nonreductive ways, lines of oppression. Yet these social movements were pictured as being based on the old logic of identity, which conceived of collective subjects in terms of stable, essential and homogeneous categories. These essentializing views attributed new collective subjects the modernist characteristics of singular actors and reduced emerging collective social identities to the model of the individual imperial self where differences became subsumed and internal conflict were eliminated. Questions of oppression within or between oppressed groups were occluded in the romanticization of collective actors who were seen to act, think, and feel as one.

Stuart Hall addresses himself to the question of a significant shift that has taken place in black politics in terms of a politics of representation, which he characterizes as "the end of the essential black subject" (1992, p. 254). By this he means that the category "black" is a politically and culturally constructed category that is never fixed but is historically articulated and contains within it a tremendous diversity of experience. A politics of representation recognizes racism as the play of identity and difference that positions the black subject not only in relation to the dimensions of class, gender and nation but also in relation to sexuality and desire. Hall explains as follows: "Just as masculinity always constructs femininity as double — simultaneously Madonna and Whore — so racism constructs the black subject: noble savage and violent avenger. . . . This double fracturing entails a different kind of politics because . . . black radical politics has frequently been stabilized around particular conceptions of black masculinity, which are only now being put into question by black women and black gay men" (1992, p. 256).

It is clear that the poststructuralist critique of the subject and of reason has been instrumental in unsettling the modernist discourse of identity and the politics that it was based on. In their introduction to a recent edited collection of essays entitled *"Race", Culture and Difference*, James Donald and Ali Rattansi indicate that the move away from essentializing "race" demands a new conceptualization of community: "a shift from the idea of inherited or imposed authority and towards the principles of difference and dialogue" (1992, p. 5). They argue that the recent theoretical advances in rethinking culture (Saussurean semiotics, Lacanian psychoanalysis, feminism, cultural studies and so forth) undermine the notion of community understood in terms of normative identity and tradition to emphasize "the contingency of *any* instituted cultural authority." They continue: "'Race' and identity are inherently contestable social and political categories: that is why it calls into question multicultural and antiracist paradigms, as well as the logic of assimilation" (p. 5).

The politics of difference is suspicious of universalist, foundationalist and essentialist kinds of thinking and now more alert to the political purposes that they serve. The emphasis of such a politics on plurality and otherness is based on understanding the subtle processes of identity formation and the ways in which modernist, Euro-centric discourses have created nations, races and classes through a series of systematic exclusions based on binary oppositions. For postcolonial countries the deconstruction of the couplets, civilized/primitive, black/white, culture/nature, colonizer/colonized, is a necessary step toward affirming a more heterogeneous public and deinstitutionalizing neocolonial values.

Yet while the new politics of identity, founded on a more profound understanding of difference, provides the basis for building new intersubjectivities and solidarities and offers the hope of reinventing through struggle the promise of participatory democracy — a promise that remains one of the central purposes of education and educational theory — there is the distinct danger, as Mark Poster (1992) states, of conflating, confusing or reducing the politics of postmodernity with the politics of the Enlightenment, a danger that comes into focus most acutely in the debate over multiculturalism. Poster argues, more generally, that the French poststructuralists are surer guides to the reconstruction of critical theory than Habermas because "they confront squarely the dilemma of the subject in the postmodern age". In particular, "The referential anchor of the [old, bourgeois, stable identity] of the individual recedes in social prominence as global communication networks (Lyotard) and human/machine combinations (Haraway) replace older figures of man versus nature and individual versus society" (1992, p. 576). And yet, in this context, as Poster points out, the easy association of multiculturalism with postmodernism is to be questioned. While the suspicion of Enlightenment universalism appears to unite multiculturalists and postmodernists, the alliance is a troubled one, troubled to the extent that both positions can extricate themselves from Enlightenment politics.

In the case of the postmodernists the difficulty concerns their repetition in denial of the Enlightenment *posture* of critique, their replication of Enlightenment *forms* of critique (the writing of discourses) and their address of universalist themes (society *at large* for Lyotard consists of differends) while at the same time denying universalist claims. . . . In the case of the multiculturalists the difficulty concerns a reliance on subject positions that reproduce Enlightenment notions of agency. . . . The colossal problem is one of asserting the emancipatory potential of multiculturalist subject positions while avoiding the essentialism or self-identity that is associated with Enlightenment forms of resistance. (Poster, 1992, p. 577)

Poster concludes by maintaining that postmodernism is still a fledgling position, one that names a set of changes (e.g., the demise of colonialism and the advent of electronically mediated communication) that will "revolutionize the structures of modernity" and that "anticipates a future in which these tendencies" become dominant (1992, p. 579). In this situation, he suggests, "multiculturalists must choose between a Habermasian universalism that denies their enunciative position altogether and postmodernist differentialism that affirms that position but cannot fully defend that affirmation" (p. 579).

NOTES

1.   Michael Geyer (1993, Spring) Multiculturalism and the Politics of General Education. *Critical Inquiry*, *19*, 507.

2.   Peter Roberts suggests that the term "political correctness" was "initially a term of approval used by Leninists to denote commitment to the party line" and was "later employed with irony by the New Left to signify excessively strict or enthusiastic adherence to party dogma" (1995, p. 1). Only in the 1990s did the term acquire a distinctly pejorative connotation. See also Roberts' (1993) discussion of Bloom in relation to questions of philosophy, education and literacy.

3.   The attack on academic theory, especially on poststructuralism and deconstructionism, is an interesting case. Poststructuralism within the American academy has had the most impact within departments of literature rather than philosophy. Derrida's reception in Britain, by contrast to the United States, can be gauged to some extent by the public controversy over the proposal at Cambridge University to award Derrida an honorary degree. For a sociological account of the legitimation of Derrida's work in "two cultural markets as different as France and the United States," see Michele Lamont's (1987) "How to Become a Dominant French Philosopher: The Case of Jacques Derrida." I find Lamont's analysis quite unconvincing and her account of Derrida's thought naïve and unsophisticated.

Joseph Margolis, in a footnote to an essay belonging to a rare philosophical collection that appraises Derrida's work, entitled *European Philosophy and the American Academy* (Smith, 1994), writes: "In the United States it has been charged in various and wild as well as temperate ways that Derrida is a philosophical anarchist and that the favourable reception of Derridean 'methods' has somehow made its way into the seeming legitimation of relativism, 'multiculturalism', and 'political correctness' that threaten the American academy" (Margolis, 1994, p. 221). Margolis is referring to the following claim by Barry Smith in his Foreword: "Many current developments in American academic life — multiculturalism, 'political correctness,' the growth of critical theory, rhetoric and hermeneutics, the crisis of scholarship in many humanities departments — have been closely associated with, and indeed inspired by, the work of European philosophers such as Foucault, Derrida, Lyotard, and others" (1994).

That Smith as a philosopher should make such a claim, in a book devoted to European philosophy, *without* argument or further discussion I find utterly preposterous. Smith, Margolis points out, was embroiled in the Cambridge University controversy, having written "a rather pointed letter" that was published in *The Times* (London) (May 9, 1992) and signed by a list of well-known philosophers.

Referring to the heated controversy at Cambridge University over Derrida, Margolis continues:

My own assessment of this event is that neither of the charges mentions [that he is not a philosopher and that his methods are professionally unacceptable] were sustained, though a good deal of criticism of Derrida's work and the opportunistic use of his methods were indeed fairly developed and justified. The linkage between Derrida and "multiculturalism" may be roughly discerned from a recent paper by John R. Searle, "Is There a Crisis in American Higher Education?" in *Bulletin: The American Academy of Arts and Sciences* XLVI (January 1993), which mentions deconstruction (but not, I think, Derrida by name) and associates deconstruction with the attack on "realism" (in the manner of T. S. Kuhn and Richard Rorty).

Margolis says that he would not have signed the letter written by Smith if asked and he takes a more "moderate" position "by not insisting on the crisis in American education and by not linking Derrida's 'methods' to that crisis" (1994, p. 195).

4. As it happens I hold views sympathetic to Taylor's "dialogical" account of identity and also find that M. M. Bakhtin's notion of inner dialogicality a useful source of insights, but Taylor, in my view, passes too readily to a universal statement about the inherent dialogical character of identity. His own Catholic background, perhaps, conditions him to accept a particular view of dialogue that emphasizes an inner, "spiritual" dimension. Paulo Freire (1972), for instance, provides an alternative dialogical account that interprets cultural identity as a product of political action. Both Taylor's and Freire's accounts, I would argue, bear the marks of a Hegelian dialectic. I find it surprising that Taylor does not take the work of poststructuralist thinkers at all seriously here, given their preoccupation with nondialectical, language-dependent accounts of identity based upon the concept of difference. See, for instance, Gilles Deleuze's (1983) now classic *Nietzsche and Philosophy*, Michel Foucault's (1983) "The Subject and Power" and Judith Butler's (1987) excellent historical account, *Subjects of Desire: Hegelian Reflections in Twentieth Century France*. For a recent dialogical account of student identity based upon the notion of difference, see Bill Readings (1995).

5. Walzer's formulation is as follows:

(1) The first kind of liberalism . . . is committed in the strongest possible way to individual rights and, almost as a deduction from this, to a rigorously neutral state, that is, a state without cultural or religious aspects or, indeed, any sort of collective goals beyond the personal freedom and the physical security, welfare, and safety of its citizens. (2) The second kind of liberalism . . . allows for a state committed to the survival and flourishing of a particular nation, culture, and religion — so long as the basic rights of citizens who have different commitments or no such commitments at all are protected. (1994, p. 99)

6. Taylor's use of the pseudoscientific word "race" is an unfortunate slippage as it falsely implies a universally valid grouping of the world's population on the basis of scientific criteria. He would acknowledge this, I think, and prefer the notion of ethnicity or ethnic group, which carries the connotation of cultural construction.

7. This denial, in practice, of the very dialogical nature of liberalism also characterizes the contributions of Amy Gutmann and Jürgen Habermas. Gutmann glosses over important differences among poststructuralists with the blanket label "deconstructionists." Given that she does not explain to whom she is referring it is difficult to take her arguments seriously. Without the mention of a single name or text she sets up a "straw man" argument, if I can use this dubious popularist, philosophical term. Deconstructionists, Gutmann asserts, "deny the desirability of shared intellectual standards," viewing them "as marks for the will to political power of dominant, hegemonic groups" (1994, p. 18). Such a view, she maintains, is logically and practically self-undermining and threatens to politicize the university more profoundly and destructively than ever before" (p. 19). Reasonable questions would be: To whom is she referring? What are the arguments involved? How can we judge these arguments and accounts in the total absence of all references?

Habermas (1994) is perhaps less directly scathing about deconstructionism, choosing to accept Gutmann's characterization of deconstructionism *as a method*; but, nevertheless, he curtly dismisses the radicals with the following remark: "We can leave this debate aside, since it contributes little to an analysis of struggles for recognition in the democratic state and virtually nothing to their political resolution" (1994, p. 120). This claim carries an extraordinary rhetorical force for someone who is deeply embroiled in the debate and has modified his own evaluation of poststructuralism considerably over time (see Peters, 1994).

Bibliography

Adorno, T. (1982). *Against Epistemology: A Metacritique*. W. Domingo (Trans.). Oxford: Blackwell.

Adorno, T. (1981). *Prisms*. Cambridge, MA: MIT Press.

Adorno, T. (1973). *Negative Dialectics*. New York: Seabury Press.

Althusser, L. (1970). *Reading Capital*. London: New Left Books.

Althusser, L. (1969). *For Marx*. Harmondsworth: Penguin.

Antonik, S. (1002, Winter). Utopian Machines: Leibniz's "Computer" and Hesse's Glass Bead Game. *The German Review*, 72, 35–45.

Appadurai, A. (1990, June). Disjuncture and Difference in the Global Cultural Economy. *Theory, Culture and Society*, 7(2–3), 295–310.

Arendt, H. (1958). *The Human Condition*. Chicago: University of Chicago Press.

Aronowitz, S. (1983). *The Crisis in Historical Materialism: Class, Politics and Culture in Marxist Theory*. New York: Bergin.

Aronowitz, S., & Giroux, H. (1985). *Education Under Siege*. Westport, CT: Bergin and Garvey.

Ascott, R. (1994, September 16). Time for a Planetary Collegium. *The Times Higher Education* (Multimedia Supplement), 4, v.

Badham, R. (1986). *Theories of Industrial Society*. London: Croom Helm.

Bakhtin, M. (1986). The *Bildungsroman* and Its Significance in the History of Realism (Toward a Historical Typology of the Novel). In M. Bakhtin (Ed.), C. Emerson & M. Holquist (Eds.), *Speech Genres and Other Late Essays*, V. W. McGee (Trans.). Austin: University of Texas Press.

Barthes, R. (1983). Writers, Intellectuals, Teachers. In Susan Sontag (Ed.), *Roland Barthes: Selected Writings* (pp. 378–403). New York: Fontana.

Baudrillard, J. (1983). *Simulations*. New York: Semiotext(e).

Baudrillard, J. (1981). Towards a Critique of the Political Economy of the Sign. In *For a Critique of the Political Economy of the Sign*. St. Louis: Telos Press.

Baudrillard, J. (1970). *La société de consommation: ses mythes, ses structures*. Paris: Gallimard.

Bauman, Z. (1989). *Modernity and the Holocaust*. Cambridge: Polity Press.

Bauman, Z. (1987). *Legislators and Interpreters: On Modernity, Post-Modernity and Intellectuals*. Cambridge: Cambridge University Press.

Beddow, M. (1982). *The Fiction of Humanity: Studies in the Bildungsroman from Weiland to Thomas Mann*. Cambridge: Cambridge University Press.

Bell, D. (1980). The Social Framework of the Information Society. In T. Forester (Ed.), *The Microelectronics Revolution*. Oxford: Basil Blackwell.

Bell, D. (1974). *The Coming of Postindustrial Society: A Venture in Social Forecasting*. Harmondsworth: Penguin.

Bell, D. (1973). *The Coming of Post-Industrial Society: A Venture in Social Forecasting*. New York: Basic Books.

Benda, J. (1969). *The Treason of the Intellectuals*. London: Norton.

Benhabib, S. (1986). *Critique, Norms and Utopia*. New York: Columbia University Press.

Bennington, G. (1988). *Lyotard: Writing the Event*. New York: Columbia University Press.

Bernd, M. (1989) Nietzsche and Postmodern Criticism. *Nietzsche-Studien, 18*, 301–316.

Bernstein, R. (1990, October 28). The Rising Hegemony of the Politically Correct. *New York Times*, p. 1:4.

Birch, C. (1988, Autumn). Eight Fallacies of the Modern World and Five Axioms for a Postmodern Worldview. *Perspectives in Biology and Medicine, 32*(1), 12–30.

Bloom, A. (1987). *The Closing of the American Mind*. New York: Simon & Schuster.

Bohm, D. (1985). *Unfolding Meaning: A Weekend Dialogue with David Bohm*, D. Factor (Ed.). Loveland, CO: Foundation House.

Bohm, D. (1980). *Wholeness and the Implicate Order*. London: Routledge & Kegan Paul.

Böhme, G., & Stehr, N. (1986). The Growing Impact of Scientific Knowledge on Social Relations. In G. Böhme and N. Stehr (Eds.), *The Knowledge Society: The Growing Impact of Scientific Knowledge on Social Relations* (pp. 7–29). Dordrecht: Reidel.

Bolter, J. D. (1991). *Writing Space: The Computer, Hypertext, and The History of Writing*. Hillsdale, NJ: Erlbaum.

Bowles, S., & Gintis, H. (1976). *Schooling in Capitalist America: Education Reform and the Contradictions of Economic Life*. London: Routledge & Kegan Paul.

Breton, A. (1978). *What is Surrealism?* F. Rosemont (Ed.). New York: Monad Press.

Burchell, G. (1993). Liberal Government and Techniques of the Self. *Economy and Society, 22*(3), 267–282.

Butler, J. (1987). *Subjects of Desire: Hegelian Reflections in Twentieth Century France*. New York: Columbia University Press.

Calvino, I. (1989). *The Literature Machine: Essays*. London: Picador.

Carroll, D. (1984, Fall). Rephrasing the Political with Kant and Lyotard: From Aesthetic to Political Judgements. *Diacritics, 14*, 74–89.

Castells, Manuel. (1989). *The Informational City*. Oxford, Basil Blackwell.

Cervigni, D. (Ed.). (1991). *Annali d'Italianistica*. Special issue on Italian postmodernism.

Chalmers, A. (1990). *Science and its Fabrication*. Minneapolis: University of Minnesota Press.

Cheney, L. V. (1987). *The Humanities and the American Promise: A Report of the Colloquium on the Humanities and the American People*. Charlottesville, VA: Colloquium on the Humanities and the American People.

Collins, J. (1987). Postmodernism and Cultural Practice: Defining the Parameters. *Screen, 28*(2), 11–27.

Conio, G. (1979). Preface. In C. Pike (Ed.), *The Futurists, the Formalists and the Marxist Critique*, C. Pike & J. Andrew (Trans.). London: Ink Links.

Danuta, C. (1990). *Auschwitz Chronicle, 1939–1945*. New York: Henry Holt.

Delany, P., & Landow, G. P. (1993). Managing the Digital Word: The Text in an Age of Electronic Reporduction. In G. Landow and P. Delany (Eds.), *The Digital*

Word: Text-Based Computing in the Humanities (pp. 3–30). Cambridge, MA: The MIT Press.

Deleuze, G. (1992). Postscript on the *Societies of Control*. *October, 59*, 3–7.

Deleuze, G. (1988). *Foucault*. London: Athlone.

Deleuze, G. (1983). *Nietzsche and Philosophy*, H. Tomlinson (Trans.). New York: Columbia University Press.

Deleuze, G., & Guattari, F. (1983). *Anti-Oedipus: Capitalism and Schizophrenia*. Minneapolis: University of Minnesota Press.

Derrida, J. (1983, Fall). The Principle of Reason: The University in the Eyes of its Pupils. *diacritics*, pp. 3–20.

Derrida, J. (1982a). The Ends of Man. In *Margins of Philosophy,* A. Bass (Trans.), Chicago: University of Chicago Press.

Derrida, J. (1982b). The Pit and the Pyramid: Introduction to Hegel's Semiology. In *Margins of Philosophy*, A. Bass (Trans.). Chicago: University of Chicago.

Derrida, J. (1982c). Différance. In *Margins of Philosophy*, A. Bass (Trans.). Chicago: University of Chicago Press.

Derrida, J. (1981). *Positions*, A. Bass (Trans.). Chicago: University of Chicago Press.

Derrida, J. (1978a). Structure, Sign and Play in the Discourse of the Human Sciences. In A. Bass (Trans.), *Writing and Difference* (pp. 278–294). Chicago: University of Chicago Press.

Derrida, J. (1978b). *Writing and Difference (L'écriture et la différence)*, A. Bass (Trans.). Chicago: University of Chicago Press.

Derrida, J. (1976). *Of Grammatology*, G. Spivak (Trans.). Baltimore: Johns Hopkins University Press.

Descombes, V. (1980). *Modern French Philosophy* L. Scott Fox and J. Harding (Trans.). Cambridge: Cambridge University Press.

D'Souza, D. (1991). *Illiberal Education: The Politics of Race and Sex on Campus*. New York: Free Press.

Diani, M., & Ingraham, C. (Eds.). (1989). *Restructuring Architectural Theory*. Evanston, IL: Northwestern University Press.

Donald, J., & Rattansi, A. (1992). Introduction. In J. Donald and A. Rattansi (Eds.), *"Race," Culture and Difference*. London: Sage.

Dreyfus, R., & Rabinow, P. (1983). *Michel Foucault: Beyond Structuralism and Hermeneutics*, 2d ed. Chicago: University of Chicago Press.

Eagleton, T. (1985). *Literary Theory*. Oxford: Basil Blackwell.

Eco, U. (1989). A Correspondence on Postmodernism. In I. Hoesterey (Ed.), *Zeitgeist in Babel: The Postmodernist Controversy* (pp. 242–254). Bloomington, Indiana University Press.

Eden, L. (1991). Bringing the Firm Back In: Multinationals in International Political Economy. *Millennium Journal of International Studies, 20*(2), 197–224.

Eisenstadt, S. (1989). Introduction: Culture and Social Structure in Recent Sociological Analysis. In H. Haferkamp (Ed.), *Social Structure and Culture*. Berlin: de Gruyter.

Erlich, V. (1969). *Russian Formalism: History-Doctrine* (rev. ed.). The Hague: Mouton.

Esping-Andersen, G. (1990). *The Three Worlds of Welfare Capitalism*. Princeton, NJ: Princeton University Press.

Eyerman, R., Svensson, L., & Söderqvist, T. (Eds.). (1987). Introduction. In *Intellectuals, Universities and the State in Western Modern Societies*. Berkeley: University of California Press.

Fairclough, N. (1992). *Discourse and Social Change*. Cambridge: Polity Press.

Featherstone, M. (1990, June). Global Culture: An Introduction. *Theory, Culture and Society, 7*(2–3), 1–14.

Featherstone, M. (1989a). Towards a Sociology of Postmodern Culture. In H.

Haferkamp (Ed.), *Social Structure and Culture* (pp. 147–171). New York: de Gruyter.

Featherstone, M. (1989b). Postmodernism, Cultural Change and Social Practice. In D. Kellner (Ed.), *Postmodernism, Jameson, Critique* (pp. 117–138). Washington, DC: Maisonneuve Press.

Finkielkraut, A. (1988). *The Undoing of Thought*. London: The Claridge Press.

Flower, J. (1991). Wherefore the Intellectuals? *French Cultural Studies*, 2(6), 275–288.

Foster, H. (1985). Postmodernism: A Preface. In H. Foster (Ed.), *Postmodern Culture*. London: Pluto Press.

Foster, H. (1983). Postmodern: A Preface. In H. Foster (Ed.), *Postmodern Culture*. Washington: Bay Press.

Foucault, M. (1991a). Governmentality. In G. Burchell, C. Gordon and P. Miller (Eds.), *The Foucault Effect: Studies in Governmentality*. London: Harvester Wheatsheaf.

Foucault, M. (1991b). Politics and the Study of Discourse. In G. Burchell, C. Gordon and P. Miller (Eds.), *The Foucault Effect: Studies in Governmentality* (pp. 51–72). London: Harvester Wheatsheaf.

Foucault, M. (1991c). *Remarks on Marx: Conversations with Duccio Trombadari*, R. Goldstein and J. Cascaito (Trans.). New York: Semiotext(e).

Foucault, M. (1990). *The History of Sexuality*: Vol. 1, *An Introduction*. Harmondsworth: Penguin.

Foucault, M. (1989a). How Much Does It Cost For Reason to Tell the Truth. In J. Johnson (Trans.), S. Lotringer (Ed.), *Foucault Live, Interviews 1966–84* (pp. 233–256). New York: Semiotext(e).

Foucault, M. (1989b). The Concern for Truth. In J. Johnson (Trans.), S. Lotringer (Ed.), *Foucault Live, Interviews 1966–84* (pp. 293–308). New York: Semiotext(e).

Foucault, M. (1989c). End of the Monarchy of Sex. In J. Johnson (Trans.), S. Lotringer (Ed.), *Foucault Live, Interviews 1966–84* (pp. 137–155). New York: Semiotext(e).

Foucault, M. (1989d). The Masked Philosopher. In J. Johnson (Trans.), S. Lotringer (Ed.), *Foucault Live, Interviews 1966–84* (pp. 193–202). New York: Semiotext(e).

Foucault, M. (1988). Technologies of the Self. In L. H. Martin, H. Gutman and P. H. Hutton (Eds.), *Technologies of the Self*. London: Tavistock.

Foucault, M. (1984a). Space, Knowledge, and Power. In P. Rabinow (Ed.), *The Foucault Reader*. New York: Pantheon.

Foucault, M. (1984b). What is Enlightenment? In P. Rabinow (Ed.), *Foucault Reader*. New York: Pantheon.

Foucault, M. (1983). The Subject and Power. In H. Dreyfus and P. Rabinow (Eds.), *Michel Foucault, Beyond Structuralism and Hermeneutics*, 2d ed., (pp. 208–226). Chicago: University of Chicago Press.

Foucault, M. (1980). *Power/Knowledge*. New York: Pantheon.

Foucault, M. (1979). *Discipline and Punish: The Birth of the Prison*, A. Sheridan (Trans.). New York: Vintage Books.

Foucault, M. (1972). Intellectuals and Power. In D. Bouchard (Ed.), *Language, Counter-Memory, Practice* (pp. 205–217). Ithaca, NY: Cornell University Press.

Frampton, K. (1989). Some Reflections on Postmodernism and Architecture. In L. Appignanesi (Ed.), *Postmodernism: ICA Documents* (pp. 75–88). London: Free Association Books.

Frampton, K. (1985). Towards a Critical Regionalism: Six Points for an Architecture of Resistance. In H. Foster (Ed.), *Postmodern Culture* (pp. 16–30). London: Pluto Press.

Frankel, B. (1987). *The Post-Industrial Utopians*. Cambridge: Polity Press.

Fraser, N. (1985). Michel Foucault: A "Young Conservative?" *Ethics*, *96*, 165–184.

Fraser, N. (1983). Foucault's Body-language: A Post-humanist Political Rhetoric? *Salmagundi, 61,* 55–70.

Fraser, N. (1981). Foucault on Modern Power: Empirical Insights and Normative Confusions. *Praxis International, 1,* 272–287.

Freedman, R. (1978). *Hermann Hesse: Pilgrim of Crisis.* New York: Pantheon.

Fritzman, J. M. (1993). Escaping Hegel. *International Philosophical Quarterly, 33*(1), 57–68.

Gargani, A. (Ed.). (1979). *Crisi della ragione: Nuovi modelli nel rapporto tasapere e attivita umane.* Torino: Einaudi.

Geyer, M. (1993, Spring). Multiculturalism and the Politics of General Education. *Critical Inquiry, 9,* 499–533.

Gibson, W. (1984). *Neuromancer.* London: Grafton.

Giroux, H. (1983). *Theory and Resistance: A Pedagogy for Opposition.* South Hadley, MA: Bergin & Garvey.

Giroux, H., & McLaren, P. (1991). Language, Schooling and Subjectivity: Beyond a Pedagogy of Reproduction and Resistance. In K. Borman, P. Swami and L. Wagstaff (Eds.), *Contemporary Issues in US Education.* Norwood, NJ: Ablex.

Goldgar, H. (1966–67). Hesse's *Glasperlenspiel* and the Game of Go. *German Life and Letters, 20,* 132–137.

Gordon, C. (1991). Government Rationality: An Introduction. In G. Burchell, C. Gordon and P. Miller (Eds.) *The Foucault Effect: Studies in Governmentality* (pp. 1–52). London: Harvester Wheatsheaf.

Gouldner, A. (1971). *The Coming Crisis of Western Sociology.* London: Heineman.

Grene, M. (1985). Perception, Interpretation and the Sciences: Toward a New Philosophy of Science. In D. J. Depew and B. H. Weber (Eds.), *Evolution at the Crossroads: The New Biology and the New Philosophy of Science.* Cambridge, MA: MIT Press.

Griffin, D. R. (Ed.). (1988). *The Reenchantment of Science: Postmodern Proposals.* New York: State University of New York Press.

Gutmann, A. (1994). *Multiculturalism: Examining the Politics of Recognition.* Princeton: Princeton University Press.

Habermas, J. (1990a). Remarks on the Discussion. *Theory, Culture and Society, 7,* 127–132.

Habermas, J. (1990b). *The Philosophical Discourse of Modernity: Twelve Lectures,* F. Lawrence (Trans.). Cambridge, MA: MIT Press.

Habermas, J. (1989). *The New Conservatism: Cultural Criticism and the Historian's Debate,* S. Nicholsen (Trans.). Cambridge: Polity Press.

Habermas, J. (1987a, Spring–Summer). The Idea of the University-Learning Processes. *New German Critique, 41,* 3–22.

Habermas, J. (1987b). *Theory of Communicative Action:* Vol. 2, *System and Lifeworld: A Critique of Functionalist Reason,* T. McCarthy (Trans.). Boston: Beacon Press.

Habermas, J. (1984). *Theory of Communicative Action:* Vol. 1, *Reason and the Rationalization of Society,* T. McCarthy (Trans.). Boston: Beacon Press.

Habermas, J. (1981a, Winter) Modernity versus Postmodernity. *New German Critique, 22,* 3–14.

Habermas, J. (1981b, Fall). New Social Movements. *Telos, 49,* 33–37.

Habermas, J. (1971). *Knowledge and Human Interests,* J. Shapiro (Trans.). Boston: Beacon Press.

Hacking, I. (1991). How Should We Do the History of Statistics? In G. Burchell, C. Gordon and P. Miller (Eds.), *The Foucault Effect: Studies in Governmentality* (pp. 181–196). London: Harvester.

Hall, S. (1990, Summer). The Emergence of Cultural Studies and the Crisis of the Humanities. *October*, pp. 11–23.

Hand, S. (1988). Translator's Introduction. In G. Deleuze, *Foucault*. London: Athlone.

Haraway, D. (1990). Manifesto for Cyborgs. In L. Nicholson (Ed.), *Feminism / Postmodernism*. New York: Routledge.

Harris, K. (1979). *Education and Knowledge*. London: Routledge & Kegan Paul.

Hayek, F. (1949). Individualism: True and False. In F. Hayek (Ed.), *Individualism and the Economic Order*. London: Routledge.

Henriques, J., Hollway, W., Urwin, C., Venn, C., & Walkerdine, V. (1984). *Changing the Subject: Psychology, Social Regulation and Subjectivity*. London: Methuen.

Hesse, H. (1970).*The Glass Bead Game (Magister Ludi)*, R. Winston and C. Winston (Trans.). London: Jonathan Cape.

Hilberg, R. (1988). The Holocaust Today. Syracuse: Syracuse University, The B. G. Rudolph Lectures in Judaic Studies.

Hilberg, R. (1961). *The Destruction of the European Jews*. Chicago: Quadrangle Books.

Hirsch, E. D. (1987). *Cultural Literacy: What Every American Needs to Know*. Boston: Houghton Mifflin.

Holland, E., & Lambropoulos, V. (1990, Summer). Introduction to a special issue of *October* (The Humanities as Social Technology), pp. 1–9.

Hood, C. (1991, Spring). A Public Management for All Seasons? *Public Aministration, 69*, 3–19.

Hood, C. (1990). De-Sir Humphreyfying the Westminster Model of Bureaucracy: A New Style of Governance? *Governance, 3*(2), 205–214.

Hood, C., & Jackson, M. (1991). *Administrative Argument*. Dartmouth, England: Aldershot.

Horkheimer, M., & Adorno, T. (1972). *Dialectic of Enlightenment*, J. Cumming (Trans.). New York: Seabury Press.

Houlgate, S. (1986). *Hegel, Nietzsche and the Criticism of Metaphysics*. Cambridge: Cambridge University Press.

Husbands, C. (1991). Militant Neo-Nazism in the Federal Republic of Germany in the 1980s. In L. Cheles, R. Ferguson and M. Vaughan (Eds.), *Neo-Fascism in Europe* (pp. 86–119). London: Longman.

Hutcheon, L. (1989). *The Politics of Postmodernism*. London: Routledge & Kegan Paul.

Illich, I. (1973). *Deschooling Society*. Harmondsworth: Penguin.

Ingram, D. (1987). *Habermas and the Dialectic of Reason*. New Haven: Yale University Press.

Jackson, R. L., & Rudy, S. (Eds.). (1985). *Russian Formalism: A Retrospective Glance*. New Haven: Yale Center of International and Area Studies.

Jakobson, R. (1973). Statement by the First Prague International Slavistic Congress. In R. Jakobson (Ed.), *Main Trends in the Science of Language*. London: George Allen and Unwin.

Jameson, F. (1990, September). Clinging to the Wreckage: A Conversation with Stuart Hall. *Marxism Today*, pp. 28–31.

Jameson, F. (1989a). Marxism and Postmodernism. *New Left Review, 176*, 31–45.

Jameson, F. (1989b). Regarding Postmodernism: A Conversation with Frederic Jameson, Anders Stephanson. In A. Ross (Ed.), *Universal Abandon? The Politics of Postmodernism*. Edinburgh: Edinburgh University Press.

Jameson, F. (1985). Postmodernism and Consumer Culture. In H. Foster (Ed.), *Postmodern Culture* (pp. 111–125). London: Pluto Press.

Jameson, F. (1984) *The Postmodern Condition* (pp. vii–xxi). Manchester: Manchester University Press.

Jameson, F. (1983). Postmodernism and Consumer Society. In H. Foster (Ed.), *Postmodern Culture*. London: Pluto Press.

Jay, M. (1984). *Adorno*. London: Fontana.

Jencks, C. (1987). *Post-Modernism: The New Classicism in Art and Architecture*. London: Academy Editions.

Johnson, R. (1986). The Story So Far: and Further Transformations. In D. Punter (Ed.), *Introduction to Contemporary Cultural Studies* (pp. 277–313). Harlow: Longman.

Keat, R., & Abercrombie, N. (Eds.). (1991). *Enterprise Culture*. London: Routledge.

Kellner, D. (Ed.). (1989). *Postmodernism, Jameson, Critique*. Washington, DC: Maisonneuve Press.

Kimball, R. (1990). *Tenured Radicals: How Politics Has Corrupted Our Higher Education*. New York: Harper & Row.

Klotz, H. (1988). *The History of Postmodern Architecture*. Cambridge, MA: MIT Press.

Kolb, D. (1990). *Postmodern Sophistications: Philosophy, Architecture and Tradition*. Chicago: University of Chicago Press.

Kristeva, J. (1986). A New Type of Intellectual: The Dissident. In T. Moi (Ed.), *The Kristeva Reader* (pp. 292–300). Oxford: Blackwell.

Kuhn, T. (1970). *The Structure of Scientific Revoltuions*, 2d ed. Chicago: University of Chicago Press.

Laclau, E., & Mouffe, C. (1985). *Hegemony and Socialist Strategy: Towards a Radical Democratic Politics*. London: Verso.

Lamont, M. (1987). How to Become a Dominant French Philosopher: The Case of Jacques Derrida. *American Journal of Sociology, 93*(3), 584–622.

Landow, G. P. (1992). *Hypertext: The Convergence of Contemporary Critical Theory and Technology*. Baltimore: Johns Hopkins University Press.

Landow, G. P., & Delany, P. (Eds.) (1993). *The Digital Word: Text Baood Computing in the Humanities*. Cambridge, MA: The MIT Press.

Lanham, R. (1993). *The Electronic Word: Democracy, Technology and the Arts*. Chicago: University of Chicago Press.

Latour, B. (1987). *Science in Action: How to Follow Scientists and Engineers through Society*. Cambridge, MA: Harvard University Press.

Lévi-Strauss, C. (1968). *Structural Anthropology (Anthropologie structurale)*, C. Jacobson and B. Schoepf (Trans.). Harmondsworth: Penguin.

Levin, C. (1981). Introduction. In J. Baudrillard, *For a Critique of the Political Economy of the Sign*, C. Levin (Trans.). St. Louis: Telos Press.

Lewis, H. (1988). *The Politics of Surrealism*. New York: Paragon House.

Lovibond, S. (1989). Feminism and Postmodernism. *New Left Review, 178*, 5–28.

Luke, T. (1991). Touring Hyperreality: Critical Theory Confronts Informational Society. In P. Wexler (Ed.), *Critical Theory Now*. London: Falmer Press.

Lyotard, J-F. (1993). Tomb of the Intellectual. In *Political Writings* (pp. 3–7), B. Readings & K. P. Geiman (Trans.). Minneapolis: University of Minnesota Press.

Lyotard, J-F. (1992). *The Postmodern Explained to Children: Correspondence 1982–1985*, J. Pefanis & M. Thomas (Trans.). Sydney: Power Publications.

Lyotard, J-F. (1989). Defining the Postmodern. In L. Appignanesi (Ed.), *Postmodernism: ICA Documents* (pp. 7–10). London: Free Association Books.

Lyotard, J-F. (1988). *The Differend: Phrases in Dispute*, G. Van Den Abbeele (Trans.) Manchester: Manchester University Press.

Lyotard, J-F. (1987). The Sign of History. In D. Attridge, G. Bennington and R. Young (Eds.), *Post-Structuralism and the Question of History* (pp. 162–180). Cambridge: Cambridge University Press.

Lyotard, J-F. (1984). *The Postmodern Condition: A Report on Knowledge*, G. Bennington and B. Massumi (Trans.). Manchester: Manchester University Press.

Lyotard, J-F. (1974, Spring). Adorno as the Devil. *Telos, 19*, 128–137.

Machlup, F. (1962). *The Production and Distribution of Knowledge in the United States*. Princeton: Princeton University Press.

Mahon, M. (1992). *Foucault's Nietzschean Genealogy: Truth, Power, and the Subject*. New York: State University of New York Press.

Maier, C. (1988). *The Unmasterable Past: History, Holocaust, and German National Identity*. Cambridge, MA: Harvard University Press.

Marginson, S. (1993). *Education and Public Policy in Australia*. Cambridge: Cambridge University Press.

Margolis, J. (1994). Differing to Derrida's Difference. In B. Smith (Ed.) *European Philosophy and the American Academy* (pp. 195–226). La Salle, IL: Monist Library of Philosophy.

Marshall, J., & Peters, M. (1995). The Governance of Educational Research. *Australian Educational Researcher, 22*, 1.

Marshall, J., & Peters, M. (1990). Empowering Teachers. *Unicorn, 16*(3), 163–168.

Mason, T. (1993). Whatever Happened to "Fascism". In T. Childers and J. Caplan (Eds.), *Reevaluating the Third Reich* (pp. 252–262). London: Holmes and Meier.

Masuda, Y. (1990). *Managing in the Information Society*. Oxford: Blackwell.

Masuda, Y. (1981). *The Information Society as Post-Industrial Society*. Washington, DC: World Future Society.

Matthews, M. (1980). *The Marxist Theory of Schooling*. London: Harvester Press.

McCarthy, T. (1989). The Politics of the Ineffable: Derrida's Deconstructionism. *The Philosophical Forum, 21*(1–2), 146–168.

McLaren, P. (1994). Multiculturalism and the Postmodern Critique: Towards a Pedagogy of Resistance and Transformation. In H. Giroux & P. McLaren (Eds.), *Between Borders: Pedagogy and the Politics of Cultural Studies*. London: Routledge & Kegan Paul.

McLaren, P. (1989). *Life in Schools: An Introduction to Critical Pedagogy in the Foundations of Education*. New York: Longman.

McLaren, P. (1985). The Politics of Student Resistance. In R. Common (Ed.), *New Forces in Educational Policy-Making* (pp. 94–107). Brock University Occasional Publications.

McLaren, P., & Hammer, R. (1989). Critical Pedagogy and the Postmodern Challenge: Towards a Critical Postmodernist Pedagogy of Liberation. *Educational Foundations, 3*(3), 29–62.

McLennan, G. (1991, Spring). Post-Marxism and Retro-Marxism: Theorising the Impasse of the Left. *Sites: A Journal for Radical Perspectives on Culture, 23*, 46–62.

Messer-Davidow, E. (1993, Fall). Manufacturing the Attack on Liberalized Higher Education. *Social Text, 36*, 40–80.

Moi, T. (1986). Introduction. In T. Moi (Ed.), *The Kristeva Reader* (pp. 1–22). Oxford: Basil Blackwell

Mommsen, H. (1991). *From Weimar to Auschwitz: Essays in German History*, P. O'Connor (Trans.). Cambridge: Polity Press.

Mouffe, C. (1988). Radical Democracy: Modern or Postmodern? In A. Ross (Ed.), *Universal Abandon? The Politics of Postmodernism* (pp. 45–52). Minneapolis: University of Minnesota Press.

Müller-Hill, B. (1988). *Murderous Science: Elimination by Scientific Selection of Jews, Gypsies, and Others, Germany 1933–1945*, G. Fraser (Trans.). Oxford: Oxford University Press.

Nolte, E. (1985). Between Myth and Revisionism? The Third Reich in the Perspective of the 1980s. In H. W. Koch (Ed.), *Aspects of the Third Reich* (pp. 19–30). London: Macmillan.

Norton, R. (1973). *Hermann Hesse's Futuristic Idealism:* The Glass Bead Game *and Its Predecessors.* Frankfurt: Peter Lang.

Odlyzko, A., M. (1994). Tragic Loss or Good Riddance? The Impending Demise of Traditional Scholarly Journals. *Surfaces, 4*(105), 1–44.

Organization for Economic Cooperation and Development. (1991). *Information Networks and the New Technologies: Emerging Economic Opportunities and Implications for IT Policies in the 1990s.* Paris: Organization for Economic Cooperation and Development.

Pavel, T. (1989). The Present Debate: News from France. *diacritics, 19*(1), 17–32.

Pecora, V. (1986). Deleuze's Nietzsche and Post-Structuralist Thought. *Sub-Stance, 48,* 34–50.

Perry, P. (1993). Deleuze's Nietzsche. *Boundary, 2*(1), 174–191.

Peters, M. (Ed.). (1995a). *Education and the Postmodern Condition.* New York: Bergin & Garvey.

Peters, M. (1995b). Radical Democracy, The Politics of Difference and Education. In B. Kanpol & P. McLaren (Eds.), *Critical Multiculturalism.* New York: Bergin & Garvey.

Peters, M. (1994, October). Habermas, Poststructuralism and the Question of Postmodernity. *Social Analysis, 36,* 3–20.

Peters, M. (1991). Postmodernism: The Critique of Reason and the Rise of the New Social Movements. *Sites: A Journal for Radical Perspectives on Culture, 24,* 142–160.

Peters, M., & Marshall, J. (1993). Beyond the Philosophy of the Subject: Liberalism, Education and the Critique of Individualism. *Educational Philosophy and Theory, 25*(1), 19–39.

Peukert, D. (1993). The Genesis of the "Final Solution" from the Spirit of Science. In T. Childers and J. Caplan (Eds.), *Reevaluating the Third Reich* (pp. 234–252). London: Holmes and Meier.

Pfohl, S. (1992). *Death at the Parasite Cafe: Social Science (Fictions) and the Postmodern.* New York: St. Martin's Press.

Piaget, J. (1971). *Structuralism,* C. Maschler (Trans. & Ed.). London: Routledge & Kegan Paul.

Pickering, M. (1991). Social Power and Symbolic Sites: In the Track of Cultural Studies. *Sites: A Journal for Radical Perspectives on Culture, 23,* 3–32.

Pike, C. (Ed.). (1979). *The Futurists, the Formalists, and the Marxist Critique,* C. Pike and J. Andrew (Trans.), (pp. 1–38). London: Ink Links.

Polan, D. (1990). The Spectacle of Intellect in a Media Age: Cultural Representations and the David Abraham, Paul de Man and Victor Farias Cases. In B. Robbins (Ed.), *Intellectuals: Aesthetics, Politics, Academics* (pp. 343–363). Minneapolis: University of Minnesota Press.

Porat, M. (1977). *The Information Economy: Definition and Measurement.* Washington, DC: U.S. Department of Commerce.

Porphyrios, D. (1989). Architecture and the Postmodern Condition. In L. Appignanesi (Ed.), *Postmodernism: ICA Documents* (pp. 89–90). London: Free Association Books.

Portoghesi, P. (1982). *After Modern Architecture,* M. Shore (Trans.). New York: Rizzoli.

Porush, D. (1994). The Rise of Cyborg Culture or The Bomb Was A Cyborg. *Surfaces, 4*(205), 1–32.

Poster, M. (1994). A Second Media Age? *Arena, 3,* 49–92.

Poster, M. (1992). Postmodernity and the Politics of Multiculturalism: The Lyotard-Habermas Debate Over Social Theory. *Modern Fiction Studies, 38*(3), 567–580.

Poster, M. (1990). *The Mode of Information: Poststructuralism and Social Context.* Cambridge: Polity Press.

Poster, M. (1981). The Future According to Foucault: The Archaeology of Knowledge and Intellectual History. In D. Lacapra and S. Kaplan (Eds.), *Modern European Intellectual History: The Appraisals and New Perpectives* (pp. 137–52). Ithaca, NY: Cornell University Press.

Poster, M. (1975). *Existential Marxism in Postwar France: From Sartre to Althusser*. Princeton: Princeton University Press.

Poster, M. (1973). The Hegel Renaissance. *Telos, 16,* 109–127.Pusey, M. (1991). *Economic Rationalism in Canberra: A Nation-Building State Changes Its Mind*. Cambridge: Cambridge University Press.

Radhakrishan, R. (1990). Toward an Effectual Intellectual: Foucault or Gramsci? In B. Robbins (Ed.), *Intellectuals: Aesthetics, Politics, Academics* (pp. 57–99). Minneapolis: University of Minnesota Press.

Radhakrishan, R. (1989). Poststructural Politics: Towards a Theory of Coalition. In D. Kellner (Ed.), *Postmodernism, Jameson, Critique* (pp. 301–332). Washington, DC: Maisonneuve Press.

Raulet, G. (1991, Spring). The New Utopia: Communication Technologies, *Telos, 87,* 39–58.

Raulet, G. (1983, Spring). Structuralism and Post-Structuralism: An Interview with Michel Foucault, J. Harding (Trans.), *Telos, 55,* 195–211.

Readings, B. (1995). From Emancipation to Obligation: Sketch for a Heteronomous Politics of Education. In M. Peters (Ed.), *Education and the Postmodern Condition*. New York: Bergin & Garvey.

Reed, E. (1992, July). Knowers Talking about the Known: Ecological Realism as a Philosophy of Science. *Synthese, 92*(1), 9–23.

Remys, E. (1983). *Hermann Hesse's* Das Glasperlenspiel: *A Concealed Defense of the Mother World*. New York: Peter Lang.

Rhinegold, H. (1994). *Virtual Community*. London: Secker & Warburg.

Richman, M. (1982). *Reading Georges Bataille: Beyond the Gift*. Baltimore: Johns Hopkins University Press.

Roberts, D. (1989). Intellectuals and Modernity: A Post-Modern Perspective. *Thesis Eleven, 24,* 142–149.

Roberts, P. (1995, Spring). Political Correctness, Great Books and the University Curriculum. *Sites, 31.*

Roberts, P. (1993). Philosophy, Education and Literacy: Some Comments on Bloom. *New Zealand Journal of Educational Studies, 28*(2), 165–179.

Rorty, R. (1985). Habermas and Lyotard on Postmodernity. In R. Bernstein (Ed.), *Habermas and Modernity*. Cambridge: Polity Press.

Rose, M. (1991). *The Post-modern and the Post-industrial*. Cambridge: Cambridge University Press.

Rose, N. (1993). Government, Authority and Expertise in Advanced Liberalism. *Economy and Society, 22*(3), 283–299.

Rosenau, P. (1992). Modern and Post-Modern Science: Some Contrasts. *Review, 15*(1), 49–90.

Ross, A. (1990). *No Respect: Intellectuals and Popular Culture*. London: Routledge.

Rosso, S. (1991). A Correspondence on Postmodernism. In I. Hoesterey (Ed.), *Zeitgeist in Babel: The Postmodernist Controversy* (pp. 242–254). Bloomington: Indiana University Press.

Rosso, S. (1990). Postmodern Italy: Notes on the "Crisis of Reason," "Weak Thought," and *The Name of the Rose*. In M. Calinescu and D. Fokkema (Eds.), *Exploring Postmodernism* (pp. 79–92). Amsterdam: John Bejamins.

Rouse, J. (1987). *Knowledge and Power: Toward a Political Philosophy of Science*. Ithaca: Cornell University Press.

Santos, B. (1992). A Discourse on the Sciences. *Review, 15*(1), 9–48.

Sarup, M. (1993). *An Introductory Guide to Post-structuralism and Postmodernism*. Hempel: Harvester Wheatsheaf.

Searle, J. (1990, December 6). The Storm Over the University. *New York Review of Books*, pp. 34, 42.

Shaffner, R. (1984). *The Apprenticeship Novel*. Frankfurt: Peter Lang.

Sheldrake, R. (1991). *The Rebirth of Nature. The Greening of Science and God*. New York: Bantam.

Slemon, S. (1989). Modernism's Last Post, *Ariel*, *20*(4), 3–17.

Smith, B. (1994). *European Philosophy and the American Academy*. La Salle, IL: Monist Library of Philosophy.

Smith, J. (1987). U-topian Hegel: Dialectic and Its Other in Poststructuralism. *The German Quarterley*, *60*(2), 237–262.

Smith, P. (1988). *Discerning the Subject*. Minneapolis: University of Minnesota Press.

Snyder, J. (1988). Translators Introduction. In G. Vattimo, *The End of Modernity: Nihilism and Hermenuetics in Post-Modern Culture* (pp. vi-lviii). Cambridge: Polity Press.

Soja, E. (1989). *Postmodern Geographies: The Reassertion of Space in Critical Social Theory*. London: Verso.

Spivak, G. C. (1976). Translator's Preface. In J. Derrida, *Of Grammatology*. Baltimore: Johns Hopkins University Press.

Steiner, P. (1984). *Russian Formalism: A Metapoetics*. Ithaca: Cornell University Press.

Steiner, P. (Ed.). (1982). *The Prague School: Selected Writings, 1926–1946*. Austin: University of Texas Press.

Striedter, J. (1989). *Literary Structure, Evolution and Value: Russian Formalism and Czech Structuralism Reconsidered*. Cambridge: Harvard University Press.

Sugimoto, Y. (1990, Winter). A Post-Modern Japan? *Arena*, *91*, 48–59.

Swales, M. (1978). *The German Bildungsroman From Wieland to Hesse*. Princeton: Princeton University Press.

Taylor, C. (1994). The Politics of Recognition. In A. Gutmann (Ed.), *Multiculturalism: Examining the Politics of Recognition*. Princeton: Princeton University Press.

Toulmin, S. (1990). *Cosmopolis: The Hidden Agenda of Modernity*. New York: The Free Press.

Toulmin, S. (1985). Pluralism and Responsibility in Post-Modern Science. *Science, Technology and Human Values*, *10*, 28–37.

Toulmin, S. (1982). *The Return to Cosmology: Postmodern Science and the Theology of Nature*. Berkeley: University of California Press.

Touraine, A. (1974). *The Post-Industrial Society: Tommorow's Social History, Classes, Conflicts and Culture in the Programmed Society*, L. Mayhew (Trans.). London: Wildwood House.

Touraine, A. (1969). *La Société Postindustrielle*. Paris: Denöel.

Trachtenberg, S. (Ed.). (1985). *The Postmodern Moment: A Handbook of Contemporary Innovation in the Arts*. London: Greenwood Press.

van Reijen, W., & Veerman, D. (1988). An Interview with Jean-François Lyotard. *Theory, Culture and Society*, *5*, 277–309.

Vattimo, G. (1992). *The Transparent Society*, D. Webb (Trans.). Baltimore: Johns Hopkins University Press.

Vattimo, G. (1991). The End of (Hi)story. In I. Hoesterey (Ed.), *Zeitgeist in Babel: The Postmodernist Controversy* (pp. 132–143). Bloomington: Indiana University Press.

Vattimo, G. (1988). *The End of Modernity: Nihilism and Hermeneutics in Post-Modern Culture*, J. Snyder (Trans.). Cambridge: Polity Press.

Vattimo, G. (1986). Nietzsche and Heidegger. *Stanford Italian Review* (Nietzsche in Italy), *6*(1-2), 19–30.

Vattimo, G., & Rovatti, P. A. (Eds.). (1983). *l Pensiero Debole*. Milan: Feltrinelli.

Wahl, J. (1929). *Le malheur de la conscience dans la philosophie de Hegel*. New York: Garland.

Walzer, M. (1994). Comment. In A. Gutmann (Ed.), *Multiculturalism: Examining the Politics of Recognition*. Princeton: Princeton University Press.

Waugh, L. R., & Monville-Burston, M. (1990). Introduction: The Life, Work and Influence of Roman Jakobson. In R. Jakobson, L. R. Waugh, & M. Monville-Bursten (Eds.), *On Language* (pp. 1–48). Cambridge, MA: Harvard University Press.

Wellbery, D. (1985). Postmodernism in Europe: On Recent German Writing. In S. Trachtenberg (Ed.), *The Postmodern Moment* (pp. 229–250). London: Greenwood Press.

West, C. (1990). The New Cultural Politics of Difference. In R. Ferguson et al. (Eds.), *Out There: Marginalization and Contemporary Culture*. Cambridge, MA: MIT Press.

Wexler, P. (1992, August). Corporatism, Identity and After Postmodernism in Education. Paper presented at the joint session of the Society for the Study of Social Problems and the American Sociological Association.

Whiteman, J., Kipnis, J., & Burdett, R. (Eds.). (1992). *Strategies in Architectural Thinking*. Cambridge, MA: MIT Press.

Wiener, N. (1948). ICybernetics, or, Control and Communication in the animal and the Machine. *New York: Wiley*.

Williams, R. (1983). *Keywords: A Vocabulary of Culture and Society*. London: Fontana.

Williams, R. (1981). *Culture*. London: Fontana.

Willis, P. (1977). *Learning to Labour*. Lexington: D. C. Heath.

Yeatman, A. (1994). *Postmodern Revisionings of the Political*. New York: Routledge & Kegan Paul.

Yeatman, A. (1992). Minorities and the Politics of Difference. *Political Theory Newsletter*, (Special Issue, Symposium on The Politics of Difference), *4*(1), 1–10.

Young, I. M. (1992). Together in Difference: Transforming the Logic of Group Political Conflict. *Political Theory Newsletter* (Special Issue, Symposium on The Politics of Difference), *4*(1), 11–26.

Young, I. M. (1990). *Justice and the Politics of Difference*. Princeton: Princeton University Press.

Young, I. M. (1988). Five Faces of Oppression. *The Philosophical Forum*, *19*(4), 270–290.

Ziman, J. (1994). *Prometheus Bound: Science in a Dynamic Steady State*. Cambridge: Cambridge University Press.

Ziolkowski, T. (1965). *Novels of Hermann Hesse: A Study in Theme and Content*. Princeton: Princeton University Press.

Zuroff, E. (1989). Recent Efforts to prosecute Nazi War Criminals Living in Western Democracies — Successes and Failures. In Y. Baner et al. (Eds.), *Remembering for the Future: Working Papers and Addenda* (pp. 2806–2809). London: Pergamon Press.

Index

ABOUT THE AUTHOR

MICHAEL PETERS is Senior Lecturer in the Department of Education at the University of Auckland in New Zealand. He is a contributor to Kanpol and McLaren's *Critical Multiculturalism: Uncommon Voices in a Common Struggle* (Bergin & Garvey, 1995) and editor of *Education and the Postmodern Condition* (Bergin & Garvey, 1995), a collection of essays on the significance of Jean-François Lyotard for the field of education.

ISBN 0-89789-418-9

EAN

HARDCOVER BAR CODE